Criminal Jurisdiction

A Nordic Perspective

Thomas Elholm & Birgit Feldtmann

Criminal Jurisdiction

A Nordic Perspective

DJØF Publishing
Copenhagen 2014

Thomas Elholm & Birgit Feldtmann
Criminal Jurisdiction. A Nordic Perspective
1. edition

© 2014 by DJØF Publishing
Jurist- og Økonomforbundets Forlag

Cover: Bo Helsted
Print: Narayana Press, Gylling

Printed in Denmark 2014
ISBN 978-87-574-2687-8

Published with support from Margot & Thorvald Dreyers fond

dreyersfond

Sold and distributed in Scandinavia by:
DJØF Publishing
Copenhagen, Denmark
Email: forlag@djoef.dk
www.djoef-forlag.dk

Sold and distributed in North America by:
International Specialized Book Services (ISBS)
Portland, USA
Email: orders@isbs.com
www.isbs.com

Sold in all other countries by:
The Oxford Publicity Partnership Ltd
Towcester, UK
Email: djof@oppuk.co.uk
www.oppuk.co.uk

Distributed in all other countries by:
Marston Book Services
Abingdon, Oxon, UK
Email: trade.orders@marston.co.uk
www.marston.co.uk

Contents

Foreword

Jurisdiction in criminal matters is one of the "classical" central issues concerning criminal justice. The question of the range of domestic criminal justice is of major relevance both from a theoretical and a practical point of view. It is not a new topic but due – among other things – to the globalisation and the emerging of the internet, it seems increasingly relevant for legislators, prosecutors and judges to consider matters of criminal jurisdiction. However, it is a topic which in the Nordic context has been, with few exceptions, somehow neglected in the academic world. This is the contextual background of the present book.

The book has been underway for quite some time. Vagn Greve, a former professor of law and dean of the Faculty of Law at University of Copenhagen, now connected to University of Southern Denmark, got the idea back in 2011. He persuaded us to publish a book on the systems of criminal jurisdiction in the Nordic countries. The relevance of doing so – of writing a comparative study about the Nordic systems – is elaborated in the last chapter of the book. Furthermore, Vagn Greve had already written a short report of the Danish system together with Karin Cornils, who is a former researcher and head of division of the Nordic Section at *Max-Planck-Institut für ausländisches und internationales Strafrecht* in Freiburg im Breisgau. Likewise, Karin Cornils had already written a short report of the Swedish system of criminal jurisdiction. In other words, two out of five country reports were already in place, when the idea emerged in 2011.

Ragnheiður Bragadóttir, who is professor of criminal law at the University of Iceland and closely related to the criminal law scholars in Denmark, was then asked to write the report of the Icelandic system. Subsequently postdoctoral research fellow and international criminal law scholar from the University of Bergen, Annika Suominen, was asked to do the Norwegian and Finnish reports. She has the rare capability of being familiar with both legal systems. Fortunately, they both agreed to do so.

The team of all six researchers met in Freiburg in 2012, at Karin Cornils house in Scheffelstrasse. Together we agreed on a structure for the country reports, which would make it possible to compare fairly easy the systems of the five countries. We also agreed that we should write the final chapter. In light of the relatively short country reports and the easy way of comparing the systems, the idea of writing a chapter summarising the five country reports was abandoned. Instead it was decided that we should write a chapter, where some central issues describing trends in the five Nordic countries were analysed.

We have got important comments on the draft from professor Gorm Toftegaard Nielsen, University of Aarhus, and Dan Helenius, doctoral student at Helsinki University. Thanks a lot!

We also owe thanks to our translators/proof-readers Rachel Ives and Mark Gallacher. Furthermore we would like to thank our student helper Jesper Kusk Markvart who has been doing a great job in connection with setting up the manuscript. Due to a heavy workload at University of Southern Denmark the publication has not been finalised until ultimo 2013. But here it is, finally.

By the way, the book is going to be published also in a German version by the same publisher later in 2014. And one more thing: We got financial support for the project by *Dreyerfonden*. We would like to thank the foundation and express our gratitude.

Thomas Elholm & Birgit Feldtmann
Fasanen, Samsø & Aarhus December 2013

CHAPTER 1

Denmark

Karin Cornils & Vagn Greve[1]

1. General Basis

1.1. Systematic classification of the rules on jurisdiction

Section 6 et seq. of the Danish Criminal Code (*straffeloven*, strl.)[2] contain provisions on the scope of national jurisdiction, that is, on the power to prosecute a criminal offence in Denmark. These are not rules on the scope of Danish criminal law; the application of Danish criminal provisions is rather a consequence which occurs where, due to the existence of jurisdiction, a criminal prosecution takes place in Denmark (Section 10 (1) strl.).

Danish jurisdictional rules have been subject to a comprehensive reform which took effect on 1 July 2008.[3] Although they are contained in the Criminal Code, it is the predominant view that they should be classified as procedural provisions, based on their content and legal effect.[4] Certain writers treat them as substantive legal norms or as a mixture of procedural and substantive

---

1. Revised and expanded version of a country report submitted by the authors in 2011 as part of the project "Jurisdiktionskonflikte bei grenzüberschreitender organisierter Kriminalität – ein Rechtsvergleich zum internationalen Strafrecht" headed by Zentrum für Europäische und Internationale Strafrechtsstudien (ZEIS), Osnabrück.
2. Act no. 126 of 15 April 1930 with changes. The version used here is that of the updated Order no. 1028 of 22 August 2013.
3. Act no. 490 of 17 June 2008. On this change of legislation see *Carsten Kristian Vollmer*, "Nye regler om dansk straffemyndighed", Juristen 2008, pp. 197-204.
4. *Vagn Greve et al.*, Kommenteret straffelov, Almindelig del, 10th edition, Copenhagen 2013, pp. 150 ff.; *Vagn Greve*, Det strafferetlige ansvar, 2nd edition, Copenhagen 2004, pp. 105 ff.; Betænkning no. 1488/2007 om dansk straffemyndighed, Copenhagen 2007, pp. 26 f.; *Knud Waaben*, Strafferettens almindelige del, I. Ansvarslæren, 5th edition, continued by Lars Bo Langsted, Copenhagen 2011, p. 259.

law.[5] However, the literature consistently draws a clear distinction between jurisdictional rules and the question of the territorial scope of Danish criminal law,[6] which undisputedly forms part of substantive law. This view was recently confirmed by the Supreme Court.[7] In place of the ambiguous *"international criminal law"*, there has, in recent years, been a preference for using the term *"inter-legal criminal law"*.[8]

1.2. Outline of the principles of the law on jurisdiction

Denmark bases its right to exercise its own criminal jurisdiction on a specific relationship between the offence and Denmark itself. Under the provisions of Section 6 et seq. strl., the *locus delicti*, the nationality of the offender or victim and the protected interest which has been violated or put at risk may all be taken into account as relevant factors. In addition, the interests of international legal cooperation in criminal matters and other obligations under international law may also play a role.

Under the *territoriality principle*, Denmark has jurisdiction over all offences committed within its territory (Section 6 no. 1 strl.). The *locus delicti* is deemed to be the place where the offender was present when he/she/it committed the offence, attempted to commit the offence or was a party thereto, as is the place where the result of the offence occurred or where the offender intended it to occur (Section 9 (1)-(3) strl.). In this regard, an offence is also deemed to be a domestic offence if only a part of it was committed in Denmark (Section 9 (4) strl.).[9]

Under the *flag state principle*, which relies on a narrower definition of the *locus delicti*, Danish criminal jurisdiction may be exercised with respect to offences committed on board Danish ships or aircraft, even those in foreign waters or airspace, or in international waters or over stateless regions (Section 6 no. 2-3 strl.).

---

5.   *Gorm Toftegaard Nielsen*, Strafferet I, Ansvaret, 4th edition, Copenhagen 2013, pp. 303 ff.; *Per Ole Träskman*, "'In dubio, pro Dania', Några reflexioner över dansk straffrättslig jurisdiktion", in: Thomas Elholm et al. (ed.), Ikke kun straf, Festskrift til Vagn Greve, Copenhagen 2008, pp. 563-590 (566 ff.).
6.   See below 1.3.
7.   U 2012.2399 H.
8.   *Greve et al.* (2013), p. 152; *Vagn Greve*, "Straffebestemmelsers interlegale gyldighed", Tidsskrift for Kriminalret (TfK) 2010, pp. 502-524 (502); *Vagn Greve* "Danske straffebestemmelsers interlegale gyldighed, Træk af en forvirret retsudvikling" in: Thomas Elholm et al. (ed.), Liber amicarum et amicorum Karin Cornils, Copenhagen 2010, pp. 161-183.
9.   On the concept of the *locus delicti* in Denmark, see 2.1.1.

With respect to offences committed abroad, the main jurisdictional basis arises under the *active personality principle*. This basically extends domestic jurisdiction to offences committed by individuals who 1) are Danish nationals or 2) are domiciled or 3) have similar permanent residence in Denmark (Section 7 (1) strl.).[10] The same applies, in this regard, to nationals and domiciled persons of one of the other Scandinavian countries (Finland, Iceland, Norway and Sweden) where the person concerned was in Denmark at the time of the charge (Section 7 (3) strl.). In general, criminal prosecution under the *active personality principle* requires that the offence also be subject to criminal sanction under the law of the *locus delicti* (double criminality[11]). With respect to offences committed in stateless regions, the principle only applies where they are punishable by more than four months' imprisonment (Section 7 (2) strl.).

Restrictive by comparison, the *passive personality principle*, allows for Danish jurisdiction over foreign offences aimed at Danish nationals or persons domiciled or with permanent residence in Denmark. In addition to double criminality, the offence must also be subject to at least six years imprisonment under Danish law and comprise one of a number of statutory offences (Section 7 a (1)–(2) strl.). Offences committed outside sovereign territories must be subject to a punishment of more than four months' imprisonment (Section 7 a (3) strl.); this rule is not restricted to specific types of offence.

The *principle of state protection* applies to domestic protected interests. It places under Danish jurisdiction offences which are directed against the Danish state, its authorities or interests or offences which violate a particular official duty (Section 8 no. 1-4 strl.).

The *principle of universal jurisdiction* arises out of the duty or right to prosecute crimes under international law. It states that Denmark has criminal jurisdiction over offences committed abroad, where international provisions impose an obligation on Denmark to provide for its own jurisdiction (Section 8 no. 5 strl.). Insofar as the offence is covered by the Rome Statute of the International Criminal Court, or constitutes an attack on air or marine traffic, the defendant must have Danish nationality, or his/her domicile or permanent residence in Denmark, or must be present in Denmark (Sections 8 a-8 b strl.).

Where Denmark refuses another country's request to extradite a defendant and, under Danish law, the offence is punishable by at least one year's im-

---

10. On Danish territory, see below 2.1.2., on the requirement of double criminality, see 1.4.
11. See below 1.4.

prisonment, Danish jurisdiction applies pursuant to the *principle of represen-tational jurisdiction* (Section 8 no. 6 strl.).[12]

Where an actual offence falls under the jurisdiction of several countries, Danish law has no rules on the extent to which its own criminal jurisdiction takes precedence over, or must give way to, the rights of other countries to effect criminal prosecution. The crucial factor is whether the Danish authorities decide to prosecute or – under the *principle of discretionary prosecution* – refrain from doing so. In practice, the country in which the offence is committed or the defendant's home country is granted precedence.[13]

1.3. The relationship between jurisdictional rules and the scope of the criminal provisions

Danish legal doctrine strictly distinguishes the question of domestic jurisdiction in criminal matters from the substantive legal aspect of the territorial limits of the national criminal statutes.[14] Even where the Danish courts have jurisdictional competence under Sections 6-9 a strl., the prosecution of an offence requires that it is in fact covered by domestic criminal provisions (Section 10 (1)).

The substantive scope of the national criminal law is not determined in Sections 6 et seq. strl. but arises from the inherent area of application of the provisions for the individual offences.[15] It is clear from the wording of many provisions that their application is limited to domestic offences or domestic protected interests (for example Section 128 strl., which makes it a criminal offence to recruit people in Denmark for foreign military service). Others expressly specify that they extend to foreign offences (thus Section 158 strl. relating to false testimony in a foreign court). In most cases, specific interpretation is required in this regard.

With respect to the offences in the Criminal Code, insofar as they safeguard protected legal interests of the individual, the traditional assumption is that they are universally applicable, i.e. they basically apply to acts and omissions irrespective of the *locus delicti*, whereas other criminal legislation only criminalises offences committed in Denmark. The latter applies to the law on tax crime, criminal provisions in the trade and healthcare sectors and to provisions on hunting, fishing and animal welfare, but not to the laws on weap-

---

12. On the requirement of double criminality, see below 1.4.
13. Cf. *Greve et al.* (2013), p. 151, and below 1.6.
14. See above 1.1.
15. Cf. *Greve et al.* (2013), pp. 129 ff.; *Greve*, TfK 2010, pp. 502 ff.; *Greve* (2010), pp. 179 f.

ons and drugs.[16] The Road Traffic Act contains express provision (Section 134) for its own application to foreign offences. Recent theory[17] and case law, though, assume that the scope must be determined by interpreting each individual provision and that it is irrelevant whether an offence is regulated within the criminal code or in special criminal laws. This theory further rejects the classic dichotomy which states that criminal provisions are either limited to the domestic arena or are universally applicable. It is argued that many provisions are only applicable in relation to certain foreign countries and not in relation to others. Thus the extraterritorial application may, for example, extend exclusively to EU Member States or to states that, along with Denmark, have ratified certain treaties.

1.4. Impact of foreign law

Where an offence is prosecuted in Denmark, the court exclusively applies Danish criminal law (Section 10 (1) strl.). Provisions from a foreign legal system may be consulted, in the case of offences with a foreign component, where this is necessary in order to clarify preliminary questions of civil or administrative law to which Danish criminal law refers.[18] Thus, in a criminal case involving embezzlement (Section 278 (1) no. 2 strl.), the existence of a loan or lending agreement under foreign civil law may have to be determined according to foreign civil law, as may third-party rights in the case of debtor's fraudulent dispositions (Section 283 (1) no. 1 strl.). The preliminary question of whether the addressee of an attempted bribe (Section 122 strl.) is a foreign official or the recipient of false testimony (Section 158 (1) strl.) is a foreign court, must be answered according to foreign public law.

In certain cases involving foreign offences, however, foreign criminal provisions must also be taken into account, such as where the Danish judge has to determine whether the act committed is a criminal offence under the applicable law of the *locus delicti*. This requirement of double criminality is provided for under the statute in conjunction with the *active and passive personality principles* and the *principle of representational jurisdiction* (Sections 7 (1) no. 1, 7 a (1), 8 no. 6 strl.).[19] It is based, inter alia, on considerations of legal certainty and foreseeability: where someone adapts their conduct to the legal system of the country in which they are staying, they should not have to fear subsequent criminal prosecution for this conduct in another country due

---

16. Cf. Betænkning no. 1488/2007, pp. 83 ff.; *Greve et al.* (2013), pp. 190 f.
17. See in particular *Greve*, TfK 2010, pp. 509 ff.; *Greve* (2010), pp. 176 f.
18. Cf. *Greve et al.* (2013), p. 188.
19. For more detail, see below 2.3., 2.4. and 2.7.

to a difference in the laws. In addition, it is asserted that conviction for a foreign offence always represents interference in the internal affairs of the country where the act was committed and as such is particularly unacceptable where the act is not a criminal offence in the country concerned.[20]

The requirement of double criminality is regarded as a requirement *in concreto*, which means that it does not depend on the general criminalisation of a particular type of conduct in the foreign legal system but on the actual ability to prosecute the offender for a concrete offence in the country in which it was committed taking account of objective or subjective defences and other grounds of impunity which apply there and any impediment of criminal procedure, particularly lapse of time.[21] On the other hand, the legal classification of an offence – such as receiving stolen goods – need not be the same in both countries.

Under Danish law, the criminal liability of legal entities is substantially the same as that of natural persons. Many other legal systems have not, however, taken this step and this could give rise to problems in relation to double criminality. Therefore, for the purpose of establishing Danish jurisdiction over a legal entity, there is no requirement for the law of the *locus delicti* to recognize the criminal liability of legal entities at all (Section 7 b strl.). It is sufficient that commission of the act in question by a natural person constitutes a criminal offence in both countries.

Offences which fall under the *principle of state protection* or the *principle of universal jurisdiction* are exempt from the requirement of double criminality. The *active personality principle*, which is based on the particular relationship of the offender to Denmark, also gives rise to an exemption applicable to certain types of case: where the offence involves the sexual exploitation of children, traffic in human beings or female circumcision, criminal liability under Danish law alone is sufficient (Section 7 (1) no. 2 (a) strl.). The same applies where the offence is directed at Danish nationals etc. (Section 7 (1) no. 2 (b) strl.).[22]

Where double criminality is a requirement for Danish jurisdiction, the principle of *lex mitior* (Section 10 (2) strl.) must also be taken into account. This states that when it comes to sentencing by the Danish court, the punish-

---

20. Betænkning no. 1488/2007, pp. 72 f. with reference to *Greve et al.* (2009), p. 114. Information on foreign law may be obtained in accordance with protocol 15 March 1978, cf. Circular no. 72 of 15 June 1988.
21. Cf. *Greve et al.* (2013), pp. 190 f.; *Toftegaard Nielsen* (2013), p. 318; Betænkning no. 1488/2007, pp. 73 f.
22. In detail, see below 2.3.

ment imposed may not be stricter than that applicable under the law of the *locus delicti*. In this regard, it is the maximum penalty applicable in the *locus delicti* which is relevant rather than the actual sentence that might be expected in the individual case.[23] This certainly does not prevent the Danish court from taking account of sentencing practice in the country where the offence took place.[24] Thus, for example, in criminal proceedings relating to drunken driving in Iceland, the Danish Eastern High Court took account of Icelandic practice when deciding the sentence.[25]

1.5. Impact of foreign Judgments

The *ne bis in idem* ban, relating to offences already decided by a foreign court, was amended following Denmark's accession to the European Convention on the International Validity of Criminal Judgments (1970).

Under Section 10 (a) strl., someone who has been sentenced for an offence in a foreign country may not be prosecuted for the same act where this conflicts with an international obligation on the part of Denmark to recognise the legal validity of criminal Judgments.[26]

In other cases, a repeat prosecution in Denmark is ruled out where the person concerned has been acquitted *res judicata*, or convicted without being sentenced, or where the sentence imposed has been enforced, is in the process of being enforced or has lapsed (Section 10 a (2) strl.).

Even where these requirements are fulfilled, a person convicted or acquitted in a foreign country may, under certain circumstances, be prosecuted again. This applies to offences committed on Danish sovereign territory or deemed, under Section 9 or 9 a strl., to have been committed in Denmark (Section 10 a (3) no. 1 (a) strl.), also to foreign offences by Danes and equivalent persons in cases involving the sexual exploitation of children, traffic in human beings or female circumcision or where the offence is aimed at a Danish national or Danish resident, and finally, to foreign offences against the state of Denmark or its interests (Section 10 a (3) no. 1 (b) strl.). All of these cases are characterized by the fact that, from a Danish point of view, it may be uncertain whether the foreign sentence satisfies the Danish need to

---

23. Cf. *Toftegaard Nielsen* (2013), p. 319; *Greve et al.* (2013), pp. 190 f.
24. See also *Vagn Greve*, "Strafzumessung im internationalen Strafrecht", in: Jörg Arnold u.a. (Hrsg.), Menschengerechtes Strafrecht, Festschrift für Albin Eser, München 2005, pp. 751-763 (753 ff.).
25. TfK 2002.467 Ø.
26. In detail, see *Andreas Laursen*, Internationale forbrydelser i dansk ret, Copenhagen 2011, pp. 57 ff.

impose punishment. However, the exemptions under sub-section (3) no. 1 (a)-(b) strl. do not apply where the criminal prosecution in the prosecuting country took place at the request of the Danish prosecution service (Section 10 a (4) strl.); in this case the *ne bis in idem* ban must be upheld.

Extreme differences of opinion between the countries on the concept of justice are warded off by an *ordre-public* clause under which the legal validity of the foreign sentence may be overridden where its recognition would clearly be incompatible with Danish legal principles (Section 10 a (3) no. 3 strl.). The *travaux préparatoires* cite as an example the case where a foreign criminal procedure is a sham carried out in order to prevent other countries from bringing a criminal prosecution.[27]

In rare cases, the retrial of an offence which has already been tried abroad is also possible under Danish procedural law (Section 10 a (3) no. 2 strl.[28]). This refers to cases where a person who is acquitted abroad later confesses, or other evidence comes to light, justifying his/her/its retrial for the offence.

Where a person is convicted in Denmark and a penalty has been imposed against that person in a foreign country for the same offence, the Danish judge must reduce the sentence to be imposed by the amount of the foreign sentence which has already been served (Section 10 b strl.).

Irrespective of whether it is lawful to re-prosecute the case in Denmark, a Danish national or resident who is convicted in another country for an offence which, under Danish law, may result in loss of office or the forfeiture of a right, may be deprived of the office or the right by way of a public court action in Denmark (Section 11 strl.). The main use of this provision is in relation to the revocation of a driving licence due to driving abroad whilst under the influence of alcohol. Since the revocation of a driving licence in the country of the offence (outside the EU) has no practical effect to prevent the offender from driving in Denmark, the provision allows for a corresponding follow-up measure by the Danish authorities without any violation of the *ne bis in idem* ban.[29]

1.6. Restrictions on prosecution

Under Danish criminal procedural law, the principle of discretionary prosecution generally applies.[30]

---

27. Bill L 16 of 28 November 2007, 2007-08 (2nd), Point 3.7.6.
28. In conjunction with Administration of Justice Act Section 985 a.
29. Cf. *Greve et al.* (2013), p. 201.
30. Cf. *Vagn Greve*, "The Criminal Justice System in Denmark", in: Vagn Greve/Karin Cornils, Studien zum dänischen Strafrecht, Studies in Danish Criminal Law, Copen-

With respect to the prosecution of foreign offences on the basis of the *principle of universal jurisdiction* and the *principle of representational jurisdiction* (Section 8 no. 5-6 strl.), the Director of Public Prosecution, as the highest prosecuting authority, has issued a circular containing a special ruling: since these offences often involve the competing jurisdictions of several countries, and the relations between states may be affected, prosecution in Denmark is only instituted on the order of the Minister of Justice.[31]

A similar restriction on prosecution applies with regard to the *territoriality principle* for offences committed inside Danish sovereign territory on board a foreign vessel or aircraft, by or against a crew member or a passenger. The Director of Public Prosecution decides whether to prosecute in such cases unless the offender is a Danish national or resident, the offence breaches public order in Denmark, the victim has requested help from the Danish authorities or the offence falls under Section 8 strl.[32]

Public prosecution of offences against the independence and security of the state, against the constitution and highest organs of state, or of terrorism offences, requires the order of the Minister of Justice (Sections 110 f, 118 a strl.). Insofar as these offences are committed from abroad, they constitute a substantial proportion of the offences which fall under the *protective principle* (Section 8 no. 1 strl.) thus here too there is a control on the exercise of domestic jurisdiction.[33]

In connection with the *passive personality principle,* it is assumed that an offence committed abroad, against a Danish national or resident, will generally only be dealt with by prosecution where the victim has pressed charges in the *locus delicti* via the foreign authorities or a body representing Denmark. In some cases, the relationship of the offence to Denmark may be only tenuous, and the legitimate claims of another country to have exclusive jurisdiction may lead the Danish authorities to forego exercising their own jurisdiction. The Ministry of Justice has stated, in this regard, that Danish courts should exercise restraint in the case of offences committed by foreigners with

hagen 2011, pp. 15-65 (33); *Lars Bo Langsted et al.*, Criminal Law in Denmark, 3rd edition, Copenhagen 2011, pp. 183 ff.; *Gorm Toftegaard Nielsen*, Straffesagens gang, 5th edition, Copenhagen 2011, pp. 109 ff.; *Birgit Feldtmann*, "Anklagemyndighedens rolle – nogle komparative tanker om legalitet og opportunitet i det danske og det tyske retssystem", Nordisk Tidsskrift for Kriminalvidenskab (NTfK) 2002, pp. 157-174.

31. RM 3/2002 (Kompetenceregler, p. 3).
32. RM 3/2002 (Kompetenceregler, p. 2); cf. *Greve et al.* (2013), pp. 176 f.
33. Cf. *Toftegaard Nielsen* (2013), p. 327.

no direct connection to Denmark against someone who may be connected in some way to Denmark but, at the same time, also has a strong connection to the *locus delicti*.[34]

2. The Rules on Jurisdiction in Detail

2.1. Territoriality principle

The main rule under the Danish law on jurisdiction is linked to the location in which the offence is committed:

Section 6 strl.
Denmark has jurisdiction over offences committed
1. in Denmark,
[…].

The sovereignty of the Danish criminal courts under Section 6 strl. is unconditional, that is, irrespective of the nationality of the offender or the victim and irrespective of foreign legal provisions.

2.1.1. Localisation

Since the *territoriality principle* is based on the location in which the offence is committed, the identification of that location, that is the localisation of the offence, is of crucial importance. The Criminal Code contains a special provision for this:

Section 9 strl.
(1) An offence is deemed to have been committed in the place where the offender was located when the offence was committed. With respect to legal entities, an offence is deemed to have been committed in the place where the act or acts are undertaken which give rise to the criminal liability of the legal entity.

(2) Where the criminal liability of an offence is dependent on or influenced by a result which occurs or is intended to occur, the offence is also deemed to have been committed in the place where the result occurs or where, in the intention of the perpetrator, it was to occur.

---

34. Betænkning no. 1488/2007, pp. 281 f.; Bill L 16, 2007/08 (2nd), Point 3.4.2.4 and 3.4.2.7; cf. *Greve et al.* (2013), p. 168.

(3) Attempt or complicity in an offence is deemed to have been committed in Denmark where the perpetrator was in Denmark when he/she carried out the act, irrespective of whether the offence is accomplished, or intended to be accomplished, abroad.

(4) Where part of an offence is committed in Denmark, the whole offence is deemed to have been committed in Denmark.

In principle, the *locus delicti* is considered to be the place where the perpetrator was present when the criminal act was carried out. Attempt and complicity are also deemed to be criminal acts; this is expressly made clear in Sub-section 3. A criminal offence committed by a legal entity is located in the place where the act ascribed to the entity was carried out (Sub-section 1, Sentence 2). Where the criminal liability of the legal entity is based on the physical act of an individual, such as the unlawful discharge of harmful substances, it is the location of this act which is the deciding factor. Where the criminal liability arises from corporate acts, the company headquarters containing the board of management, who have, for example, breached their managerial duties, may be considered to constitute the *locus delicti*.[35] The company headquarters is determined in accordance with company law rules.

Where the location of the act is different to that in which the result occurs, both are deemed to be *locus delicti* (Sub-section 2). This rule is referred to as the *principle of ubiquity*. Classic examples are the gunshot across the border between two countries, the letter bomb sent abroad and the transportation of the dying victim of a crime over the border. It is sufficient to establish Danish jurisdiction if the act is carried out in Denmark or the result occurs, or was intended to occur there. This applies to intentional and negligent offences, but neither intent nor negligence is required as regards the country in which the result occurs. Result within the meaning of this provision is only deemed to be the effect of the act implied in the definition of the offence. Indirect consequences, such as pecuniary loss by the insurer of the victim, are irrelevant.

Section 9 strl. does not cover transit cases, such as where the dying victim is transported from Germany via Denmark to Sweden. The most common transit case, in practice, that of the drugs courier who is caught while passing though Denmark, does however fall under Sub-section 1 because possession of drugs itself is a criminal offence in Denmark.

Under Sub-section 4, the offence is deemed to have been wholly committed in Denmark even if just part of it has been committed there. This provision applies, for example, where acts preparatory to an offence are carried out

---

35. Cf. *Greve et al.* (2013), p. 181.

on Danish soil and the offence is accomplished abroad.[36] In this case, the perpetrator is prosecuted by the Danish authorities not only for the attempt but also for the accomplished act, and indeed, even where the act is not a criminal offence in the country in which it is accomplished – which may quite easily be the case due to the extremely broad definition of attempt under Danish criminal law.[37]

The Criminal Code contains no express provision on localisation for offences of omission. Legal doctrine considers the act to have been committed in the place where the omitted act – the feeding of animals for example – should have been carried out, or where the perpetrator was present at the time he/she/it should have acted.[38] In the case of result crimes, the location where the (unobstructed) result takes place is also relevant (Section 9 (2) strl.). In practice, Section 9 strl. has been applied against a father who travelled to the USA with his daughter. After the mother was granted sole custody of the child, he failed to return to Denmark for a period of several weeks. Only with the intervention of the US authorities could the child be returned to the care of her mother. The father was convicted by the Danish Western High Court of violating parental custody rights.[39]

Internet crimes, in which text, sound or images are made generally available in Denmark from abroad, are deemed to have been committed in Denmark insofar as the material has a particular connection to Denmark (Section 9 a strl.). The particular connection may be, for example, that the Danish language is used or that the material relates to a specific target group in Denmark, such as students at a specific educational establishment.[40] This provision was introduced under the reform of 2008 in order to restrict Danish jurisdiction in relation to Section 9 strl.[41]

2.1.2. Definition of Denmark

Denmark within the meaning of Section 6 no. 1 strl. also includes the Faroe Islands, which since 1948 have constituted an autonomous region under the

---

36. This is true even for the case of two foreign tourists who in Denmark conspire the offence to be committed abroad.
37. See *Karin Cornils*, "Straffelovens § 21 – Rechtsvergleichende Überlegungen zur Versuchsstrafbarkeit im dänischen Recht", in: Thomas Elholm et al. (eds.), Ikke kun straf, Festskrift til Vagn Greve, Copenhagen 2008, pp. 89-106.
38. Cf. *Toftegaard Nielsen* (2013), p. 307; *Greve* (2004), p. 103.
39. TfK 2011.440 V.
40. Cf. *Greve et al.* (2013), p. 187; see also *Karin Cornils*, "Om lokalisering av brott på internet", NTfK 1999, pp. 194-205.
41. Cf. Betænkning no. 1488/2007, pp. 351 f.

sovereignty of Denmark, and Greenland, which also gained political autonomy in 1979, as part of, and on an equal footing with, Denmark.

The national sovereign territory encompasses the land and sea territory as well as the airspace above. Danish coastal waters extend up to 12 nautical miles, the fishing area and exclusive economic zone up to 200 nautical miles, from the baseline. The height of the airspace claimed is not precisely defined.[42] Denmark does not regard the continental shelf as part of its national territory but domestic jurisdiction has been extended by special law[43] to cover crimes committed on installations used for research or for the exploitation of natural resources in the area of the continental shelf, such as drilling platforms. This applies irrespective of the nationality of the installation, as in the case of crimes committed on board a ship or an aircraft situated in Danish waters or airspace, which may be prosecuted as domestic offences without consideration for the respective flag.[44]

2.2. Flag state principle

The *territoriality principle* is supplemented and extended by the *flag state principle* as set down in Section 6 no. 2 and 3 strl.

Section 6 strl.
Denmark has jurisdiction over offences committed

1. [...]
2. on a Danish vessel or aircraft situated in foreign sovereign territory, by someone belonging to the crew or travelling as a passenger, or
3. on a Danish vessel or aircraft situated outside a sovereign territory.

Whilst the law of the flag state is not recognised in the domestic prosecution of offences committed on board a foreign vessel or aircraft within Danish sovereign territory,[45] Denmark does claim jurisdiction over ships and aircraft registered under its own flag. This applies without restriction to offences committed in international waters or over stateless areas (No. 3), for example where a Danish ship is attacked by pirates. Where the vessel or aircraft is situated within foreign sovereign territory, however, Danish jurisdiction is limited to offences committed by crew members or persons travelling as passengers (No. 2). It does not apply where the perpetrator is only on board tempo-

42. Cf. *Greve et al.* (2013), pp. 155 ff.
43. Order no. 1101 of 18 November 2005.
44. However, for restriction of prosecution, see above 1.6.; cf. *Greve et al.* (2013), p. 156.
45. See above 2.1.2.

rarily, for example as a pilot in shipping traffic or as ground staff to clean a Danish aircraft during a stop-over in a foreign airport.[46] Where a Danish ship is attacked by pirates within foreign sovereign waters, Danish jurisdiction may however arise under Section 7 a strl.; in addition, Section 8 b strl. contains a special provision for attacks on air or sea traffic.[47]

According to the wording of the statute, the provision covers acts "on board" the craft. Under case law, however, offences committed from the ship or aircraft against an object situated off-board are also covered.[48]

2.3. Active personality principle

Using the perpetrator himself/herself/itself as a basis for the application of domestic jurisdiction under the *active personality principle* has a comparatively broad scope under Danish law:

Section 7 strl.

(1) Denmark has jurisdiction over acts committed on foreign sovereign territory by a person who, at the time of the charge, had Danish nationality or domicile or similar permanent place of residence in Denmark, provided
1. the act is also a criminal offence under the law applicable in the *locus delicti* (double criminality) or
2. the perpetrator also had the aforesaid connection to Denmark when the act was committed and the act
   a) involves the sexual exploitation of children, traffic in human beings or female circumcision, or
   b) is aimed at someone who had the said connection to Denmark when the act was committed.

(2) Denmark also has jurisdiction over acts committed outside a sovereign territory by a person who, at the time of the charge, had the connection to Denmark referred to in subsection 1, provided such acts are punishable by more than 4 months' imprisonment.

(3) Sub-section 1, no. 1 and Sub-section 2 apply mutatis mutandis to acts by a person who, at the time of the charge, had either Finnish, Icelandic, Norwegian or Swedish nationality, or residence in one of these countries, and is staying in Denmark.

Since 1960, in addition to foreign offences by Danish nationals and foreigners with domicile in Denmark, acts committed by the nationals and residents

46. Cf. *Greve et al.* (2013), pp. 157 f.; Betænkning no. 1488/2007, p. 52.
47. See below 2.4. respectively 2.6.
48. Cf. Betænkning no. 1488/2007, p. 51, with reference to the decision of the Danish Western High Court U 1957.610 V (Sinking of fishing stakes into the seabed for bottom trawling).

of the other Scandinavian countries have also been included (today Sub-section 3). This already relatively large group of people was further extended by the reform in 2008 to include foreigners with permanent residence in Denmark. In this regard, it is not relevant whether they are staying in the country legally.[49] The new provisions also cover persons who have been waiting for a long time for a decision on their residency permit petition or against whom extradition has been ordered but not yet executed.[50] Foreign students who are staying for a long period are also covered, but not tourists or business travellers, even where they often stay in Denmark or their stay is of longer duration.[51] The new provisions have been criticized by international law experts.[52]

Prosecution under the *active personality principle* generally requires the act also to be a criminal offence under the law applicable in the *locus delicti* (Sub-section 1, no. 1), and the maximum penalty applicable there may not be exceeded.[53] In some cases, however, the requirement of double criminality is waived, that is, firstly in the case of offences involving the sexual exploitation of children, traffic in human beings and female circumcision (Sub-section 1, no. 2 (a)). This provision has been criticised in the literature as a sort of crusade against sex tourism and circumcision. In the case of sexual offences against children it depends solely on whether the provision is formulated as a criminal offence against a child not on whether the victim in the actual case is in fact a child.

Secondly, double criminality is not required if the offence is directed at a person who has a connection to Denmark under Sub-section 1 (Sub-section 1 no. 2 (b)). The situation where both perpetrator and victim are "Danish" has been expressly regulated since 2008 and is referred to as the so-called *combined personality principle* (active/passive) for the purpose of "internal Danish matters".[54] It is unclear whether the victim's connection to Denmark must be known to the perpetrator. Intentional bodily harm inflicted on a Danish person whilst abroad by another Danish person is cited as an example of its application. On the other hand, the provision does not cover the case where a

49. Cf. Betænkning no. 1488/2007, pp. 252 f.
50. Thus, Bill L 16 of 28 November 2007, 2007-08 (2nd), Point 3.3.3.
51. Cf. *Greve et al.* (2013), pp. 160 f.
52. *Ole Spiermann*, "Dansk straffemyndighed i folkeretlig belysning", Ugeskrift for Retsvæsen 2007 B, pp. 219-228 (222 f.).
53. For the requirement of double criminality and the principle of *lex mitior*, see above 1.4. According to Danish law, offences committed in an area outside sovereign territory must be punishable with a sentence higher than four months' imprisonment (Section 7, Sub-section 2).
54. Betænkning no. 1488/2007, pp. 262 ff.

Danish national, whilst abroad, commits fraud against a foreigner who, for his part, claims compensation from a Danish insurance company; this constitutes an indirect consequence of the offence so the fraud is not considered to have been directed at the Danish company.

The waiver of the requirement of double criminality is intended to simplify the proceedings and at the same time allow for domestic prosecution or an appropriate sentence even where the act is not a criminal offence in the country in which it was committed or is subject to a far more lenient sentence.[55]

An additional peculiarity of the cases covered by Sub-section 1, no. 2, is the fact that the personal connection of those involved in the offence to the state of Denmark must also exist at the time the offence was committed. Otherwise, as regards the perpetrator's connection to Denmark under the active personality principle, it basically depends on the time of the charge, which means that it is sufficient if the person concerned only obtains Danish nationality or takes up domicile or residence in Denmark after the offence has been committed. This is intended to avoid Denmark becoming a haven for criminals. Thus, for example, an asylum seeker can also be convicted for acts which he/she committed prior to fleeing his/her country. This has been criticised by international law experts.[56]

2.4. Passive personality principle

By comparison with the jurisdictional regulations in other countries, Danish jurisdiction under the *passive personality principle*, which is based on the victim's relationship to Denmark, is rather restrictively regulated:

Section 7 a strl.

(1) Denmark has jurisdiction over offences committed on foreign sovereign territory which are directed against someone who, at the time of the offence, had Danish nationality or domicile or similar permanent residence in Denmark provided the act also constitutes a criminal offence under the law applicable in the country where the offence took place (double criminality) and, under Danish law, is punishable by at least 6 years imprisonment.

(2) Danish jurisdiction under Sub-section 1 requires the act to fall within one of the following types of offence:
1. murder,
2. grievous bodily harm, unlawful imprisonment or robbery,
3. offences endangering public safety,

---

55. Bill L 16 of 28 November 2007, 2007-08 (2nd), Point 3.3.6.
56. Cf. *Greve et al.* (2013), p. 161.

4. sexual offences or incest or
5. female circumcision.

(3) Denmark also has jurisdiction over offences committed outside a sovereign territory which are directed against someone who at the time of the offence had the connection to Denmark referred to in Sub-section 1, provided offences of this type are punishable by more than 4 months imprisonment.

Sub-sections 1 and 2 were not brought in until the 2008 reform. Prior thereto, the *passive personality principle* only applied to offences committed outside sovereign territory (now Sub-section 3). The earlier restriction on domestic jurisdiction was based on the effort to avoid what looked like a vote of no confidence in a foreign country's administration of justice. It was feared that extending national jurisdiction to offences committed abroad by foreigners against Danish citizens could run counter to international solidarity by showing a lack of confidence in the level of criminal protection offered by the law of the *locus delicti*.

Such concerns have now been overridden by the legislator in a range of different offences. In its advisory opinion on the reform, the Jurisdiction Committee, which proposed the expansion, did not rule out the possibility that the application of the new jurisdictional rules may in certain cases be "difficult to reconcile with international law principles".[57] In the literature on international law, this statement was later described as an "extraordinary understatement" and the expansion of the *passive personality principle* has been strongly criticised.[58]

The victim of the offence must be a Danish national or have domicile or similar permanent residence in Denmark. These requirements of a connection to Denmark correspond with those applicable to the offender under the *active personality principle*.[59] In this respect, the status at the time of the offence is the decisive factor. There is also a requirement for double criminality[60] and the additional qualification that the offence be punishable under Danish law by at least six years imprisonment. Finally, the offence must be one of the types of offence listed under Sub-section 2.

There is a fundamental principle that the offender must have had reason and opportunity to acquaint himself/herself with the substance of Danish law. This will not be the case where, for example, a Somali national, in Somalia,

57. Betænkning no. 1488/2007, p. 182.
58. Cf. *Spiermann* (2007), p. 225.
59. See above 2.3.
60. In detail, see above 1.4.

circumcises a girl of Danish nationality. The Jurisdiction Committee's advisory opinion on the reform, submitted in 2007, espouses the view that, in this case, the Somali could not be prosecuted under the passive personality principle.[61]

2.5. Principle of state protection

According to the *principle of state protection*, Danish sovereign jurisdiction covers acts directed against the Danish state, its authorities or interests or acts which violate a specific official duty:

Section 8 strl.
Denmark has jurisdiction over offences committed abroad, irrespective of the offender's nationality or place of residence, where
1. the offence violates the independence, security, constitution or public authorities of the state of Denmark or breaches an official duty owed to the state,
2. the act violates interests whose legal protection, within the state of Denmark, implies a specific connection to Denmark, or
3. the offence violates a duty which the offender is obliged by law to fulfil in a foreign country,
4. the offence violates a duty which the offender is obliged to fulfil in relation to a Danish vessel or aircraft,
[…].

State interests are not generally protected by foreign legal systems. Danish jurisdiction over foreign offences against Denmark and its interests is therefore subject to regulation irrespective of the law in the *locus delicti*.[62]

Denmark's legally protected interests within the meaning of no. 2 may be violated, for example, by breaches of legislative provisions on health or the environment and breaches of tax or customs law. In such cases, however, localisation of the offence in Denmark based on the result which occurs or is intended to occur there, may also arise pursuant to Section 6 strl. in conjunction with Section 9 (2) strl.

Traditionally, the term duty pursuant to no. 3 is given a restrictive interpretation and, in practice, is applied, for example, to contravention of statutory employment protection provisions by Danes abroad. Another example of its application, provided by the literature, would be in relation to an attack by Danish soldiers on a foreign civil population.[63] In the context of the prepara-

---

61. Betænkning no. 1488/2007, p. 283. For the general restrictive attitude of the Ministry of Justice in this context, see above 1.6. and below 2.5.
62. Cf. *Greve* (2004), p. 109.
63. *Ole Spiermann*, Moderne folkeret, 3rd edition, Copenhagen 2006, p. 284.

tions for the 2008 reform, the Jurisdiction Committee spoke out in favour of a broader interpretation of jurisdiction under no. 3;[64] however, the Ministry of Justice intended to keep to the restrictive interpretation.[65] It was emphasised, during preparation of the bill, that the threat of punishment is aimed principally at Danish nationals. The liability of foreigners for an act which corresponds to the definition of the offence may also be limited under Section 12 strl. if it is contrary to a recognized principle of international law.

2.6. Principle of universal jurisdiction

In the context of the *principle of universal jurisdiction*, domestic jurisdiction applies unconditionally, that is, irrespective of the nationality of offender and victim and irrespective of whether the act is a criminal offence in the place where it was committed:

Section 8 strl.
Denmark has jurisdiction over acts carried out abroad, irrespective of the offender's nationality or place of residence, where
[…]
5. the act falls within an international provision under which Denmark is obliged to provide for its own jurisdiction,
[…].

The term *"international provision"* means that customary international law is not sufficient in this respect but that the obligation must arise from codified international law such as an international convention, an EU legal instrument (e.g. a framework decision) or a resolution of the UN Security Council.[66] Translated literally it also states in no. 5 "… under which Denmark is obliged to have jurisdiction". This formulation, brought in in 2008, is, according to the *travaux préparatoires*, intended to make it clear that the relevant international provision does not need to contain a specific duty to effect prosecution.[67]

---

64. Betænkning no. 1488/2007, pp. 273 ff.; predominantly similar also *Toftegaard Nielsen* (2008), pp. 320 f.
65. Cf. *Greve et al.* (2013), pp.172 ff., inter alia with further references for criticiscm under international law of the broad interpretation.
66. Cf. Betænkning no. 1488/2007, p. 394; *Greve et al.* (2013), pp. 175 f.
67. Betænkning no. 1488/2007, p. 394.

A provision which was also brought in under the 2008 reform relates to offences by "Danes"[68] or by foreigners who are in Denmark at the time of the charge:

Section 8 a strl.
Denmark has jurisdiction over offences committed abroad provided offences of this type are covered by the Rome Statute of the International Criminal Court and the offence is committed by a person, who at the time of the charge,
1. has Danish nationality or his/her domicile or similar permanent residence in Denmark or
2. is in Denmark.

Denmark secures, by way of this provision, primary jurisdiction with respect to the International Criminal Court. It goes beyond the Rome Statute in its content, however, in that it even applies to the offences contained therein (currently genocide, crimes against humanity and serious war crimes) where the act has been committed on the territory and by the citizens of a country that has not ratified the Statute.[69]

Another provision aimed at the same target group as Section 8 a strl., relates to air and sea piracy (Section 183 a strl.):

Section 8 b
(1) Denmark has jurisdiction over acts committed abroad insofar as they are covered by Section 183 a and committed by a person who at the time of the charge
1. has Danish nationality or his/her domicile or similar permanent residence in Denmark or
2. is in Denmark.

(2) Criminal prosecution for an offence under Sub-section 1 may at the same time extend to an offence under Sections 237 or 244-248, committed in connection with the offence under Section 183 a.

The provision was originally brought in to implement the 1970 Hague Convention for the suppression of the unlawful seizure of aircraft. Subsequently, the scope of Section 183 a strl. was extended to cover attacks against ships and other collective means of transport as well as fixed and mobile marine platforms, so that corresponding offences now also fall under Danish jurisdic-

---

68. See above 2.3.
69. Cf. *Greve et al.* (2013), p. 178; see also *Laursen* (2011), pp. 50 ff.

tion in accordance with the *principle of universal jurisdiction*.[70] Sub-section 2 also covers offences of homicide and assault committed in unity of crime with the main offence.

2.7. Principle of representational jurisdiction

The *principle of representational jurisdiction* is expressed in Section 8 no. 6 strl:

Section 8 strl.

Denmark has jurisdiction over acts committed abroad irrespective of the nationality or residence of the offender where

[...]

6. the extradition of the offender for prosecution in another country has been refused and the act, insofar as it was committed on another sovereign territory, is a criminal offence under the law of the *locus delicti* (double criminality) and is punishable by at least 1 year's imprisonment under Danish law.

In addition to double criminality, an actual extradition request must also have been submitted by the foreign country. It is not sufficient to say that Denmark would reject such a request.[71]

3. Abbreviations

H	Højesterets dom (Judgment of the Danish Supreme Court)
L	Lovforslag (Draft law)
NTfK	Nordisk Tidsskrift for Kriminalvidenskab (Scandinavian Journal of Criminal Law and Criminology)
RM	Rigsadvokatens meddelelse (Notices from the Director of Public Prosecutions)
strl.	straffeloven (The Danish Criminal Code)
TfK	Tidsskrift for Kriminalret (Danish Criminal Law Periodical with Law Reports)

---

70. Thus *Greve et al.* (2013), p. 179; cf. Bill L 16 of 28 November 2007, 2007/08 (2nd), Point 3.4.3.6. See also *Birgit Feldtmann*, "Er strafferet et effektivt middel i kampen mod sørøveri? Et dansk indblik i strafferetlige udfordringer på baggrund af kapringen af CEC Future", in: Thomas Elholm et al. (eds.), Liber amicarum et amicorum Karin Cornils, Copenhagen 2010, pp. 101-120.
71. Cf. *Spiermann* (2007), pp. 226 f.

U	Ugeskrift for Retvæsen (Danish Legal Periodical with Law Reports)
V	Vestre Landsrets dom (Judgment of the Danish Western High Court)
Ø	Østre Landsrets dom (Judgment of the Danish Eastern High Court)

4. The Jurisdictional Rules of the Danish Criminal Code in English translation

Section 6
Denmark has jurisdiction over offences committed
1. in Denmark,
2. on a Danish vessel or aircraft situated in foreign sovereign territory, by someone belonging to the crew or travelling as a passenger, or
3. on a Danish vessel or aircraft situated outside a sovereign territory.

Section 7
(1) Denmark has jurisdiction over acts committed on foreign sovereign territory by a person who, at the time of the charge, had Danish nationality or domicile or similar permanent place of residence in Denmark, provided
1. the act is also a criminal offence under the law applicable in the *locus delicti* (double criminality) or
2. the perpetrator also had the aforesaid connection to Denmark when the act was committed and the act
   a) involves the sexual exploitation of children, traffic in human beings or female circumcision, or
   b) is aimed at someone who had the said connection to Denmark when the act was committed.

(2) Denmark also has jurisdiction over acts committed outside a sovereign territory by a person who, at the time of the charge, had the connection to Denmark referred to in Sub-section 1, provided such acts are punishable by more than 4 months' imprisonment.

(3) Sub-section 1, no. 1 and Sub-section 2 apply mutatis mutandis to acts by a person who, at the time of the charge, had either Finnish, Icelandic, Norwegian or Swedish nationality, or residence in one of these countries, and is staying in Denmark.

Section 7 a
(1) Denmark has jurisdiction over offences committed on foreign sovereign territory which are directed against someone who, at the time of the offence, had Danish nationality or domicile or similar permanent residence in Denmark provided the act also constitutes a criminal offence under the law applicable in the country where the offence took place (double criminality) and, under Danish law, is punishable by at least 6 years imprisonment.

(2) Danish jurisdiction under Sub-section 1 requires the act to fall within one of the following types of offence:
1. murder,
2. grievous bodily harm, unlawful imprisonment or robbery,
3. offences endangering public safety,
4. sexual offences or incest or
5. female circumcision.

(3) Denmark also has jurisdiction over offences committed outside a sovereign territory which are directed against someone who at the time of the offence had the connection to Denmark referred to in Sub-section 1, provided offences of this type are punishable by more than 4 months imprisonment.

Section 7 b
Where Danish jurisdiction with respect to a legal entity requires double criminality, it is not necessary for the criminal liability of legal entities to be provided for under the law of the *locus delicti*.

Section 8
Denmark has jurisdiction over offences committed abroad, irrespective of the offender's nationality or place of residence, where
1. the offence violates the independence, security, constitution or public authorities of the state of Denmark or breaches an official duty owed to the state,
2. the act violates interests whose legal protection, within the state of Denmark, implies a specific connection to Denmark, or
3. the offence violates a duty which the offender is obliged by law to fulfil in a foreign country,
4. the offence violates a duty which the offender is obliged to fulfil in relation to a Danish vessel or aircraft,
5. the act falls within an international provision under which Denmark is obliged to provide for its own jurisdiction,
6. the extradition of the offender for prosecution in another country has been refused and the act, insofar as it was committed on another sovereign territory, is a criminal offence under the law of the *locus delicti* (double criminality) and is punishable by at least 1 year's imprisonment under Danish law.

Section 8 a
Denmark has jurisdiction over offences committed abroad provided offences of this type are covered by the Rome Statute of the International Criminal Court and the offence is committed by a person, who at the time of the charge,
1. has Danish nationality or his/her domicile or similar permanent residence in Denmark or
2. is in Denmark.

Chapter 1. Denmark

Section 8 b

(1) Denmark has jurisdiction over acts committed abroad insofar as they are covered by Section 183 a and are committed by a person who at the time of the allegation
1. has Danish nationality or his/her domicile or similar permanent residence in Denmark or
2. is in Denmark.

(2) Criminal prosecution for an offence under Sub-section 1 may at the same time extend to an offence under Sections 237 or 244-248, committed in connection with the offence under Section 183 a.

Section 9

(1) An offence is deemed to have been committed in the place where the offender was present when the offence was committed. With respect to legal entities, an offence is deemed to have been committed in the place where the act or acts are undertaken which give rise to the criminal liability of the legal entity.

(2) Where the criminal liability of an offence is dependent on or influenced by a result which occurs or is intended to occur, the offence is also deemed to have been committed in the place where the result occurs or where, in the intention of the perpetrator, it was to occur.

(3) Attempt or complicity in an offence is deemed to have been committed in Denmark where the perpetrator was in Denmark when he/she carried out the act, irrespective of whether the offence is accomplished, or intended to be accomplished, abroad.

(4) Where part of an offence is committed in Denmark, the whole offence is deemed to have been committed in Denmark.

Section 9 a

An offence involving inter alia text, sound or images which, by way of acts carried out abroad, are made generally available in Denmark via the internet or similar system for the distribution of information, are deemed to have been committed in Denmark insofar as the material has a particular connection to Denmark.

Section 10

(1) Where an offence is prosecuted in Denmark, the decision as to both the punishment and other legal consequences of the offence must be reached according to Danish law.

(2) Where Danish jurisdiction requires double criminality, the punishment imposed may not be stricter than that applicable under the law of the *locus delicti.*

Section 10 a

(1) Someone who has been sentenced for an offence in a foreign country may not be prosecuted for the same act where this conflicts with an international obligation on the part of Denmark to recognize the legal validity of criminal Judgments.

(2) In other cases, a person who has been convicted of an offence abroad may not be prosecuted for the same offence in Denmark where,
1. the person concerned has been acquitted res judicata,
2. the sentence imposed has been enforced, is in the process of being enforced or has lapsed under the law of the country of Judgment, or
3. the person concerned has been convicted without being sentenced.

(3) Sub-section 2 does not apply where
1. the foreign conviction relates to offences which
    a)   are deemed to have been committed in Denmark pursuant to Section 9 or Section 9 a, or
    b)   fall under Section 7 (1) no. 2 or Section 8 no. 1 or 2,
2. a criminal prosecution takes place in Denmark pursuant to Section 985 a Judicial Procedure Act, or
3. recognition of the foreign conviction is clearly incompatible with Danish legal principles.

(4) In the cases referred to under Section 3 no. 1, a criminal prosecution may not take place in Denmark where the prosecution in the country of Judgment took place at the request of Danish prosecution service.

Section 10 b
Where a person is prosecuted in Denmark against whom a penalty has been imposed in a foreign country for the same offence, the sentence to be imposed in Denmark must be reduced by the amount of the foreign sentence already served.

Section 11
Where a person with Danish nationality, domicile or similar permanent residence in Denmark, is convicted in another country for an offence which, under Danish law, may result in loss of office or the forfeiture of a right to exercise a profession or the loss of other rights, such denial of rights may take place by way of a public court action in Denmark.

Section 12
Sections 6-11 do not apply where they conflict with recognized exemptions under international law.

CHAPTER 2

Finland

Annika Suominen[1]

1. General Basis

1.1. Systematic classification of the rules on jurisdiction

The Finnish provisions on criminal jurisdiction are found in the first chapter of the Finnish Criminal Code (*Strafflagen*, SL).[2] The starting point is that the provisions on criminal jurisdiction are part of substantive criminal law, and part of the general part of Finnish criminal law.[3] The rules on jurisdiction are considered part of national law, and not of international procedural law.[4] The international dimension is obviously present, but as a starting point the criminal jurisdiction is considered part of national criminal law. This means that in cases of lack of jurisdiction, the person will be acquitted, as no offence is considered having taken place.[5] In some situations however, the provisions are also considered part of procedural law, but this applies only in situations of derivative jurisdiction.

The Finnish norms on criminal jurisdiction prescribe the scope of application of Finnish criminal law. They also prescribe the international competence of Finnish courts. Finnish courts only apply Finnish criminal law and

1. Postdoctoral research fellow, Faculty of Law, University of Bergen. The author wishes to thank PhD researcher Dan Helenius who has been of great help in writing this article. Any errors are however the author's own. When Finnish legislation is cited in English, the unofficial translations of the Ministry of Justice are used.
2. Act 1889/39, Strafflagen.
3. *Dan Frände*, Allmän straffrätt, Helsingfors 2004, p. 327.
4. *Brynolf Honkasalo*, Suomen rikosoikeus – Yleiset opit, Helsinki 1948, p. 67 and *Per Ole Träskman*, Straffrättsliga åtgärder med främmande inslag, I. En granskning av den finska straffrättens tillämpningsområde, Borgå 1977, p. 27.
5. *Frände* (2004), p. 327.

therefore generally, if the offence falls within the scope of application of Finnish criminal law, the Finnish courts are competent to handle the case.[6]

The Criminal Code starts with the provisions on the scope of application of Finnish criminal law. Section 1(1) of the first chapter states the main rule, that Finnish law applies to an offence committed in Finland. The application of Finnish law to an offence committed in Finland's economic zone is subject to the Act on the Economic Zone of Finland[7] and the Act on the Environmental Protection of Seafaring.[8]

The provisions in the first chapter of the Finnish Criminal Code were revised thoroughly in 1996.[9] This revision restricted the scope of application of Finnish criminal law, amongst other by requiring double criminality and a separate prosecution order to a greater extent for offences committed outside Finland. This last revision was motivated by previous provisions being problematic in relation to international law and the possibilities for conflicts of jurisdiction with other states.

1.2. Outline of the principles of the law on jurisdiction

The *territoriality principle* constitutes the starting point for the application of the Finnish provisions of criminal law. The state where the offence has been committed is considered having jurisdiction of the offence. This is clear from the main rule in section 1(1) of chapter one SL. The *locus delicti* constitutes the substantial link between the state and the offence. The place of commission of the offence is specified in section 10 of chapter one SL. This section concerns firstly offences committed through active conduct. It also applies for offences of omission and has further rules on attempt and on incitement and abetting.

Finnish jurisdiction has been considered necessary for Finnish vessels and aircrafts. The *flag state principle* is therefore applicable and section 2 of chapter one SL regulates offences connected with a Finnish vessel or aircraft.

Finnish law applies to an offence committed outside of Finland by a Finnish citizen (and some other groups of persons considered equal to Finnish citizens). The *active personality principle* is laid down in section 6 of chapter one SL. Pursuant to section 9 of chapter one of the Finnish Constitution, Finnish citizens shall not be prevented from entering into Finland or deported

6. The Finnish courts may have to take foreign law into account, as prejudicial arguments.
7. Act 1058/2004, Lag om Finlands ekonomiska zon.
8. Act 1672/2009, Miljöskyddslag för sjöfarten.
9. See Government Bill, Regeringens Proposition till Riksdagen med förslag till revidering av lagstiftningen om tillämpningsområdet för finsk straffrätt, RP 1/1996.

or extradited (except for other Member States of the EU and the Nordic States) from Finland to another country. This has led to the *active personality principle* being applied for offences Finnish citizens commit abroad.

Before the revision of 1996, the *passive personality principle* was unrestricted and did not require double criminality or any minimum in relation to punishability. Today it applies pursuant to section 5 of chapter one SL to offences committed outside Finland if these are directed at a Finnish citizen, a Finnish legal entity or a foreigner permanently resident in Finland. This applies only if the offence under Finnish law is punishable by imprisonment for more than six months. This provision protects private Finnish interests.

Another provision protects important interests of the Finnish State. Section 3 of chapter one SL expresses the *principle of state protection* (*statsskyddsprincipen* in Swedish). This section states that Finnish law is applicable to offences committed outside Finland when these are directed at Finland. An offence is directed at Finland when it is an offence of treason or high treason, it otherwise seriously endangers national, military or economic rights or interests of Finland or it is directed at a Finnish authority.

The *principle of representational jurisdiction* (also called the *principle of vicarious jurisdiction*) is laid down in section 8 of chapter one SL. Finnish criminal law can therefore be applied to an offence where the alleged offender is present in Finland, even if the offence lacks a further link to Finland and the other jurisdictional principles mentioned above do not apply.

The *principle of universal jurisdiction* is laid down in section 7 of chapter one SL. Finnish law applies for offences where the punishability of the act is based on an international agreement binding on Finland. This principle, concerning international offences, is based on several international treaties demanding States to extend the applicability of their criminal law in the extent of the treaties.

1.3. The relationship between jurisdictional rules and the scope of the criminal provisions

Contrary to the general departing point in the SL, which considers the offences possible to be committed anywhere and by anyone and does not have requirements in relation to the object of the offence, there are some offences that require a closer connection to Finland. The starting point for offences outside the SL is that Finnish jurisdiction is not applicable, unless the offences have a connection to Finland. As an example, Finnish jurisdiction does not apply for tax offences against Spanish tax laws. These offences can be categorised in three different groups.[10]

First of all, some offences require special circumstances in relation to the *offender*. The offender has to be a debtor (chapter 39 SL), a public official (chapter 40 SL), a soldier (chapter 45 SL) or an employer (chapter 47 SL). These offences all have the fact in common that the offender shall be Finnish, for the provisions to apply. Abuse of public office pursuant to section 7 of chapter 40 SL therefore requires that the public official, the offender, is Finnish. The offence can be committed abroad. There are some exceptions to these special circumstances in relation to the offender, such as that some provisions of offences in office also apply for foreign public officials, in situations of the public official being based in Finland doing preliminary investigation, which again is based on international agreements.

Secondly, some offences have specific requirements in relation to the *place of commission* of the offence. Offences such as border offence, territorial violation and illegal immigration (sections 7, 7b and 8 of chapter 17 SL) all require that the offence is related to the Finnish border. The same applies for smuggling (section 4 of chapter 46 SL), in relation to import and export.

Thirdly, some objects of the offence constitute a Finnish phenomenon. Offences against the administration of justice (chapter 15 SL) apply in relation to the Finnish judicial system. A false denunciation given in a German court cannot therefore be punished pursuant to section 6 of chapter 15 SL in Finland. There are some exceptions in relation to legal assistance given by a foreign court to a Finnish court (section 12 of the same chapter). The provisions on offences against public authorities (chapter 16 SL) should generally be applied when offences are directed at Finnish public authorities. There are however some exceptions to this, such as in relation to bribery, where the public authority can be a foreign one. Furthermore are electoral offences (*valbrott*), offences against public finances (when not directed against the EU), business offences and data and communications offences (respectively chapters 14, 29, 30 and 38 SL) considered offences which constitute a Finnish phenomenon and therefore these provisions are applicable only in relation to Finnish society.[11]

---

10. The division of groups is based on *Frände* (2004), pp. 329-332.
11. See further *Frände* (2004), pp. 329-332 on more details.

1.4. Impact of foreign law

The *double criminality principle* is relevant in relation to the *active and passive personality principles* and the *principle of representational jurisdiction* (sections 5, 6 and 8 of chapter one SL). Pursuant to section 11(1) of chapter one SL, if the offence has been committed in the territory of a foreign state, the application of Finnish criminal law pursuant to sections 5, 6 or 8 can take place only if the offence is punishable also under the law of the place of the commission. This requires that a sentence could have been passed for the offence in a court in that foreign state. In such a situation, the sanction in Finland shall not be more severe than what is provided by the law of the place of commission.

Double criminality is required as a general principle when applying Finnish law to an offence committed outside Finland by a Finnish citizen, to offences directed at a Finn and to offences committed outside Finland pursuant to section 8 of chapter one SL. The *double criminality principle* applies *in concreto*. The provision 11(1) expressly requires that the offender could have been sentenced for the offence in the place of commission. When examining the double criminality, a Finnish court should take criminal and procedural norms (such as grounds of excuse and time limitation of the offence) into account, as well as case law of the place of commission.

The *double criminality principle* should be assessed in accordance with the *lex mitior* principle. If the legislation in the place of commission has been amended between the time of the offence and court proceedings, the more lenient legislation should be applied.

Furthermore is the principle of *poena mitior* applicable. No sanction more severe than prescribed in the place of commission should be imposed. This means that a Finnish court must take into account not only the prescribed penalty, but also the relevant circumstances that would have affected the penalty scale, which would have been relevant for a court in the place of commission.[12] Possibly the Finnish court should also compare different forms of penalties in order to determine the most lenient sanction.[13]

---

12. Government Bill RP 1/1996 p. 26, where it is stated: "Om t.ex. straff för brottet skall dömas ut enligt en lindrigare straffskala på grund av en omständighet som nämns i lagen på gärningsorten, bestämmer denna lindrigare straffskala det maximistraff som kan dömas i Finland, även om motsvarande omständigheter inte enligt finsk lag anses som en förmildrande omständighet."
13. *Frände* (2004), p. 339. An example of this is where the offender would have been sentenced only to a financial penalty at the place of commission, and the normal

An exception is stated in section 11(2). Even if the offence is not punishable under the law of the place of commission Finnish law applies to the offence, if it has been committed by a Finnish citizen or a person permanently resident in Finland. This applies if the offence is:

- a war crime or aggravated war crime referred to in article 15 of the second protocol to the 1954 Hague Convention for the Protection of Cultural Property in the Event of Armed Conflict or an act of participation into said acts
- an offence against administration of justice (e.g. false statement, false denunciation, falsification of evidence and threatening a person to be heard in the administration of justice) by the International Criminal Court
- distribution of sexually obscene pictures, aggravated distribution of sexually obscene pictures depicting children and possession of sexually obscene pictures depicting children
- sexual abuse of a child, aggravated sexual abuse of a child and purchase of sexual services from a young person
- pandering and aggravated pandering, if the act is directed at a person below the age of eighteen years.

In relation to sexual offences directed at children, Finland has, as the other Nordic countries tried to be a forerunner in relation to prosecution of such offences. Double criminality is therefore not required. Before the revision of 1996, the *double criminality principle* was only required to a limited extent, and the limitation has now been extended.

1.5. Impact of foreign judgments
Before the revision in 1996, foreign judgments did not have a *res judicata* effect in Finnish criminal proceedings. In relation to legal certainty, it was considered important that foreign judgments would have similar effects as national ones. Foreign judgments should function as obstacles for repeated proceedings of the same offence.[14]

Section 13 of chapter one SL states that:

Finnish penalty would be a suspended sentence. In such a situation, the Finnish court should impose a financial penalty.

14. Government Bill RP 1/1996 pp. 28-29.

(1) Charges may not be brought in Finland if a judgment has already been passed and has become final in the State where the act was committed or in another member state of the European Union and
1. the charge was dismissed,
2. the defendant was found guilty but punishment was waived,
3. the sentence was enforced or its enforcement is still in progress or
4. under the law of the State where the judgment was passed, the sentence has lapsed.

(2) The provisions of subsection 1 notwithstanding, the Prosecutor-General [Director of public prosecution] may order that the charge be brought in Finland if the judgment passed abroad was not based on a request of a Finnish authority for a judgment or on a request for extradition granted by the Finnish authorities and
1. under section 3, the offence is deemed to be directed at Finland,
2. the offence is an offence in public office or a military offence referred to in section 4,

(3) the offence is an international offence referred to in section 7, or

(4) pursuant to section 10, the offence is deemed to have been committed also in Finland. However, the Prosecutor-General [Director of public prosecution] shall not order charges to be brought for an offence that has been partially committed in the territory of that member state of the European Union where the judgment was passed.

The main rule is that charges may not be brought in Finland if a judgment has been passed and become final in the state where the offence was committed. This applies also if the judgment has become final in another Member State of the EU. A foreign judgment has this effect if the case has been decided on its merits, and also in situations where the charge was dismissed or the prosecution was waived.[15] If the case has been dismissed on procedural grounds, it does not have this effect. The exception listed in paragraph 2 makes it possible for the Prosecutor-General to order that charges be brought in Finland although a foreign final judgment exists. An example of such a situation is if a foreign trial has not taken Finnish interests into account to a reasonable extent or the trial has been a mock trial.[16] The second paragraph of section 13 then enumerates the cases in which a prosecution order can be given. These correspond to article 55 CISA and the relevant provisions in the European conventions on the international validity of criminal judgments and the transfer of proceedings in criminal matters.[17]

---

15. See section 12 of chapter six SL on waiver of prosecution.
16. Government Bill RP 1/1996 p. 29.
17. Finland has not ratified these conventions, see   http://conventions.coe.int/Treaty/-Commun/ChercheSig.asp?NT=070&CM=8&DF= 07/10/ 2011&CL=ENG and

It is furthermore possible pursuant to section 14 of chapter six SL to make a deduction of punishment imposed abroad. If the person in Finland is sentenced for an offence for which he has already served a sanction imposed abroad fully or partly, a reasonable amount shall be deducted from the sentence to be imposed. If the sanction served was a custodial sentence, the court shall deduct the corresponding time to the loss of liberty. This section corresponds to article 56 CISA.

1.6. Restrictions on prosecution

The scope of application of the provisions of Finnish criminal jurisdiction is rather extensive. Finnish jurisdiction can apply even if the connection to Finland is not close. In such situations another state usually also has jurisdiction. The *principle of legality* applies in Finnish criminal procedure. A procedure has therefore been deemed necessary for determining if individual cases are to be prosecuted in Finland. The highest prosecutorial agency in Finland, the Prosecutor-General, (*Riksåklagaren*) does this examination.

Pursuant to section 12 of chapter one SL:

(1) A criminal case may not be investigated in Finland without a prosecution order by the Prosecutor-General, where
1. the offence was committed abroad, or
2. a foreigner has committed an offence on board a foreign vessel when the vessel was in Finnish territorial waters or on board a foreign aircraft when the aircraft was in Finnish air space and the offence was not directed at Finland, a Finnish citizen, a foreigner permanently resident in Finland or a Finnish corporation, foundation or other legal entity.

(2) However, the order by the Prosecutor-General is not be required, if
1. the offence was committed by a Finnish citizen or a person who, under section 6, is equivalent to a Finnish citizen and it was directed at Finland, a Finnish citizen, a foreigner permanently resident in Finland, or a Finnish corporation, foundation or other legal entity,
2. the offence was committed in Denmark, Iceland, Norway or Sweden and the competent public prosecutor of the place of commission has requested that the offence be tried in a Finnish court,
3. the offence was committed aboard a Finnish vessel while on the high seas or in territory not belonging to any State or aboard a Finnish aircraft while it was in or over such territory,
4. the offence was committed aboard a vessel or aircraft while it was in scheduled traffic between points in Finland or between a point in Finland and a point in Denmark, Iceland, Norway or Sweden,

http://conventions.coe.int/Treaty/Commun/ChercheSig.asp?NT=073&CM =8&DF-=07/10/ 2011 &CL=ENG.

5. the offence is to be tried as a criminal case in accordance with the Military Court Procedure Act (326/1983), or
6. there is a statutory provision to the effect that the President of the Republic or Parliament is to order any charges to be brought.

The principal rule is therefore that a prosecution order by the Prosecutor-General is required for prosecution in Finnish courts of offences committed abroad. The exceptions are listed in section 12(2). The first exception concerns situations where both the offender and the object of the offence have internationally recognised connections to Finland. The second situation is based on the Nordic agreement of 1970 on the proceedings of bringing charges in another Nordic country than the one where the offence was committed.[18] The third situation does not require a prosecution order as the offence has strong connections to Finland and a conflict or jurisdiction seems unlikely. The fourth situation completes the third, as this one covers offences committed in the territory of another state or on board a non-Finnish vessel or aircraft. The fifth situation of military court proceedings does not require a prosecution order due to the special circumstances in such cases. Lastly, the sixth situation can for example be based on section 114 of the Finnish Constitution. According to this section, the decision to bring a charge against a Member of the Government for unlawful conduct in the office is made by the Parliament, after having obtained an opinion from the Constitutional Law Committee (*grundlagsutskottet*). As the power to initiate proceedings or not is reserved to the Parliament, it was not considered possible to restrict this through a prosecution order.[19]

From the statistics from the Office of the Prosecutor-General, we can see that in the recent years, the Prosecutor-General has issued prosecution orders for offences committed abroad mainly in situations of sexual abuse of children or buying sexual services from children, aggravated drug offences, assaults and concealment offences. In some situations prosecution orders were issued in relation to genocide, environmental offences in the Finnish Economic Zone and firearms offences.[20]

18. Nordiskt samarbetsavtal om lagföring i annat nordiskt land än det där brottet förövats, Oslo 6 February 1970.
19. Government bill RP 1/1996 pp. 26-28.
20. See the Annual reports of the Office of the Prosecutor General from years 2005 to 2009 (Valtakunnansyyttäjän vuosikertomus, available in Finnish on http://www.vksv.oikeus.fi/Etusivu /Julkaisut/Vuosikertomus).

2. The Rules on Jurisdiction in Detail

2.1. Territoriality principle

The *territoriality principle* is, as mentioned above, laid down in section 1(1) of chapter one SL: "Finnish law applies to an offence committed in Finland."

2.1.1. Localisation

The place of commission is defined in section 10 of chapter one SL. According to this section:

(1) An offence is deemed to have been committed both where the criminal act was committed and where the consequence contained in the statutory definition of the offence became apparent. An offence of omission is deemed to have been committed both where the perpetrator should have acted and where the consequence contained in the statutory definition of the offence became apparent.

(2) If the offence remains an attempt, it is deemed to have been committed also where, had the offence been completed, the consequence contained in the statutory definition of the offence either would probably have become apparent or would in the opinion of the perpetrator have become apparent.

(3) An offence by an inciter and abettor is deemed to have been committed both where the act of complicity was committed and where the offence by the offender is deemed to have been committed.

(4) If there is no certainty as to the place of commission, but there is justified reason to believe that the offence was committed in the territory of Finland, said offence is deemed to have been committed in Finland.

The place of commission is defined based on the *principle of ubiquity*. It firstly concerns offences committed through active conduct. Both the place where the offence was committed and where the consequence contained in the statutory definition (and only then) of the offence are considered as places of commission. The definition of the place of commission includes offences of omission. This is considered firstly taking place where the perpetrator should have acted and secondly where the consequence contained in the statutory definition of the offence became apparent. It should be noted that Finnish criminal law makes a distinction between genuine and non-genuine offences of omission.

Genuine offences of omission are punishable pursuant to section 3(1) of chapter 3 SL, if this is specifically provided in the statutory definition of an offence. This applies for example for situations of neglect of rescue. Non-genuine offences of omission are punishable not based on specific statutory obligations to act, but on a person's legal duty to avoid consequences resulting from others. Pursuant to section 3(2) of the same chapter such a duty may be based on:

1. an office, function or position,
2. the relationship between the perpetrator and the victim,
3. the assumption of an assignment or a contract,
4. the action of the perpetrator in creating danger, or
5. another reason comparable to these.

An example of a non-genuine offence of omission is a situation where a domestic servant responsible for the care of elderly persons neglects to take care of these, which results in one or more elderly persons dying.

As can be seen in section 10(2) regulating attempt, the provision is based on the provision of completed offences. The place of commission is deemed as the place where the attempted offence was committed. The place of commission can also be the place where, had the offence been completed, the consequence contained in the statutory definition probably would have become apparent or would in the opinion of the offender have become apparent. When assessing where the consequences of the offence would become apparent, two criteria are applicable. Either an objective probability calculation is applied or a subjective, based on the offenders perception. The subjective perception of the offender should be taken into account also in situations where the consequences were intended to become apparent in Finland, but by chance these become apparent in another state. An example of this is if the offender intended to kill his victim with placing a bomb on a train destined for Finland, which is to detonate in Finland, and the bomb detonates in a foreign country due to the train being delayed. In such a situation, it is justified to regard Finland also as the place of commission.[21]

Section 10(3) regulates the place of commission in relation to complicity. Finnish criminal law applies the principle of accessory, which entails that the criminal responsibility for complicity is dependant on the punishability of the completed offence. Section 10(4) contains a complementary provision for cases where the place of commission cannot be established with certainty. For this to apply there needs to be a justified reason to believe that the offence was committed in Finland.

There are no specific rules in the SL in relation to so called cybercrimes, where the offence is committed on the internet. This is primarily solved by defining the place where the server is, as the place of commission.

---

21. Government Bill RP 1/1996 p. 24.

2.1.2. Definition of Finland

Finnish state territory is defined in international agreements and legislation other than criminal legislation. The state territory consists of its land and sea regions. Finnish jurisdiction is also extended to the airspace above these territories and the space below the surface and the seabed. This is done in accordance with the Convention on International Civil Aviation and the Convention on the Territorial Sea and the Contiguous Zone.[22] How high a state's airspace reaches is not clear, but it is considered to reach as high as customary air crafts can fly.[23]

Finland has retained the right to use and utilise its continental shelf. There are however no specific criminal law provisions regulating the application of Finnish criminal law on this area. Finland has also on an international level extended its criminal law to the continental shelf. Some offences committed on the continental shelf can fall under Finnish criminal jurisdiction in accordance with the provisions in chapter one SL.[24]

2.2. Flag state principle

Section 2 of chapter one SL regulates offences connected with a Finnish Vessel. It expresses the *flag state principle* and states the following:

(1) Finnish law applies to an offence committed on board a Finnish vessel or aircraft if the offence was committed
1. while the vessel was on the high seas or in territory not belonging to any State or while the aircraft was in or over such territory, or
2. while the vessel was in the territory of a foreign State or the aircraft was in or over such territory and the offence was committed by the master of the vessel or aircraft, a member of its crew, a passenger or a person who otherwise was on board.

(2) Finnish law also applies to an offence committed outside of Finland by the master of a Finnish vessel or aircraft or a member of its crew if, by the offence, the perpetrator has violated his or her special statutory duty as the master of the vessel or aircraft or a member of its crew.

Pursuant to international law and treaties, the flag state is to effectively exercise its jurisdiction over vessels sailing under its flag. Then again, the coastal state might in some situations have jurisdiction for offences committed

22. Convention on International Civil Aviation, known as Chicago Convention, signed on 7 December 1944 and Convention on the Territorial Sea and the Contiguous Zone, signed on 29 April 1958. UN Treaty Series, vol. 516, p. 205.
23. Government Bill RP 1/1996 p. 16.
24. Ibid.

aboard foreign vessels or aircrafts in the coastal state's territory. The Finnish legislator has considered it necessary to include a provision on this. There is no explicit definition of vessels or aircrafts in criminal law, but this was not considered necessary in relation to section 2 of chapter one SL. When interpreting this provision, not all smaller means of conveyance are to be considered equal to vessels and the criminal policy objectives should furthermore be relevant in this interpretation.[25]

Determining whether a vessel or aircraft is Finnish is primarily based on if the vessel or aircraft is registered in the Finnish ship or aircraft register. In situations of registration being unnecessary or omitted, the determination of a necessary connection to Finland should be made on a case by case evaluation.

The *flag state principle* applies first of all when the vessel or aircraft is on the high seas or in territory not belonging to any state. In situations of the vessel or aircraft being in or over a foreign state's territory, Finnish jurisdiction only applies for persons with a strong connection to Finland, such as the master of the vessel or aircraft or a member of its crew. Finnish jurisdiction is furthermore extended to cover offences committed outside of Finland by such persons with a strong connection to Finland, if the perpetrator by the offence has violated his special statutory duty. Some particular statutory duties have been assigned to the master and crew of aircrafts and vessels through special legislation. This concerns for example the safety of the ship and rescuing people at distress at sea.[26]

2.3. Active personality principle

This principle is laid down in section 6 of chapter one SL, which states that:

(1) Finnish law applies to an offence committed outside of Finland by a Finnish citizen. If the offence was committed in territory not belonging to any State, a precondition for the imposition of punishment is that, under Finnish law, the act is punishable by imprisonment for more than six months.

(2) A person who was a Finnish citizen at the time of the offence or is a Finnish citizen at the beginning of the court proceedings is deemed to be a Finnish citizen.

(3) The following are deemed equivalent to a Finnish citizen:
1. a person who was permanently resident in Finland at the time of the offence or is permanently resident in Finland at the beginning of the court proceedings, and

---

25. Government bill RP 1/1996 pp. 16-17.
26. Ibid. pp. 17-18.

2. a person who was apprehended in Finland and who at the beginning of the court proceedings is a citizen of Denmark, Iceland, Norway or Sweden or at that time is permanently resident in one of those countries.

The scope of application of Finnish criminal law is extended to offences committed by Finns in the territory of a foreign state. This is based on the Constitutional ban to extradite or deport Finnish citizens (mentioned above in chapter 1.2.). The *double criminality principle* further restricts the principle of active personality (mentioned above in chapter 1.4). The *principle of active personality* is today more based on international solidarity than an expression of Finnish citizens' allegiance to Finnish legislation when abroad. In situations where the offence has been committed in territory not belonging to any state, a precondition is that the act is punishable by imprisonment for more than six months under Finnish law. This extension of Finnish law has been considered necessary only for more serious offences.[27]

In relation to citizenship, both the time of the offence and the beginning of the court proceedings is taken into account. The idea here is that no one shall avoid criminal prosecution by changing citizenship. The provision further states that persons permanently resident in Finland at either of these situations should be considered equivalent to a Finnish citizen. It further states that Nordic citizens are considered equivalent to Finnish citizens, which is based on the Nordic countries considering persons domiciled in the Nordic countries as equal to their own nationals.[28]

There are specific provisions regulating offences in public office and military offences. Pursuant to section 4 of chapter one SL,

(1) Finnish law applies to an offence referred to in chapter 40 of this Code that has been committed outside of Finland by a person referred to in chapter 40, section 11, paragraphs (1), (2), (3) and (5).

(2) Finnish law also applies to an offence referred to in chapter 45 that has been committed outside of Finland by a person subject to the provisions of that chapter.

To extend Finnish jurisdiction to offences committed in public office and military offences was considered necessary due to the offences being directed directly at the state or a public body. A specific provision was needed, as these offences are nationally restricted which could signify that the double criminality principle would not be fulfilled.

27. Government Bill RP 1/1996 p. 21.
28. Ibid.

Chapter 40 SL concerns offences in office and offences committed by employees of public bodies. The specific persons mentioned in section 4(1) SL are public officials, persons elected to a public office (however excluding members of Parliament), employees of a public corporation and persons exercising public authority. Chapter 45 concerns military offences. These apply for soldiers, which are defined in section 27 of that chapter. Generally and according to international law, the criminal law (of the state of commission) cannot be applied for military offences committed by soldiers of a foreign country. It was regarded justified nevertheless to extend the applicability of Finnish criminal law to military offences committed by persons referred to in chapter 45 due to sustaining order and general preventive reasons.[29]

2.4. Passive personality principle

The *passive personality principle* is expressed in section 5 of chapter one SL:

Finnish law applies to an offence committed outside of Finland that has been directed at a Finnish citizen, a Finnish corporation, foundation or other legal entity, or a foreigner permanently resident in Finland if, under Finnish law, the act may be punishable by imprisonment for more than six months.

The previous broad scope of this principle was in 1996 considered problematic from an international law perspective. In the *travaux préparatoires* it was stated that the legislation in the place of commission in most cases offers a sufficient and effective protection for Finnish citizens, persons permanently residing in Finland and Finnish entities. For situations where fairly serious offences directed at these groups of interest would go unpunished, the provision laying down the *passive personality principle* was considered justified.[30]

The scope of application of Finnish jurisdiction is however restricted to fairly serious offences directed at Finns. The requirement of six months refers to the maximum punishment imposed for the act, not to the concrete punishment in a particular case. The *double criminality principle* (mentioned in chapter 1.4.) further restricts the application of the *passive personality principle*.

2.5. Principle of state protection

As mentioned earlier, the *passive personality principle* concerns private interests. The *principle of state protection* concerns particular interests of the

29. Ibid., p. 19.
30. Government Bill RP 1/1996 p. 20.

Finnish state. Section 3 of chapter one SL regulates offences directed at Finland, and it states:

(1) Finnish law applies to an offence committed outside of Finland that has been directed at Finland.

(2) An offence is deemed to have been directed at Finland
1. if it is an offence of treason or high treason,
2. if the act has otherwise seriously violated or endangered the national, military or economic rights or interests of Finland, or
3. if it has been directed at a Finnish authority.

This provision was considered necessary in order to sufficiently protect Finnish public or state interests, as foreign states cannot be presumed to offer such protection.[31] Most of the cases falling under section 3(1) will also fall under the scope of application of Finnish criminal law as the consequences of the offence becomes apparent in Finland (in such cases Finnish criminal law applies based on section 1 of chapter one SL). To further stipulate, the *principle of state protection* was however considered necessary in order to apply Finnish criminal law in situations where the offence cannot be deemed to have been committed in Finland. The application of the provision does not require that the offence is criminalised in the place of commission, and therefore double criminality is not required.[32]

According to the second paragraph of section 3 an offence is deemed to have been directed at Finland firstly if it is an offence of treason or high treason. The definition of treason offences is found in chapter 12 SL. These include: compromising the sovereignty of Finland, incitement to war, treason and aggravated treason, espionage and aggravated espionage, disclosure of a national secret and negligent disclosure of a national secret, unlawful intelligence operations, violation of the rules of neutrality and treasonable conspiracy. Offences of high treason are defined in chapter 13 SL. These include: high treason and aggravated high treason, preparation of high treason and unlawful military operations.

An offence is secondly considered to be directed at Finland if it otherwise has seriously violated or endangered the national, military or economic rights or interests of Finland. This applies only for serious violations of these interests. The assessment of the seriousness of the offence is to be made on a case

31. Ibid., p. 18.
32. Ibid.

by case evaluation. Examples of offences falling under the scope of this provision are giving bribes, some forgery offences and environmental offences.[33]

An offence is thirdly deemed to have been directed at Finland if it has been directed at a Finnish authority. An example of this is a Finnish diplomat abroad. The purpose of this provision is to safeguard important state interests, which was not considered possible without an explicit provision. Otherwise some difficulties might arise when interpreting whether or not the conditions for applying other provisions on the application of Finnish criminal law are present.[34]

2.6. Principle of universal jurisdiction

The *principle of universal jurisdiction* is laid down in section 7 of chapter one SL. This section states:

(1) Finnish law applies to an offence committed outside of Finland where the punishability of the act, regardless of the law of the place of commission, is based on an international agreement binding on Finland or on another statute or regulation internationally binding on Finland (international offence). Further provisions on the application of this section shall be issued by Decree.

(2) Regardless of the law of the place of commission, Finnish law applies also to a nuclear explosive offence or the preparation of an endangerment offence that is to be deemed an offence referred to in the Comprehensive Nuclear Test Ban Treaty (Treaties of Finland 15/2001)

(3) Regardless of the law of the place of commission, Finnish law applies also to trafficking in persons, aggravated trafficking in persons and an offence referred to in chapter 34a committed outside of Finland. (650/2004).

The first paragraph of section 7 lays down the *principle of universal jurisdiction*. This is based on several international treaties requiring states acceding to them to extend their application of criminal law to offences defined in the treaties. Some treaties also require the *principle of universal jurisdiction* to be applied to offences in the treaties. In relation to the *principle of legality*, it is considered important that the offences, for which the *principle of universal jurisdiction* applies, are listed in the legislation. Before the revision of 1996, the offences were listed in the provision. After the revision, and due to the

---

33. Government Bill RP 1/1996, p. 18.
34. Ibid., pp. 18-19.

constantly changing nature of international law, to include the relevant offences in a Decree that is easier to amend, was considered sufficient.[35]

Therefore, the first paragraph of section 7 is a general clause stating that Finnish law applies to international offences regardless of the law of the place of the commission and that further provisions are found in a Decree.[36] This Decree then lists the types of offences that are to be considered as international offences. Today these are the following:

(1) counterfeiting currency, the preparation of the counterfeiting of currency, or the use of counterfeited currency, referred to in the International Convention for the Suppression of Counterfeiting Currency (Treaties of Finland 47/1936) and counterfeiting of the euro referred to in article 7, paragraph 2 of the Council framework decision of 29 May 2000, on increasing protection by criminal penalties and other sanctions against counterfeiting in connection with the introduction of the euro (Official Journal L 140, 14 June 2000), (370/2001)

(2) a crime against humanity, aggravated crime against humanity, war crime and aggravated war crime defined in the Charter of Rome of the International Criminal Court (Treaties of Finland 56/2002) or other corresponding punishable criminal act which should be deemed a grave breach of the Geneva Conventions for the Amelioration of the Condition of the Wounded and Sick in Armed Forces in the Field, for the Amelioration of the Condition of the Wounded, Sick and Shipwrecked Members of Armed Forces at Sea, Relative to the Treatment of Prisoners of War, and Relative to the Protection of Civilian Persons in Time of War (Treaties of Finland 8/1955), as well as the Protocol Additional to the Geneva Conventions, and relating to the protection of victims of international armed conflicts (Treaties of Finland 82/1980), (286/2008)

(3) genocide and the preparation of genocide referred to in the Convention on the prevention and Punishment of the Crime of Genocide (Treaties of Finland 5/1960)

(4) a narcotics offence, aggravated narcotics offence, preparation of a narcotics offence, promotion of a narcotics offences, promotion of an aggravated narcotics offence, and concealment offence as referred to in the Single Convention on Narcotic Drugs of 1961 (Treaties of Finland 43/1965), the Protocol amending the Single Convention on Narcotic Drugs of 1961 (Treaties of Finland 42/1975), the Convention on psychotropic substances (Treaties of Finland 60/1976), and the United Nations Convention against illicit traffic in narcotic drugs and psychotropic substances (Treaties of Finland 44/1994), (1014/2006)

(5) such seizure of aircraft or other punishable act by which the perpetrator unlawfully, by force or threat thereof, seizes or exercises control of an aircraft, that is to be deemed an of-

---

35. Government Bill RP 1/1996 p. 22.
36. Decree on the application of chapter 1, section 7 of the Criminal Code (627/1996).

fence referred to in the Convention for the suppression of unlawful seizure of aircraft (Treaties of Finland 62/1971),

(6) such criminal traffic mischief or aggravated criminal mischief, preparation of an endangerment offence or other punishable act that is to be deemed an offence referred to in the Convention for the Suppression of Unlawful Acts Against the Safety of Civil Aviation (Treaties of Finland 56/1973),

(7) murder, assault or deprivation of liberty directed against the person of an internationally protected person, or violent attack upon the official premises, the private accommodation or the means of transport of such a person, or a threat thereof, referred to in the Convention on the Prevention and Punishment of Crimes against Internationally Protected Persons, including Diplomatic Agents (Treaties of Finland 63/1978),

(8) taking of a hostage or other deprivation of liberty referred to in the International Convention against the Taking of Hostages (Treaties of Finland 38/1983),

(9) such torture for the purpose of obtaining a confession, assault, aggravated assault or other punishable act that is to be deemed torture referred to in the Convention against Torture and Other Cruel, Inhuman or Degrading Treatment or Punishment (Treaties of Finland 60/1989),

(10) such nuclear device offence, endangerment of health, nuclear energy use offence or other punishable act directed at or committed by using nuclear material that is be deemed an offence referred to in the Convention on the Physical Protection of Nuclear Material (Treaties of Finland 72/1989),

(11) such deprivation of liberty, aggravated deprivation of liberty, abduction, sabotage, endangerment or other punishable act that is to be deemed an offence referred to in the European Convention on the Suppression of Terrorism (Treaties of Finland 16/1990), (353/1997)

(12) homicide, assault, deprivation of liberty or robbery directed at a person on board a vessel or aircraft, or seizure, theft or damage of a vessel, aircraft or property on board a vessel or aircraft that is to be deemed piracy as referred to in the United Nations Convention on the Law of the Seas (Treaties of Finland 50/1996), (118/1999)

(13) such violation of the prohibition of chemical weapons referred to in the Convention on the Prohibition of the Development, Production, Stockpiling and Use of Chemical Weapons and on their Destruction (Treaties of Finland 19/1997), (118/1999)

(13a) such violation of the prohibition of biological weapons referred to in the Protocol for the Prohibition of the Use in War of Asphyxiating, Poisonous or other Gases, and of Bacteriological Methods of Warfare (Treaties of Finland 23/1929) and the Convention on the Prohibition of the Development, Production and Stockpiling of Bacteriological (Biological) and Toxin Weapons and on their Destruction (Treaties of Finland 15/1975), (286/2008)

(13b) such violation of the prohibition of the use, stockpiling, production and transfer of anti-personnel mines and on their destruction as referred to in the Convention Treaties of Finland 13/2012, in force from 1.7.2012)

(14) such unlawful act directed against the safety of maritime navigation that is referred to in the Convention for the Suppression of Unlawful Acts against the Safety of Maritime Navigation (Treaties of Finland 11/1999), (537/2000)

(15) such unlawful act that is directed against the safety of fixed platforms located on the continental shelf as is referred to in the Protocol for the Suppression of Unlawful Acts against the Safety of Fixed Platforms Located on the Continental Shelf (Treaties of Finland 44/2000), (739/2001)

(16) such crime against United Nations and associated personnel as is referred to in the Convention on the Safety of United Nations and Associated Personnel (Treaties of Finland 2-3/2001), (510/2002)

(17) such offence against a place of public use, state or government facility, a public transportation system or an infrastructure facility as is referred to in the International Convention for the Suppression of Terrorist Bombings (Treaties of Finland 60/2002),

(18) such financing of terrorism as is referred to in the International Convention for the Suppression of the Financing of Terrorism (Treaties of Finland 74/2002), (859/2003)

(19) such willful killing or causing of serious injury to civilians as is referred to in the Protocol on Prohibitions or Restrictions on the Use of Mines, Booby-traps and other Devices as amended on 3 May 1996 (Treaties of Finland 91/1998), (859/2003).

(20) nuclear terrorism referred to in the International Convention for the Suppression of Acts of Nuclear Terrorism (Treaties of Finland 6/2009).

Punishable attempt of and punishable participation in such an offence is also considered an international offence.

The second and third paragraphs of section 7 list some further situations of when the principle of universal jurisdiction applies. For these offences the principle of universality applies, regardless of the law of the place of commission. Based on international customary law, certain crimes are to be subjected to the principle of universal jurisdiction. These are the core crimes of international law, which can be punished regardless of international conventions or national legislation. Such offences are e.g. piracy, war crimes and crimes against humanity.[37] These offences are not included in section 7, as it was not considered necessary.[38]

2.7. Principle of representational jurisdiction

The *principle of representational jurisdiction* is prescribed in section 8 of chapter one SL. This section states:

Finnish law applies to an offence committed outside of Finland which, under Finnish law, may be punishable by imprisonment for more than six months, if the State in whose territory the offence was committed has requested that charges be brought in a Finnish court or that the offender be extradited because of the offence, but the extradition request has not been granted.

Finnish criminal law can therefore be applied to offences, which have no further link to Finland (pursuant to sections 1 to 7 of chapter one SL), when the alleged offender is present in Finland. This applies, as the perpetrator could otherwise avoid criminal responsibility. This is connected to the fact that the perpetrator cannot be extradited or the state where the offence was committed has requested a transfer of criminal proceedings.[39] The *principle of representational jurisdiction* is considered a form for international legal assistance and is based mainly on international solidarity in crime combating.[40] The *double criminality principle* (see chapter 1.D.) applies to section 8. The requirement can be considered forming the basis for applying the *principle of representational jurisdiction*. Section 8 applies only when the state where the offence

---

37. The first case where a Finnish court has tried a foreign national for core crimes committed abroad is the Bazaramba case. Bazaramba, a Rwandan national was prosecuted in Finland for genocide committed in Rwanda. The Appellate Court sentenced, as did the District Court Bazaramba to a life sentence for genocide. A leave of appeal (*besvärstillstånd*) to the Supreme Court was not granted, and the sentence of the Appellate Court is legally binding. See *Minna Kimpimäki*: Sotarikollisia ja merirosvoja – Suomen rikosoikeudellisen toimivallan rajat, Lakimies 5/2011, pp. 890-898, and *Mikaela Heikkilä*: Ajatuksia laillisuusperiaatteen merkityksestä universaalitoimivaltapatauksissa: Bazaramba-tapaus ja Suomen kansainvälinen rikosoikeus, Lakimies 5/2011, pp. 912-932 on the case.
38. Government Bill RP 1/1996 p. 22.
39. Ibid., pp. 22-23.
40. *Minna Kimpimäki*, Universaaliperiaate kansainvälisessä rikosoikeudessa, Jyväskylä 2005, p. 73. Examples of relevant international conventions are the UN Convention on the Prevention and Punishment of Crimes against Internationally Protected Persons, including Diplomatic Agents of 14 December 1973. UN Treaty Series, vol. 1035, p. 167 (article 3(2)) and the UN International Convention against the Taking of Hostages, adopted 17 December 1979, UN Treaty Series 1983, p. 206 (article 5(2)).

was committed has requested that charges are to be brought in a Finnish court or that the offender is to be extradited but the extradition request has not been granted.

3. Abbreviations

CISA	Convention Implementing the Schengen Agreement, Official Journal L 239/19, 22.09.2000.
IAEA	International Atomic Energy Agency
RP	Government Bill (Regeringens Proposition)
SL	Finnish Criminal Code, Act 1889/39

4. The Jurisdictional Rules of the Finnish Criminal Code in English translation. The Penal Code of Finland Chapter 1 – Scope of application of the criminal law of Finland

Section 1 – Offence committed in Finland
(1) Finnish law applies to an offence committed in Finland.

(2) The application of Finnish law to an offence committed in Finland's economic zone is subject to the Act on the Economic Zone of Finland (1058/2004) and the Act on the Environmental Protection of Seafaring (1672/2009).

Section 2 – Offence connected with a Finnish vessel
(1) Finnish law applies to an offence committed on board a Finnish vessel or aircraft if the offence was committed
1. while the vessel was on the high seas or in territory not belonging to any State or while the aircraft was in or over such territory, or
2. while the vessel was in the territory of a foreign State or the aircraft was in or over such territory and the offence was committed by the master of the vessel or aircraft, a member of its crew, a passenger or a person who otherwise was on board.

(2) Finnish law also applies to an offence committed outside of Finland by the master of a Finnish vessel or aircraft or a member of its crew if, by the offence, the offender has violated his/her special statutory duty as the master of the vessel or aircraft or a member of its crew.

Section 3 – Offence directed at Finland
(1) Finnish law applies to an offence committed outside of Finland that has been directed at Finland.

(2) An offence is deemed to have been directed at Finland
1. if it is an offence of treason or high treason,
2. if the act has otherwise seriously violated or endangered the national, military or economic rights or interests of Finland, or
3. if it has been directed at a Finnish authority.

Section 4 – Offence in public office and military offence
(1) Finnish law applies to an offence referred to in chapter 40 of this Code that has been committed outside of Finland by a person referred to in chapter 40, section 11, paragraphs 1, 2, 3 and 5 (604/2002).

(2) Finnish law also applies to an offence referred to in chapter 45 that has been committed outside of Finland by a person subject to the provisions of that chapter.

Section 5 – Offence directed at a Finn
Finnish law applies to an offence committed outside of Finland that has been directed at a Finnish citizen, a Finnish corporation, foundation or other legal entity, or a foreigner permanently resident in Finland if, under Finnish law, the act may be punishable by imprisonment for more than six months.

Section 6 – Offence committed by a Finn
(1) Finnish law applies to an offence committed outside of Finland by a Finnish citizen. If the offence was committed in territory not belonging to any State, it is a precondition for the imposition of punishment that, under Finnish law, the act is punishable by imprisonment for more than six months.

(2) A person who was a Finnish citizen at the time of the offence or is a Finnish citizen at the beginning of the trial is deemed to be a Finnish citizen.

(3) The following are deemed equivalent to a Finnish citizen:
1. a person who was permanently resident in Finland at the time of the offence or is permanently resident in Finland at the beginning of the trial, and
2. a person who was apprehended in Finland and who at the beginning of the trial is a citizen of Denmark, Iceland, Norway or Sweden or at that time is permanently resident in one of those countries.

Section 7 – International offence
(1) Finnish law applies to an offence committed outside of Finland where the punishability of the act, regardless of the law of the place of commission, is based on an international agreement binding on Finland or on another statute or regulation internationally binding on Finland (international offence).

(2) Further provisions on the application of this section shall be issued by Decree.

(3) Regardless of the law of the place of commission, Finnish law applies also to an offence referred to in chapter 34a committed outside of Finland. (17/2003)

Chapter 2. Finland

Section 8 – Other offence committed outside of Finland

Finnish law applies to an offence committed outside of Finland which, under Finnish law, may be punishable by imprisonment for more than six months, if the State in whose territory the offence was committed has requested that charges be brought in a Finnish court or that the offender be extradited because of the offence, but the extradition request has not been granted.

Section 9 – Corporate criminal liability

If, under this chapter, Finnish law applies to the offence, Finnish law applies also to the determination of corporate criminal liability.

Section 10 – Place of commission

(1) An offence is deemed to have been committed both where the criminal act was committed and where the consequence contained in the statutory definition of the offence became apparent. An offence of omission is deemed to have been committed both where the offender should have acted and where the consequence contained in the statutory definition of the offence became apparent.

(2) If the offence remains an attempt, it is deemed to have been committed also where, had the offence been completed, the consequence contained in the statutory definition of the offence either (i) would probably have become apparent or (ii) would in the opinion of the offender have become apparent.

(3) An offence by an inciter and abettor is deemed to have been committed both where the act of complicity was committed and where the offence by the offender is deemed to have been committed.

(4) If there is no certainty as to the place of commission, but there is justified reason to believe that the offence was committed in the territory of Finland, said offence is deemed to have been committed in Finland.

Section 11 – Requirement of dual criminality

(1) If the offence has been committed in the territory of a foreign State, the application of Finnish law may be based on sections 5, 6 and 8 only if the offence is punishable also under the law of the place of commission and a sentence could have been passed for it also by a court of that foreign State. In this event, a sanction that is more severe than what is provided by the law of the place of commission shall not be imposed in Finland.

(2) Even if the offence is not punishable under the law of the place of commission, Finnish law applies to it if it has been committed by a Finnish citizen or a person referred to in section 6(3)(1), and the penalty for it has been laid down in
1. sections 1-9 of chapter 15, by virtue of section 12a of the same chapter;
2. sections 1-3 of chapter 16 and even if the object of the offence is a person referred to in chapter 40, section 11, paragraph 2, 3 or 5 of a foreign public official who is in the service of the International Criminal Court;

3. sections 13, 14 and 14a of chapter 16 and even if the provisions are applied on the basis of section 20 of the same chapter;
4. section 18 or 19 of chapter 17;
5. sections 6-8 of chapter 20;
6. section 9 of chapter 20, where the act is directed at a person younger than eighteen years of age; or
7. sections 1-4 of chapter 40, where the offender is a member of Parliament, a foreign public official or a member of a foreign parliament. (604/2002)

Section 12 – Prosecution order by the Prosecutor-General [Director of public prosecution] (205/1997)

(1) A criminal case shall not be investigated in Finland without a prosecution order by the Prosecutor-General [Director of public prosecution], where
1. the offence was committed abroad, or
2. a foreigner has committed an offence on board a foreign vessel when the vessel was in Finnish territorial waters or on board a foreign aircraft when the aircraft was in Finnish air space and the offence was not directed at Finland, a Finnish citizen, a foreigner permanently resident in Finland or a Finnish corporation, foundation or other legal entity.

(2) However, the order by the Prosecutor-General [Director of public prosecution] is not be required, if
1. the offence was committed by a Finnish citizen or a person who, under section 6, is equivalent to a Finnish citizen and it was directed at Finland, a Finnish citizen, a foreigner permanently resident in Finland, or a Finnish corporation, foundation or other legal entity,
2. the offence was committed in Denmark, Iceland, Norway or Sweden and the competent public prosecutor of the place of commission has requested that the offence be tried in a Finnish court,
3. the offence was committed aboard a Finnish vessel while on the high seas or in territory not belonging to any State or aboard a Finnish aircraft while it was in or over such territory,
4. the offence was committed aboard a vessel or aircraft while it was in scheduled traffic between points in Finland or between a point in Finland and a point in Denmark, Iceland, Norway or Sweden,
5. the offence is to be tried as a criminal case in accordance with the Military Court Procedure Act (326/1983), or
6. there is a statutory provision to the effect that the President of the Republic or Parliament is to order any charges to be brought.

Section 13 – Foreign judgment

(1) A charge shall not be brought in Finland if a judgment has already been passed and has become final in the State where the act was committed or in another member state of the European Union and
1. the charge was dismissed,
2. the defendant was found guilty but punishment was waived,
3. the sentence was enforced or its enforcement is still in progress or

4. under the law of the State where the judgment was passed, the sentence has lapsed. (814/1998)

(2) The provisions of paragraph (1) notwithstanding, the Prosecutor-General [Director of public prosecution] may order that the charge be brought in Finland if the judgment passed abroad was not based on a request of a Finnish authority for a judgment or on a request for extradition granted by the Finnish authorities and

1. under section 3, the offence is deemed to be directed at Finland,
2. the offence is an offence in public office or a military offence referred to in section 4,
3. the offence is an international offence referred to in section 7, or
4. under section 10, the offence is deemed to have been committed also in Finland. However, the Prosecutor-General [Director of public prosecution] shall not order a charge to be brought for an offence that has been partially committed in the territory of that member state of the European Union where the judgment was passed. (814/1998)

(3) If a person is sentenced in Finland for an offence for which he/she has already served in full or in part a sanction imposed abroad, a reasonable amount shall be deducted from the sentence. If the sanction that has been imposed has been a custodial sentence, the court shall deduct from the sentence the time corresponding to the loss of liberty. The court may also note that the sanction that has been served is to be deemed a sufficient sanction for the offence.

Section 14 – Reference provision
Separate provisions apply to extradition on the basis of an offence and to other international legal assistance and to the immunity in certain cases of persons participating in a trial or a criminal investigation.

Section 15 – Treaties and international custom binding on Finland
If an international treaty binding on Finland or another statute or regulation that is internationally binding on Finland in some event restricts the scope of application of the criminal law of Finland, such a restriction applies as agreed. The provisions in this chapter notwithstanding, the restrictions on the scope of application of Finnish law based on generally recognised rules of international law also apply.

CHAPTER 3

Iceland

Ragnheiður Bragadóttir

1. General Basis[1]

1.1. Systematic classification of the rules on jurisdiction

The rules on the criminal jurisdiction of the Icelandic State are in Chapter I of the Icelandic Criminal Code (almenn hegningarlög, hgl.),[2] which is called the Basis of Criminal Liability, Scope of Criminal Law, etc. Criminal jurisdiction entails the power to enact criminal statutes and enforce them by investigation, Judgment and execution of punishment.[3] The provisions on criminal jurisdiction are in Sections 4-11 hgl., which primarily cover the place where offences are committed *(territorial jurisdiction)*. In some instances the provisions also cover by whom and against whom offences are committed *(active and passive personality principles)*. Also, Section 8 hgl. states that when a criminal case is commenced before an Icelandic court, the Judgment of the court regarding punishment and other consequences of an act shall be governed by Icelandic law. The same applies to the procedure of a case.[4]

Although these provisions deal with the limits respecting foreign criminal statutes and criminal courts, they are deemed to be Icelandic, not international, rules. These rules are therefore part of Icelandic criminal law. Despite this

---

1. Professor emeritus Jonatan Thormundsson read this article and made valuable comments on it. The author thanks him warmly for his contribution. Any errors are entirely the author's own.
2. The Icelandic Criminal Code, Act no. 19 of 12 February 1940, as amended.
3. *Jonatan Thormundsson*: Íslensk refsilögsaga, alþjóðlegar refsireglur og réttaraðstoð, Refsiréttur Almenni hlutinn I. (Icelandic jurisdictional law, international criminal law and legal assistance, Criminal Law General Part I), Reykjavik 1989, p. 9.
4. Ibid.

they have to be in harmony with the rules of jurisdiction of other states and international agreements on the subject, to facilitate communication with other countries in this area. Section 11 hgl. therefore states that the provisions of Sections 4-6 shall be applied subject to the limitations deriving from rules of international law. Also, the Icelandic State has the power to decide whether and to what extent it takes into account foreign statutes and criminal Judgments.[5] Thus, the State can limit its power by legislation, cf. Section 4, Section 8, Section 8 (a) and Section 8 (b), or by international agreements that have been implemented into Icelandic law. An example of such an agreement is the Bilateral Defence Agreement between Iceland and the United States and an Agreement on the Legal Status of the United States' forces and their property, cf. Act no. 110/1951; the agreement is legally valid in Iceland while the Bilateral Defence Agreement is in force. Upon the departure of the United States' Defence Force in 2006, amendments were made to the content of the agreement, based on changed circumstances.

Researchers writing about criminal jurisdiction in Icelandic law have not directly stated whether the rules are considered to be substantive or procedural rules. Criminal law doctrine considers criminal jurisdiction to be part of general criminal law. To that degree they are substantive rules. It is not completely clear whether failure to fulfil the conditions for criminal jurisdiction constitutes grounds for acquittal or dismissal from court, but it is more likely that it will lead to acquittal. The provisions of hgl. on criminal jurisdiction apply to all violations punishable under Icelandic law, whether the provisions are contained in the hgl. or in special criminal statutes.[6]

No comprehensive revision of the hgl.'s rules on criminal jurisdiction has been done since the enactment of the hgl. in 1940. The rules have therefore not been amended to the same extent as in other Nordic countries. Various amendments have nevertheless been made to the provisions of the act, first in 1973 and the last in 2012. These amendments will be discussed below in the appropriate places, but only two kinds of amendments are mentioned here. Firstly, many sub-clauses have been added to Section 6 hgl. relating to the interests rule.[7] The first is from an act passed in 1993 and the last from an act passed in 2012. Secondly, amendments were made to the act in 1993 because

---

5. Ibid.
6. Record of Althingi, Department A, 1939 (exposition accompanying the beginning of Chapter I).
7. Section 6 is a kind of catchall, i.e., on protective principle, principle of universal jurisdiction based on international conventions, and passive personality principle.

of the ratification of the European Convention on the International Validity of Criminal Judgments of 28 May 1970.

1.2. Outline of the principles of the law on jurisdiction

The *territoriality principle* is a fundamental principle on territorial jurisdiction; it is set out in Section 4 hgl. It states there that punishment shall be carried out in accordance with Icelandic criminal statutes for violations committed within the Icelandic State. Thus, the Icelandic State has jurisdiction over its sovereign territory, and Icelandic rules apply to everyone and everything in the State's domain. Icelandic criminal law covers all offences committed in Iceland, whether perpetrators and victims are Icelandic citizens or foreign citizens. This principle is based on the State's right of sovereignty and reasons of efficiency. From this main principle there are a few exceptions under national or international law.

Punishment should be carried out in accordance with Icelandic criminal statutes for offences committed on board Icelandic ships or aircraft wherever they were located when the offences were committed. This principle, the *flag state principle*, is stated in Section 4, no. 2 hgl.

The *active personality principle* (Section 5 hgl.) entails that the criminal jurisdiction of the Icelandic State extends to offences that Icelandic citizens or people residing in Iceland have committed abroad. If the defendant is a citizen or resident of Denmark, Finland, Norway or Sweden and is temporarily dwelling in Iceland, the principle can be applied, and he can be punished in accordance with Icelandic law even though he has committed an offence outside Iceland (Section 5 (2) hgl.). The rule of international law, *aut dedere aut judicare*, applies here, i.e., an offender must either be punished in the state where he is located or be extradited to the state where the offence was committed. This principle, by contrast with all the other principles, is based on the *principle of double criminality*, with exceptions in Section 5 (3).

The *passive personality principle* has limited application in Icelandic law. In Icelandic law there is no general rule on criminal proceedings in Iceland arising from punishable offences committed abroad against Icelandic interests. One exception to this is in Section 6, no. 3 hgl. In accordance with this provision, Icelandic criminal jurisdiction covers offences that, under the circumstances, are directed against the interests of Icelandic citizens or people residing in Iceland if committed outside the criminal jurisdiction of other States under International Law.

Important interests of the Icelandic State are protected under the *protective principle* (Section 6, no. 1 and 2 hgl.). These provisions state that punishment shall be in accordance with Icelandic criminal statutes for offences committed outside the Icelandic State, irrespective of who the perpetrator is: First, if offences are directed against the independence of the Icelandic State, its security, Constitution and government, official or administrative duties to the Icelandic State and against interests protected by Icelandic law because of close connection to the Icelandic State (Section 6, no. 1). Second, if the offence is in violation of duties that the perpetrator was obliged under Icelandic law to perform abroad, or is in violation of duties of employment on board an Icelandic vehicle, aircraft or vessel.

The *principle of universal jurisdiction* is generally entailed in Section 6, no. 4-22 hgl. Under these provisions punishment in accordance with Icelandic criminal statutes is possible for various offences where criminal liability is based on international agreements to which Iceland is a party. This principle applies even though the offence is committed outside the Icelandic State, irrespective of who the perpetrator is. The numbers in this article have increased greatly in recent years in an effort to ensure that Icelandic law meets the requirements for criminal jurisdiction in these agreements.

A rule based on the *principle of representational jurisdiction* is indirectly contained in Section 8 (a) (2) hgl. Sub-section 1 of the provision says that if a person has received a punitive sentence in a state where an offence was committed (Section 5 (1), no. 2), or in a state that is a party to the Convention on the International Validity of Criminal Judgments of 1970 or international agreements within the Schengen collaboration, upon fulfilment of certain conditions, an action against him shall not be commenced; he shall not be sentenced or penalties executed in Iceland for the same offence as he was convicted of in that state. Under Section 8 (a) (2), the provisions of Sub-section 1 do not pertain to offences falling under Section 4 and Section 6, no. 1 unless a criminal case has been commenced in the other state at the request of the Icelandic government.

1.3. The relationship between jurisdictional rules and the scope of the criminal provisions

The main rule is that Icelandic criminal provisions shall cover both foreign and domestic interests and foreign as well as Icelandic citizens. This pertains especially when offences are directed against life or limb, personal liberty, peace, honour or property.

On the other hand, some offences require closer connection to Iceland. Thus, criminal liability for an offence can be limited to Icelandic interests or Icelandic citizens. Such applies to various offences contrary to the provisions of Chapters X-XIV hgl. on treason, offences in violation of the State's Constitution or the highest level of government, offences against the authorities, disturbance of the peace and general rules on public order, as well as offences in public office. In Sections 86-88 hgl., dealing with treason, the Icelandic State is the object of the offence. Also, jurisdiction may be tied to location; thus, the offence must be committed in Icelandic territories, e.g., Section 114 hgl. making it a criminal offence to recruit people within the Icelandic State for foreign military service. The jurisdiction can also be tied to specified victims or interests, e.g., Section 125 hgl. making it a criminal offence to publicly deride or dishonour religious beliefs or the worship of legal religious organisations in Iceland. There are provisions requiring a perpetrator to be an Icelandic citizen, e.g., Section 89 hgl. making it a criminal offence for an Icelandic citizen to bear arms against the Icelandic State or its allies in times of war. On the other hand, Sections 109 and 128 hgl., on active and passive bribery, state that the party committing the offence and the recipient of bribes can be foreign government employees.

When Act no. 43/2001 on implementing the Rome Treaty for an International Criminal Court was passed, a special rule on jurisdiction was incorporated in Section 9 of the act. It states that the provisions of Chapters XII, XV and XVII hgl. apply to conduct directed at the International Court or its employees. These chapters of the hgl. deal with offences against the authorities, incorrect testimony or false criminal charges and forgery and other offences pertaining to visible evidence. It was considered necessary to enact this provision into law since many provisions in these chapters were limited to offences against the Icelandic courts and government.[8]

Jurisdiction can also be tied to Icelandic territories in accordance with specialised criminal statutes involving rules on special administrative dispositions applicable to social or administrative circumstances, e.g., the Act on Support, health legislation, acts on fishing and hunting, the Conservation Act and Tax Act and legislation on individuals' rights, where mutuality between states is stipulated, or rules on minor offences, e.g., in violation of police regulations.[9] The Act on Habituating Substances and Narcotics is not tied to Icelandic territories in this way, and punishment under it is possible for offences committed abroad.

---

8. Record of Althingi, Department A. 126th legislative session 2000-2001, Parliamentary Document 641, Case 391. See the legislative history regarding Section 9.
9. *Jonatan Thormundsson*: Íslensk refsilögsaga, alþjóðlegar refsireglur og réttaraðstoð, Refsiréttur Almenni hlutinn I. (Icelandic jurisdictional law, international criminal law and legal assistance, Criminal Law General Part I) (1989), p. 14, *Stephan Hurwitz*: Den danske Kriminalret, Almindelig del, 4. reviderede udgave ved Knud Waaben, København 1971, pp, 114-117.

If Icelanders commit traffic violations abroad, the substance and nature of the relevant provisions must be evaluated. Provisions regarding punishment for drunken driving and speeding are set in respect to citizens' safety. If an Icelander commits such a violation abroad, it would be possible to punish him for it in Iceland. On the other hand, if an Icelander violates rules on the inspection of automobiles while abroad, he would probably not be punished for it in Iceland.

1.4. Impact of foreign law

Icelandic criminal jurisdiction requires that the handling of a case and its conclusion are in full compliance with Icelandic legal rules *(lex fori)*. When a criminal case is commenced before an Icelandic court, the Judgment of the court regarding punishment and other consequences of an act shall be governed by Icelandic law (Section 8 (1) hgl.). Exceptions to this can be made if the law specifically allows foreign legislation and foreign criminal sentences to be taken into account, cf. especially Section 4, no. 1, Section 8, Section 8 (a) and Section 8 (b) hgl. The State can therefore decide whether and to what extent it takes into account foreign legislation, foreign criminal sentences and the serving of sentences.[10]

The rule on double criminality is important in connection with the *active personality principle* in Section 5 hgl. In order to punish an Icelandic citizen and a person residing in Iceland in accordance with Icelandic law for an act he committed abroad, the act must also have been punishable under the law of the relevant country. This means the home state of the accused if the offence is committed outside the criminal jurisdiction of other states under International Law, but otherwise in accordance with the law of the country where the offence was committed. This means that it would have been possible to sentence the accused in the foreign state. However, punishment in excess of the maximum punishment allowed *in concreto* for the offence in the home state of the accused or the state where the offence was committed may not be administered (Section 8 (2) hgl.).

When courts in Iceland determine the maximum punishment allowed in the foreign state under Section 8 (2) hgl., they must keep in mind all of the circumstances surrounding the act, check whether reasons for excluding or terminating punishment apply, and whether circumstances exist which increase or decrease the sentence thereby affecting the maximum punishment. If it is a condition for taking legal proceedings in the foreign state that the vic-

---

10. *Thormundsson* (1989), p. 17.

tim requests the proceedings, Icelandic courts will probably have to take this into account even though it would not be a condition under Icelandic law.

If the Icelandic State has obtained the extradition of a person from another state for the purpose of imposing a penalty, he may not be sentenced for any offences, committed prior to the extradition, other than those for which he is extradited, if the foreign state sets such a condition, nor be given a sentence which is more severe than that stipulated (Section 10 hgl.).

There are more examples in Icelandic law of the effect of foreign law and Judgments on Icelandic judicial remedies. The provision of Section 71 hgl. deals with the condition that the previous conviction of a person for an offence may be taken into account when deciding the punishment for an offence committed later by the same person. Sub-section 2 states that courts may allow punitive sentences handed down abroad to be taken into account, in the same way as they would if they had been handed down in Iceland. Also, the Supreme Court of Iceland has deemed that a foreign Judgment could affect the punishment imposed in Icelandic court proceedings under Section 78 hgl. relating to supplementary sentencing, even though foreign Judgments are not mentioned in this provision, see H 1982:1718 and H 1983:10. The ruling is based on Section 78 being regarded as advantageous to the defendant.[11]

Exceptions to the rule of double criminality in the area of the *active personality principle* are contained in Section 5 (3) hgl. For certain offences, including female genital mutilation pursuant to Section 218 (a), punishment shall be in accordance with Icelandic criminal statutes if an Icelandic citizen or person residing in Iceland has committed the offence abroad even though the act is not punishable under the laws of that state.

Under Icelandic law legal persons can be criminally liable and be fined for offences under the hgl. as well as special criminal statutes. There are no rules in Icelandic law on how criminal jurisdiction shall be determined when legal persons are involved, nor does the subject seem to have been the subject of academic discourse.

1.5. Impact of foreign Judgments

Rules on the validity of foreign criminal Judgments endeavour to prevent double penalties for the same conduct (ne bis in idem). After the ratification of the European Convention on the International Validity of Criminal Judgments of 28 May 1970, the provisions of Section 8 hgl. were amended, and two new articles, Section 8 (a) and Section 8 (b) were added, authorising

---

11. *Thormundsson* (1989), p. 18.

criminal trials to be conducted in Iceland after an offender has been sentenced or acquitted in another state for the same offence, cf. Act no. 72/1993 and substantially extending the power to take foreign Judgments and the execution of punishment into account.

Section 8 (a) (1) hgl. deals with the validity of a criminal Judgment that a person has received in specified places outside Iceland. If a person has received a Judgment in a state where the offence was committed, cf. Section 5 (1), no. 2 hgl., or in a state that is a party to the above mentioned European Convention or international agreements within the Schengen collaboration, he shall not be prosecuted in Iceland; nor shall he be sentenced or incur penalties for the same offence as he was convicted of in that state, provided that any of the following conditions are fulfilled: – 1. The offender has been acquitted. This can be because the act was not punishable in the other state; the offence had expired, or the defendant was incompetent to stand trial, e.g., because of mental illness, and this applies even though the remedies of Section 62 hgl. regarding measures used for offenders who have been acquitted because of mental illness were applied. – 2. Sentenced penalties have already been carried out or are being carried out or were cancelled, i.e., expired or pardoned under the law of the state where the Judgment was rendered, i.e., the offender has been granted a pardon, or amnesty has been granted. – 3. The person was convicted without punishment or other penalties having been determined. Included here is when a decision on punishment has been postponed on probation, or punishment is considered ineffective according to the laws of the state of conviction. However, if security arrangements are exercised in such instances, the provisions of no. 3 do not apply.

The provisions of Section 8 (a) (1) hgl. do not pertain to an offence falling under Section 4 hgl. *(territoriality principle)* and Section 6 (1) hgl. (*protective principle* because of offences against the independence and security of the Icelandic State), unless a criminal case has been commenced in the other state at the request of the Icelandic government.

If a person has been prosecuted in Iceland for an offence for which he has already been subject to penalty in another state, the penalties imposed in Iceland shall be milder or allowed to lapse to the extent that they have already been carried out abroad (Section 8 (b) hgl.). This rule provides more latitude than before because sanctions are now to be taken into account and not solely the sentence. It is therefore now allowed to take into account, for example, security measures, confiscation of property, etc., that the sentenced person has undergone in the other state.

The Traffic Act, no. 50/1987, contains a provision aimed at increasing efficiency and coordination between states regarding penalties. Section 105 states that if an Icelandic citizen or person residing in Iceland has his driver's license revoked or has undergone punishment abroad for an act that would have meant revocation of a driver's license under the Icelandic Traffic Act, he may be deprived of this right in a special criminal case, and the Traffic Act's provisions on revocation of a driver's license will be applied.

1.6. Restrictions on prosecution

The *legality principle* applies broadly in Icelandic law. A holder of prosecutorial authority shall commence a case if he deems there to be sufficient or probable cause for a conviction. Despite this, however, he has some statutory leeway to drop prosecution even though conditions of culpability are fulfilled, and proof is sufficient in his view. The Prosecutor General is the highest holder of prosecutorial authority. Several provisions of hgl. on criminal jurisdiction, on the other hand, contain limited authorisation providing that court action is only instituted on the order of a minister.

The first example of a minister's prosecutorial authority is related to the *territoriality principle*. The main rule is that foreign ships and aircraft fall under Icelandic criminal jurisdiction when they are in the Icelandic territories. If Icelandic law is violated when the ship is in Iceland's territorial waters, the offence falls within Icelandic jurisdiction. Section 4, no. 1 hgl. contains an exception to this rule. It states that if an offence is committed by an employee or passenger of a foreign ship or aircraft travelling through Icelandic jurisdiction, against a person travelling with the ship/aircraft or against interests that are closely linked to the craft, penalty shall, however, only be imposed in Iceland if a minister has ordered investigation and prosecution. This rule is in accordance with rules of international law and requirements of efficiency since it would often be difficult to arrange investigation and commencement of a case in Iceland except by stopping the ship or aircraft. In addition, it can be assumed that the offence will be investigated and adjudged in the ship/aircraft's home state.

The next example of a minister's prosecutorial authority is in Section 6 hgl. The article contains 22 numbers, and four of them provide for a case only being commenced when directed by a minister. These offences are as follows: – no. 4: An offence against the provisions of the hgl. on hijacking aircraft, as well as manslaughter, bodily harm, deprivation of liberty and other acts of violence committed in connection with offences against these provisions and those of the Convention for the Suppression of Unlawful Acts against the Safety of Civil Aviation of 23 September 1971 and a protocol to it of 24 February 1988. – no. 6: Conduct specified in Section 1 of the European Convention on the Suppression of Terrorism of 27 January 1977. – no. 7:

Conduct specified in the International Convention against the Taking of Hostages of 18 December 1979. – no. 9: Conduct specified in the Convention against Torture and Other Cruel, Inhuman or Degrading Treatment or Punishment of 10 December 1984. These jurisdictional provisions have in common that they are based on international agreements directed against various international or transnational criminal activities.

Third, there are two provisions in other chapters of the hgl. that require a minister's prosecutorial authority. Chapter X of the hgl. deals with treason. Section 97 states that cases stemming from offences in violation of the chapter's provisions shall only be commenced at the minister's direction. The same kind of provision is in Chapter XI on offences against the State's Constitution and the highest level of government, cf. Section 105, which cites offences against the President of Iceland and his relatives or holders of the presidential power.

2.   The Rules on Jurisdiction in Detail

2.1.   Territoriality principle
The *territoriality principle* is a fundamental principle of Icelandic law; it is set out in Section 4 hgl.:

Section 4 hgl.
Penalties shall be imposed in accordance with the Icelandic Penal Code[12] on account of the following:
1. Offences committed within the Icelandic State...
[...]

2.1.1.   Localisation
Section 7 hgl. has a provision on the identification of the location in which the offence is committed. This rule entails a broadening of the criminal jurisdiction of the Icelandic State.

---

12. This is the translation of Section 4 hgl. obtained from the website of the Ministry of the Interior. The Icelandic concept "hegningarlög" in Section 4 is translated literally as "Penal Code", but in Section 4 it really means "criminal statutes". The same applies to Section 5 and Section 6 hgl.

Section 7 hgl.
If the penalty to be ordered is under Law to some extent contingent upon the consequences of an act, the act shall be deemed also to have been committed at the place where the consequences occur or are intended to occur.

From this wording it is clear that Section 7 hgl. does not state directly where an offence is deemed to be committed, i.e., what the location of an act is. However, it may be concluded from the section that the main rule is that an offence is deemed to be committed where the beginning of the act occurred, cf. the wording "also". Assault in Iceland is deemed to be committed there even though the consequences surface after a victim has arrived in another country. It is not necessary for all substantive elements of an offence to be manifested in Icelandic territories. It is sufficient that a substantial portion of the act occurred in Icelandic territories, and then Icelandic criminal jurisdiction covers the entire act, also the part of it occurring outside the territory.

Section 7 deals with determining the place of an offence regarding its consequences. Some offences are such that the original act may have been committed in one place, but the consequences emerge in another place. If the consequences of an act affect its liability to punishment or are related to its culpability according to law and emerge in Iceland or are intended to emerge there, Icelandic criminal jurisdiction covers the offence although it is committed abroad.[13] It is not a condition for criminal liability in Iceland that the act is also punishable in the foreign state where it is committed. Section 8 (2) and Section 5 (1) therefore do not apply.[14] Section 7 can be put to the test when the consequences of an act surface or are intended to surface in a place other than the one where the act was committed. The offence is then deemed to have been committed in both places. With Section 7, therefore, the consequences and the beginning of the act are of equal weight in determining the place of an offence.

The wording of Section 7 indicates that the broadened jurisdiction under the provision solely covers offenses involving damage. It also covers offences involving damage that are fully committed on commencement of the act. In such situations a perpetrator's intent must cover the entire series of events, both the commencement of the act and consequences, but the offence is deemed fully committed on commencement of the act. If Icelandic paper money were counterfeited in Britain but planned for distribution in Iceland, the offence would also be deemed to be committed in Iceland and would be

13. *Thormundsson* (1989), p. 15.
14. Record of Althingi, Department A, 1939, p. 356.

punished under Section 150 hgl. on counterfeiting money, cf. Section 7 hgl. On the other hand, it is doubtful that the wording of Section 7 allows the construction that the rule also be used regarding symmetrical offences, i.e., offences completed with the original act without regard to the consequences.[15]

The concept "act" in Section 7 covers criminal attempts. If a criminal attempt is committed abroad and is intended to have consequences in Iceland, the act is also deemed to be committed in Iceland. Icelandic law distinguishes between acts of preparation and acts of implementation, and both are deemed to be criminal attempts. It could sometimes be considered doubtful whether distant acts of preparation carried out abroad are deemed to constitute offences in Iceland, but this would probably be the case when the intention is to wholly commit the offence in Iceland. An act of punishable complicity also falls under Section 7, e.g., subversive activity or instigation to commit an offence.

Direct offences of omission are offences of negligence entailing that a person does not perform a legal duty to act, and criminal liability is then attributed to the negligence as such without regard to its possible consequences. The hgl. contains only a few direct offences of omission; they aim primarily at avoiding or unveiling egregious offences that are planned or begun.[16] The provisions of Section 7 do not pertain literally to direct offences of omission because it cannot be said that consequences are involved that can be differentiated from the punishable act. However, it has been argued that a perpetrator's residence can have as much weight as the place where the duty to act ought to have been performed. Direct offences of omission are then deemed to be committed not only in the perpetrator's place of residence but also in the place where the duty to act ought to have been fulfilled.[17]

The indirect offence of omission is punishable omission that is deemed equivalent to acts described or entailing prohibitive provisions of criminal statutes. Criminal liability for indirect offences of omission is thus derived from statutes banning specified acts that are subject to punishment. Special connection is required between an offender and the disruption of interests against which the punitive provisions are aimed. This can be based on a preceding damaging act, monitoring duties, duties to provide care, contractual duties or official and work-related duties.[18] Regarding indirect offences of

---

15. *Thormundsson* (1989), p. 15.
16. *Jonatan Thormundsson*: Afbrot og refsiábyrgð I. (Offences and Criminal Liability I), Reykjavik 1999, p. 86.
17. *Hurwitz* (1971), p. 105.
18. *Thormundsson* (1991), pp. 88-102.

omission, the same applies as regarding active offences, i.e., punishment is according to Icelandic law when the consequences of the omission surface within the Icelandic State without regard to where the person obligated to act was when he ought to have begun acting.[19]

"Consequences" in Section 7 hgl. pertains primarily to direct consequences. If A in Norway sends a letter bomb to B in Iceland who dies from the explosion, the offence is deemed to be committed in Iceland in addition to Norway. Nevertheless, indirect consequences can also fall under Section 7. If B receives the package with the bomb in Greenland, is injured there by it and is transported to Iceland and dies there from his wounds, the consequences in Greenland are direct but indirect (final) in Iceland. Since manslaughter is completed upon death, the offence would also be deemed to have been committed in Iceland under Section 7 hgl. A Judgment of the Supreme Court of Iceland in 2009 tested the construction of Section 7 hgl.:

H 3. December 2009 (No. 509/2009): P, R and A, along with three other people, were indicted for a large-scale narcotics violation, in that they conspired to import a large quantity of amphetamine, cannabis and MDMA pills, intended for sales distribution in Iceland for profit. The narcotics were transported to Iceland from Belgium in a cutter; an inflatable boat came out to meet the cutter, and the boats met at sea less than 30 nautical miles south-east of Iceland, where the substances were transferred between the boats, and the inflatable boat was then sailed with the substances to land. The accused were convicted in District Court; their offences were deemed punishable under Section 173 (a) hgl. on large-scale narcotics offences. P, a citizen of the Netherlands, appealed to the Supreme Court, demanding that the case be dismissed from District Court since the Icelandic State lacked jurisdiction over him under the facts of the case. P was the charterer and skipper of the cutter, which was registered in Belgium. It was undisputed that the cutter had not sailed into Iceland's 12-mile territorial waters. It was deemed that the conduct of the six people indicted in the case as conspirators in the importation of narcotics had to be regarded as a single whole. In the meaning of Section 173 (a) hgl., the offence had been wholly committed when the substances were transported into Iceland's territorial waters. P's alleged offence could not be separated from the part of the others indicted in the case. For that reason, it formed part of conduct intended to have consequences in Iceland, and Icelandic criminal jurisdiction therefore extended to it under Section 7 hgl. It was also deemed that the conditions for arresting the cutter in the open sea

---

19. *Hurwitz* (1971), p. 105.

were fulfilled, taking into account Section 111 of the United Nations Convention on the Law of the Sea. Thereunder pursuit can be commenced, even if a ship has not entered a coastal state's territorial waters, provided one of the ship's boats is located within them. In this regard, a boat sent from a coastal state to meet the foreign ship in order to commit an offence within the state's territorial waters in cooperation with those aboard the ship is deemed to constitute the foreign ship's boat. P's motion to dismiss was therefore rejected. With reference to the District Court's premises, the Judgment was confirmed, and P and R were each sentenced to 10 years in prison and A to 9 years.

No. 3 of Section 4 hgl. is a provision put into the hgl. to fulfil obligations under the Council of Europe's Convention on Laundering, Search, Seizure and Confiscation of the Proceeds from Crime of 8 November 1990. Under the provision, an offence committed within the Icelandic State in breach of Section 264 hgl., regarding subsequent complicity to gain from a criminal offence, ought to be punished in accordance with Icelandic criminal statutes even though the original offence from which the profit stemmed was committed abroad and irrespective of who is the cause of it. Therefore it does not matter who committed the original offence, e.g., whether it was an Icelandic citizen or foreign citizen.[20]

The limits of the criminal jurisdiction deriving from rules of international law on the basis of mutuality, must be kept in mind, cf. Section 11 hgl. In this regard the rules on immunity can be mentioned and unrestricted passage through Icelandic territorial waters and airspace.

The hgl. have no provisions on the localisation of cybercrime, i.e., where the offence is committed on the internet. Therefore Section 7 would be applied in the cases of cybercrime.

2.1.2. Definition of Iceland

Under Section 4 hgl. penalties shall be imposed in accordance with Icelandic criminal statute law for offences committed within the Icelandic State, i.e., on land, in its territorial waters or its airspace. Act no. 41/1979 on territorial waters, the Exclusive Economic Zone and the continental shelf states that the general law enforcement territory is 12 nautical miles from a baseline drawn between the outermost peninsulas and skerries. Iceland's sovereign rights extend to its territorial waters, the ocean floor below them and the airspace above. Despite the State's dominion over the territorial waters, foreign ships,

---

20. Record of Althingi, Department A, 121st legislative session, Case 183, Parliamentary Document 204.

both merchant ships and military ships, may pass freely through the territorial waters, provided their passage is peaceful. The Act of 1979 also has a definition of the Exclusive Economic Zone; it is an area outside the territorial waters demarcated by a line that is always 200 nautical miles from the baseline of the territorial waters. Where the distance is less than 400 nautical miles between the baselines of the Faroe Islands and Greenland, on one hand, and Iceland, on the other, Iceland's Exclusive Economic Zone and continental shelf are demarcated by the midline. Within the Exclusive Economic Zone, the Icelandic State has sovereign rights in a limited area, i.e., regarding exploration, utilisation, protection and management of resources on and in the ocean floor and in the ocean above it. This right of the State covers fisheries and conservation of fishing grounds, and the criminal jurisdiction is limited to offences in breach of these rights. If a foreign ship violates Icelandic rules on fisheries in this area, Icelandic criminal jurisdiction covers those offences. In addition, the jurisdiction for law enforcement measures extends beyond the limit of 200 nautical miles if the conditions of the rules of international law are fulfilled, for example, rules on hot pursuit if a foreign ship is given a clear signal to halt, and pursuit begins while the ship is within jurisdictional limits. The airspace is the volume of air above the land and the 12-nautical-mile territorial waters. The vertical limits of the airspace are not clear but are thought to reach far above the area currently given to aeroplanes.

2.2. Flag state principle

No. 2 of Section 4 of hgl. is a special rule for ships and aircraft; it entails a broadening of the territoriality principle. It builds on the *flag state principle* and is as follows:

Section 4 hgl.
Penalties shall be imposed in accordance with the Icelandic Penal Code on account of the following:
1. [...]
2. Offences committed on board Icelandic ships or Icelandic aircraft, irrespective of a craft's position at the time of commission. If an offence has been committed in a place subject to the criminal jurisdiction of another State under International Law, by a person neither permanently employed on board the craft nor a passenger thereon, penalty shall not be imposed in Iceland unless this is provided for in Articles 5 or 6.

An Icelandic ship or aircraft is an extension of Icelandic territory and therefore falls under the *territoriality principle*. This is of course directly relevant when a ship is in Icelandic territorial waters, but also when the ship has left Icelandic territorial waters and is in an area that is not a subject to the criminal jurisdiction of another State under International Law, i.e., in the open ocean. Icelandic law covers any kind of offence committed there aboard the ship. If an Icelandic ship, on the other hand, has entered an area controlled by a foreign state, and an offence is committed, Icelandic criminal jurisdiction covers the offence only if it is committed by a permanent employee or passenger on the ship. If someone else commits an offence, a penalty will generally be imposed in the relevant state. However, a penalty can be imposed in Iceland if Section 5 or Section 6 applies. Under International Law, the law of the home state applies to a ship even though it is located in a port or within the territorial waters of another state. On the other hand, it is not possible to exercise the jurisdiction before the ship has returned to the open ocean or a port in the home state.

The broadening of Icelandic jurisdiction entailed in Section 4, no. 2 hgl. corresponds to the limits to criminal jurisdiction regarding foreign ships and aircraft in Icelandic territories, cf. Section 4, no. 1 hgl. It states that if an offence is committed within the Icelandic State by a person employed on board, or a passenger of, a foreign ship or aircraft travelling in Icelandic territories, against a person travelling with that craft or against interests closely linked to the craft, penalty shall, however, only be imposed in Iceland if the minister has ordered an investigation and prosecution. This rule is in accordance with rules of International Law and requirements of efficiency. It is often difficult to arrange investigation and prosecution of a case in Iceland under these circumstances, except by arresting the ship or seizing the aircraft, and it is likely that the offence will be investigated and tried in the home state of the craft.

2.3. Active personality principle
The main principle of Icelandic criminal jurisdiction (the *territoriality principle*) is broadened by the *active personality principle* and covers offences that Icelandic citizens and people residing in Iceland commit abroad. The *active personality* principle is stated in Section 5 of hgl.

Section 5 hgl.
(1) Penalties shall be imposed in accordance with the Icelandic Penal Code on account of offences committed [abroad][21] by Icelandic citizens or residents of Iceland:
1. If the offence was committed in a place outside the criminal jurisdiction of other States under International Law, provided that it was also punishable under the Law of the offender's home State;

21. The word "abroad" is lacking in the English translation of the hgl. but is in the Icelandic text (Icelandic: erlendis).

2. If the offence was committed in a place under the criminal jurisdiction of another State under International Law, provided it was also punishable under the Law of that State.

(2) The provisions of the first para. may be applied to an act committed by a Danish, Finnish, Norwegian or Swedish citizen or resident there and who stays in Iceland.

(3) In cases referred to in Sub-section 1, no. 2, offences which fall under Section 206 (2)-(4), 210b (1), Sections 218a and 227a (1) no. 2 and have been committed abroad by a person of Icelandic nationality or, who at the time was residing in Iceland, are punishable under Icelandic criminal law even if the acts committed are not a criminal offence under the law of the locus delicti. The same applies to the offence, falling under Sections 194, 197-198, 200-201 and 202 (1), by a person against a child under 15 and to the offence by a person, falling under Section 210a (1), insofar as it concerns the manufacture of material within the meaning of this provision.

The argument for the rule in Section 5 is not only that the duty to obey Icelandic law was broken. There are also arguments of efficiency and prevention that Icelandic citizens and people residing in Iceland shall be subject to criminal liability in Iceland rather than be extradited to a foreign state to be subjected to liability there. There is also the general principle that Icelandic citizens are not extradited, and that penalties must therefore be imposed on them in Iceland.

An offender must be an Icelandic citizen or resident in Iceland when prosecuted, cf. the wording "have committed". The criterion is therefore citizenship or residence upon prosecution, not upon commission of an offence. "Home state" means either the state of citizenship or the state of residence, whichever is relevant. "Residence" means a stay of a somewhat fixed and permanent duration.

Section 5 (1) is a general jurisdictional rule, but under Sub-section 2 jurisdiction is broader than in Sub-section 1. The persons mentioned there can be punished in accordance with Icelandic law for offences committed abroad although they are only staying in Iceland. The provision results from Nordic cooperation in the 1960s and 1970s, as there is now extensive mutual criminal jurisdiction between the Nordic countries. Under Section 66 (2) of the Constitution of the Republic of Iceland, no. 33/1944, as amended, an Icelandic citizen will not be barred from coming to the country, nor will he be expelled from the country. However, this does not apply between the Nordic countries. With the Act no. 12/2010 on the arrest and extradition of people between the Nordic countries for punishable acts (Nordic Arrest Warrant) arrest and extradition between the Nordic countries is made easier and more efficient than was the case under older law. Thus, the requirement regarding double criminality was dropped, and no distinction is made between a country's own citizens and other Nordic citizens.[22]

To avoid the risk that people will be punished for an act that is not punishable in the state where it was committed, the condition is set in Section 5 (1), no. 2 that an act shall also be punishable under the law of the state where it was committed.

An exception to the requirement of double criminality is stated in Section 5 (3), cf. Act no. 83/2005. Under that provision penalties shall be imposed in accordance with the Icelandic Penal Code for a specified bodily injury offence committed by a person who was an Icelandic citizen or a resident of Iceland at the time of the act if the offence was committed abroad, even though the act was not punishable under the law of that state. This offence is female circumcision under Section 218 (a) hgl.

Following Iceland's ratification of the Council of Europe Convention on the Protection of Children against Sexual Exploitation and Sexual Abuse, the hgl. has been amended accordingly. The amendment provides for an addition to Section 5 (3), so that the following offences will be subject to the same rule as female genital mutilation: – Having recourse to prostitution from children under the age of 18 or alluring, encouraging or assisting a child under 18 to engage in prostitution, be employed in prostitution of others or derive a livelihood therefrom. – Hire a child to participate in exhibitions of nakedness or pornography, organise or otherwise cause or profit from a child's participation in such exhibitions. – Procure, transport, deliver, house or receive an individual younger than 18 years for the purpose of sexually abusing him/her or forcing the individual to work or removing his/her organs. – Rape of children under the age of 15 and other serious offences against children's sexual freedom. – Production of photographs, films or comparable items exhibiting children in a sexual or pornographic manner. – Production of photographs, films or comparable items exhibiting individuals, aged 18 or older, in a sexual or pornographic manner, provided that they are in the role of a child, or if a child is imitated in such material even though it is not realistic, such as in animated films or other virtual images.

In recent years great emphasis has been placed in Iceland on fighting against sexual offences against children. Part of that fight is the implementation of the above-mentioned rules, making it possible to punish Icelandic citi-

---

22. On the other hand, Iceland is not a full-fledged party to the European Arrest Warrant of 2002, see *Björg Thorarensen and Pétur Dam Leifsson*: Þjóðaréttur (International law), Reykjavik 2011, p. 125

zens or people residing in Iceland at the time of an act for the offences under Icelandic law even though they are not punishable where they are committed.

2.4. Passive personality principle

As previously mentioned, the *passive personality principle* has limited application in Icelandic law. Icelandic law does not generally authorise trying criminal cases in Iceland because of punishable offences committed abroad against Icelandic citizens or Icelandic interests. There is a limited exception to this in Section 6 no. 3 hgl.

Section 6 hgl.
(1) Penalties shall also be imposed in accordance with the Icelandic Penal Code on account of the following offences, even if these have been committed outside the Icelandic State and irrespective of who the offender is:
1. [...]
2. [...]
3. Offences against the interests of Icelandic citizens or persons resident in Iceland, if committed outside the criminal jurisdiction of other States under International Law.

Under Section 6 hgl. penalties shall be imposed in accordance with Icelandic criminal statutes for offences committed outside the Icelandic State, irrespective of who the perpetrator is. Most of the numbers under Section 6 deal with jurisdiction regarding offences against the Icelandic State or offences described in international agreements to which Iceland is a party (the *protective principle*, the *principle of universal jurisdiction*). The provision of no. 3 is different in nature because it protects private interests of Icelandic citizens and people residing in Iceland. The rule pertains to most offences in the chapters on manslaughter and bodily harm, sexual offences, offences against people's freedom, defamation and offences against the right of privacy. The same probably applies to property offences.[23] However, it is a condition that the offence is committed in a place not covered by the criminal jurisdiction of other States under International Law, which would most likely be the open ocean, and this provision therefore has little actual validity.

2.5. Principle of state protection

Section 6, no. 1 and 2 hgl. contain rules based on the *principle of state protection*. These provisions in the act have not changed since the Penal Code

---

23. *Hurwitz* (1971), p. 101.

was enacted in 1940, and criminal jurisdiction here aims at quite extensive protection of the interests of the Icelandic State.

Section 6 hgl.

(1) Penalties shall also be imposed in accordance with the Icelandic Penal Code on account of the following offences, even if these have been committed outside the Icelandic State and irrespective of who the offender is:

1. Offences against the independence of the Icelandic State, its security, Constitution and public authorities; offences committed in violation of [official or administrative][24] duty to the Icelandic State and offences against interests protected by Icelandic Law on account of close relationship to the Icelandic State.
2. Offences in violation of a duty on the part of the perpetrator to be performed abroad according to Icelandic Law and also offences in violation of a duty of employment on board an Icelandic craft.

The *principle of state protection* entails the rule to impose penalties in accordance with Icelandic law even though an offence is committed outside Iceland and without respect to whether the perpetrator is an Icelandic or foreign citizen. These provisions protect important Icelandic interests, wherever offences against them are committed. This pertains especially to foreigners' offences committed abroad that the Icelandic courts can deal with because of the proximity or residence of the foreigner in Iceland. There is no requirement of double criminality, and it is therefore not stipulated that an offence shall be punishable in accordance with both Icelandic law and the law of the relevant foreign state. However, the rule in Section 6 is not applied solely to foreigners' offences. It can also pertain to Icelanders' offences abroad against Iceland's security interests because the *active personality principle* would generally not be applicable due to its requirement of double criminality.[25]

Section 6, no. 1 contains two rules. The provision of sentence 1 of Section 6, no. 1 contains a rule called the protective principle in International Law. In accordance with this sentence, offences against Chapter X hgl. on treason and Chapter XI on offences against the State's Constitution and the highest level of government fall under Icelandic jurisdiction and, also, probably violations against Chapter XII on offences against the authorities and Chapter XIV on offences in governmental work. Exceptions to this are offences where criminal liability depends on the violation having been committed in Iceland, e.g., Section 114 hgl. regarding hiring a person within the Icelandic State for for-

---

24. The words "official or administrative" is lacking in the English translation of the hgl. but are in the Icelandic text (Icelandic: embættis- eða sýslunarskyldum).
25. See also: *Thormundsson* (1989), p. 13.

eign military service (the *territoriality principle*). Offences against individual provisions in other chapters of the hgl. can also be considered, e.g., offences against Section 149 on making false complaints to public authorities stating that punishable acts have been committed that have actually not been committed at all.

Under sentence 2, Section 6, no. 1 hgl., the jurisdiction principle applies if an offence is committed against interests protected by Icelandic law because of close connection with the Icelandic State. These are interests particularly tied to Icelandic circumstances and local conditions, e.g., provisions in the law on territorial waters, agricultural legislation, the acts on foreign currency, tax law and health legislation. The provision could be relevant regarding offences committed abroad by Icelandic citizens and people residing in Iceland who are not criminally liable under Section 5 hgl. because the conduct was not criminal in the country where it was committed.[26]

The provision of Section 6, no. 2 hgl. also has two parts. Sentence 1 refers to the violation being a breach of special duties under Icelandic law by the person who was supposed to perform the duties abroad. This can, for example, involve a diplomat who, without authority, signed an agreement, thereby violating his duties. Sentence 2 refers to a violation of special duties abroad and arising from employment on an Icelandic aircraft or vessel. An example of this would be Section 80 of the Seamen's Act, no. 35/1985, on the desertion of crew members from a ship.

2.6. Principle of universal jurisdiction

Section 6, no. 4-22 hgl. are rules based on the *principle of universal jurisdiction*. These provisions have been added to the hgl. little by little over the last 40 years. The provisions on jurisdiction are based on international conventions that Iceland has ratified that are directed against various kinds of international or transnational criminal activities. The Icelandic State has obligated itself to implement rules on criminal jurisdiction covering these offences.

Section 6 hgl.
(1) Penalties shall also be imposed in accordance with the Icelandic Penal Code on account of the following offences, even if these have been committed outside the Icelandic State and irrespective of who the offender is:
[...]
4. For violations of para. 2, 3 and 4 of Article 165, and also for homicide, bodily harm, deprivation of freedom and other acts of violence committed in connection with viola-

---

26. *Thormundsson* (1989), p. 14.

tions of these provisions and for conduct to which the International Convention of 23 September 1971 for the Suppression of Unlawful Acts of Violence at Airports Serving International Civil Aviation and a Protocol thereto of 24 of February 1988 applies. Legal action under this clause shall, however, only be taken if ordered by the Minister of Justice.

5. For conduct to which the Convention of 14 December 1973 on the Prevention and Punishment of Crimes Against Internationally Protected Persons, including Diplomatic Agents, applies.
6. For conduct to which Article 1 of the European Convention of 27 January 1977 on the Suppression of Terrorism applies. Legal action under this clause shall, however, only be taken if ordered by the Minister of Justice.
7. For conduct to which the International Convention of 18 December 1979 against the Taking of Hostages applies. Legal action under this clause shall, however, only be taken if ordered by the Minister of Justice.
8. For incorrect sworn testimony before the Court of the EFTA States, provided the Court has required prosecution.
9. For conduct to which the Convention of 10 December 1984 against Torture and Other Cruel, Inhuman or Degrading Treatment or Punishment applies. Legal action under this clause shall, however, only be taken if ordered by the Minister of Justice.
10. For conduct described in the Convention of 21 November 1997 on Combating Bribery of Foreign Public Officials in International Business Transactions.
11. For conduct to which the Comprehensive Nuclear-Test-Ban Treaty of 10 September 1996 applies.
12. For conduct to which the Convention on the Safety of the United Nations and Associated Personnel of 9 December 1994 applies.
13. For conduct specified in the Convention to Prevent Illegal Activities Against Safety in Sailing at Sea of 10 March 1988.
14. For conduct specified in Protocol on Preventing Illegal Activities Against Seabed Fixed Constructions on the Continental Shelf of 10 March 1988.
15. For conduct specified in a Convention on the Custody of Nuclear Reactor Substances of 3 March 1980.
16. For conduct specified in the International Convention on Preventing Terrorist Explosions (Bombings) of 15 December 1997.
17. For conduct specified in the International Convention on Preventing the Financing of Terrorism Activities of 9 December 1999.
18. For conduct specified in an Agreement in the field of Criminal Law on Corruption of 27 January 1999.[27]
19. For conduct specified in the United Nations Convention against Transnational Organized Crime of 15 November 2000 and in a Protocol to that Convention to Prevent, Fight Against and Punish for Trafficking in Persons, Especially Women and Children of 15 November 2000.
20. For conduct specified in the Council of Europe Convention on Action Against Trafficking in Human Beings of 3 May 2005.

27. These are the provisions as translated and published at the website of the Ministry of the Interior. No.19-22 have not been translated by the Ministry.

21. For conduct specified in the United Nations Convention Against Corruption of 31 October 2003.
22. For conduct specified in the Council of Europe Convention on the Protection of Children against Sexual Exploitation and Sexual Abuse of 25 October 2007.

The above international conventions declare that it is in the interest of the parties to the conventions, and actually of the entire world, to prevent and punish these offences with the most extensive jurisdictional rules possible. An example of jurisdiction under the rules would be the fact that it is authorised to conduct criminal trials before Icelandic courts against a skyjacker caught in Iceland for a skyjacking in the United States of an Air France jet.[28] Regarding the numbers of Section 6 hgl., the general rule in Section 11 hgl. applies, i.e., that the rules must be applied subject to the limitations deriving from rules of International Law.

Act no. 162/2010 amended various acts because of the merger of ministries. These included the amendment that instead of the words "Minister of Justice" in Section 6 hgl. is the word "minister". Act no. 126/2011 amended Section 4 in the same way.

The amendment to the hgl. due to Iceland's ratification of the Council of Europe Convention on the Protection of Children against Sexual Exploitation and Sexual Abuse means that the rule in Section 6 hgl. covers these offences, and it has been supplemented accordingly by an additional paragraph no. 22.

2.7. Principle of representational jurisdiction

A rule based on the *principle of representational jurisdiction* appears indirectly in Section 8 (a) (2) hgl., as discussed in Chapter 1.2. above. Subsection 1 states that if a person has received a punitive sentence in another specified state, upon fulfilment of certain conditions, a case shall not be commenced against him, and he shall not be sentenced or penalties imposed in Iceland for the same offence as he was sentenced for in that state. Under Section 8 (a) (2) the provisions of Sub-section 1 do not apply when the criminal jurisdiction of the Icelandic state is based on Section 4 or Section 6, no. 1 unless a criminal case has been commenced in the other state at the request of the Icelandic government. These provisions are based on the argument that a state where an act was committed and a state having governmental interests at stake ought to be authorised to prosecute a person even though he has stood trial in another state for the same offence. The proviso that the Icelandic government shall not have requested case proceedings in the foreign state is an

---

28. *Thormundsson* (1989), p. 13.

innovation in Icelandic criminal law enacted in 1993 and is based on the Convention on the International Validity of Criminal Judgments.[29] An example of the use of this rule is where a skyjacker from another country ends his skyjacking in Iceland but escapes to Germany. The Icelandic government could then request the German authorities to commence a criminal trial against the skyjacker, and thus give up its own right to prosecute the skyjacker in Iceland.

3. Abbreviations

H: Hæstaréttardómur (Judgment of the Supreme Court of Iceland)

4. The Jurisdictional Rules of the Icelandic Criminal Code in English translation[30]

General Penal Code no. 19, 12 February, 1940

Art. 4
Penalties shall be imposed in accordance with the Icelandic Penal Code on account of the following:

1. Offences committed within the Icelandic State. If an offence is committed by a person employed on board, or a passenger of, a foreign ship or aircraft travelling here, against a person travelling with that craft or against interests closely linked to the craft, penalty shall, however, only be imposed if the Minister of Justice has ordered investigation and prosecution.
2. Offences committed on board Icelandic ships or Icelandic aircraft, irrespective of a craft's position at the time of commission. If an offence has been committed in a place subject to the criminal jurisdiction of another State under International Law, by a person neither permanently employed on board the craft nor a passenger thereon, penalty shall not be imposed in Iceland unless this is provided for in Articles 5 or 6.

29. Record of Althingi, Department A, 116th legislative session, Case 449, Parliamentary Document 775.
30. The English translation was obtained from the website of the Ministry of the Interior at: http://www.innanrikisraduneyti.is/log-og-reglugerdir/enska/

3. Offences against Art. 264 committed within the Icelandic State, even if the original offence from which the gain has been derived, was committed abroad and irrespective of who caused it[1].[1] *Act 10/1997, Art. 1.*

Art. 5
Penalties shall be imposed in accordance with the Icelandic Penal Code on account of offences committed by Icelandic citizens or residents of Iceland:

1. If the offence was committed in a place outside the criminal jurisdiction of other States under International Law, provided that it was also punishable under the Law of the offender's home State;
2. If the offence was committed in a place under the criminal jurisdiction of another State under International Law, provided it was also punishable under the Law of that State.

The provisions of the first para. may be applied to an act committed by a Danish, Finnish, Norwegian or Swedish citizen or resident there and who stays in Iceland[1].[1] *Act 101/1976, Art. 2.*

Art. 6
Penalties shall also be imposed in accordance with the Icelandic Penal Code on account of the following offences, even if these have been committed outside the Icelandic State and irrespective of who the offender is:

1. Offences against the independence of the Icelandic State, its security, Constitution and public authorities; offences committed in violation of duty to the Icelandic State and offences against interests protected by Icelandic Law on account of close relationship to the Icelandic State.
2. Offences in violation of a duty on the part of the perpetrator to be performed abroad according to Icelandic Law and also offences in violation of a duty of employment on board an Icelandic craft.
3. Offences against the interests of Icelandic citizens or persons resident in Iceland, if committed outside the criminal jurisdiction of other States under International Law.[1]
4. For violations of para. 2, 3 and 4 of Art. 165 and also for homicide, bodily harm, deprivation of freedom and other acts of violence committed in connection with violations of these provisions and for conduct to which the international Convention of 23 September 1971 for the Suppression of Unlawful Acts of Violence at Airports Serving International Civil Aviation and a Protocol thereto of 24 February 1988 applies. Legal ac-

tion under this clause shall, however, only be taken if ordered by the Minister of Justice.[2)]

5. For conduct to which the Convention of 14 December 1973 on the Prevention and Punishment of Crimes Against Internationally Protected Persons, including Diplomatic Agents, applies.[3)]

6. For conduct to which Article 1 of the European Convention of 27 January 1977 on the Suppression of Terrorism applies. Legal action under this clause shall, however, only be taken if ordered by the Minister of Justice.[4)]

7. For conduct to which the International Convention of 18 December 1979 against the Taking of Hostages applies.[5)] Legal action under this clause shall, however, only be taken if ordered by the Minister of Justice.[6)]

8. For incorrect sworn testimony before the Court of the EFTA States, provided the Court has required prosecution.[7)]

9. For conduct to which the Convention of 10 December 1984 against Torture and Other Cruel, Inhuman or Degrading Treatment or Punishment applies. Legal action under this clause shall, however, only be taken if ordered by the Minister of Justice.[8)]

10. For conduct described in the Convention of 21 November 1997 on Combating Bribery of Foreign Public Officials in International Business Transactions.[9)]

11. For conduct to which the Comprehensive Nuclear-Test-Ban Treaty of 10. September 1996 applies.[10)]

12. For conduct to which the Convention on the Safety of the United Nations and Associated Personnel of 9 December 1994 applies.[11)]

13. For conduct specified in the Convention to Prevent Illegal Activities Against Safety in Sailing at Sea of 10 March 1988.[12)]

14. For conduct specified in Protocol on Preventing Illegal Activities Against Seabed Fixed Constructions on the Continental Shelf of 10 March 1988.[12)]

15. For conduct specified in a Convention on the Custody of Nuclear Reactor Substances of 3 March 1980.[12)]

16. [13)]For conduct specified in the International Convention on Preventing Terrorist Explosions (Bombings) of 15 December 1997.

17. [13)]For conduct specified in the International Convention on Preventing the Financing of Terrorism Activities of 9 December 1999.[14)]

18. For conduct specified in an Agreement in the field of Criminal Law on Corruption of 27 January 1999.[15)]

[1] Act 72/1993, Art. 2. [2] Act 16/1990, Art. 1. [3] Act 24/1976, Art. 1. [4] Act 52/1980, Art. 1. [5] Act 72/1993, Art. 3. [6] Act 69/1981, Art. 1. [7] Act 133/1993, Art. 3. [8] Act 142/1995, Art. 1. [9] Act 147/1998, Art. 1. [10] Act 25/2001, Art. 6. [11] Act 44/2001, Art. 1. [12] Act 70/2002, Art. 1. [13] In the Government Gazette these clauses are given the numbers 13 and 14, but will be Nos. 16 and 17, cf. amendments of the Article by means of Art. 1. of Act 70/2002. [14] Act no. 99/2002, Art. 1. [15] Act 125/2003, Art. 1.

Art. 7
If the penalty to be ordered is under Law to some extent contingent upon the consequences of an act, the act shall be deemed also to have been committed at the place where the consequences occur or are intended to occur.

Art. 8
When criminal action is brought before an Icelandic Court the penalty to be imposed and other consequences of the offence shall be determined in accordance with Icelandic Law.

The penalty imposed on account of an offence subject to prosecution according to Art. 5 shall not exceed the maximum provided for by the Law of the offender's home State, cf. clause 1, or by the Law of the State of commission, cf. clause 2.
... [1] [1] Act 72/1993, Art. 4.

Art. 8 a
A person who has been sentenced in a State where his/her offence was committed, cf. Art. 5, para.1, clause 2, or in a State being party to the Convention on the International Validity of Criminal Judgments of 28 May 1970 or international agreements applying to the Schengen co-operation[1] shall not be indicted or sentenced in Iceland, or any sentence enforced against such person on account of the offence in respect of which Judgment was rendered in that State, if

1. the person was acquitted;
2. the sanctions ordered have already been enforced, these are being enforced, have been cancelled or abandoned in accordance with the Law of the State where the Judgment was rendered;
3. the person has been found guilty without a penalty or other sanctions having been ordered.

The provisions of the para.1 shall not apply to offences to which the provisions of Art. 4 and clause 1 of Art. 6 apply, except if criminal action has been initiated in the other State upon the request of Icelandic authorities.[2] [1] *Act 15/2000, Art. 1.* [2] *Act 72/1993, Art. 5.*

Art. 8 b
If criminal action is brought in Iceland on account of an offence for which a person has already been subjected to sanctions in another State, the sanctions determined in Iceland shall be correspondingly reduced or, as applicable, cancelled to the extent the sanctions may already have been enforced in that State. [1][1]*Act 72/1993, Art. 6.*

Art. 9
... [1][1]*Act 13/1984, Art. 28.*

Art. 10
If the Icelandic State has obtained extradition of a person from another State for the purpose of imposing a penalty, that person can only be sentenced for offences committed prior to extradition on account of which this takes place, if the foreign State has imposed such condition and the penalty cannot be ordered heavier than stipulated.

Art. 11
The provisions of Articles 4-6 of this Act[1] shall be applied taking into account the limitations resulting from International Law. [1]*Act 42/1985, Art. 1.*

CHAPTER 4

Norway

Annika Suominen[1]

1. General Basis

1.1. Systematic classification of the rules on jurisdiction

The rules for the scope of Norwegian criminal law (*den norske strafferetts virkekreds*) are given in sections 12, 12a and 13 in the first chapter of the Norwegian Criminal Code (*Straffeloven*, SL).[2] The point of origin is clear from section 12(1)(1): Norwegian criminal law applies to acts committed in Norway.[3] Contrary to other Nordic States' systematic approach to rules on jurisdiction, the Norwegian rules are less systematised and mainly consist of listing relevant parts of jurisdiction principles and referring to other national legislation.[4] Due to this, the presentation of the Norwegian provisions in this chapter suffers to some extent from a lack of coherence. The lack of systematisation is to some extent remedied in the new Criminal Code (new SL).[5] Although the new SL was already established in 2005, it has due to technical reasons yet to enter into force.[6]

---

1. Postdoctoral research fellow, Faculty of Law, University of Bergen, Norway. The author wishes to thank especially Professor Erling Johannes Husabø and PhD researcher Dan Helenius for insightful comments on the text.
2. Almindelig borgerlig straffelov, Act 22 May 1902 no. 10.
3. The unofficial English translation of the Norwegian SL uses the term "*felony*" for "*forbrytelse*" and "*misdemeanor*" for "*forseelse*". For the purposes of this article, the term "*offence*" is used and because "*misdemeanor*" is relatively outdated, it has been replaced by "*summary offence*".
4. Also highlighted in Straffrättslig jurisdiktion i Norden, Nord 1992:17, p. 23.
5. Lov om straff (straffeloven), Act 20 May 2005 no. 28.
6. As an exception to this, the provisions on the general part are already in force in relation to chapter 16 of the new Criminal Code, which regulates genocide, crimes

Moreover, it is systematically somewhat unclear as to whether jurisdictional rules are considered part of substantive or procedural criminal law in Norway. Jurisdictional rules are mainly considered part of substantive criminal law but at the same time, it is admitted that these provisions could also be considered part of criminal procedural law.[7] This position is in line with current case law of the Norwegian Supreme Court, although there is some previous case law from the Supreme Court stating otherwise.[8] The lack of jurisdiction is to be a ground for acquittal, and not for dismissal of the case.[9]

The Norwegian rules on jurisdiction prescribe both the scope of application of Norwegian substantive criminal law and the international/transnational competence of Norwegian courts. Norwegian courts only apply Norwegian criminal law. Norwegian jurisdiction (*straffemyndighet*) cannot be applied outside of Norway and Norwegian prosecutors and courts are restricted to applying their competence within Norwegian territory.[10] Foreign law may be taken into account at a prejudicial stage, but the basis for criminal responsibility must be rooted in Norwegian law. This is based on section 96 of the Norwegian Constitution,[11] which in essence states that a person may only be convicted according to law or punished in accordance with a court judgment.

against humanity and war crimes, see FOR 2008-03-07 nr 225: Delvis ikraftsetting av lov om straff (straffeloven) Act 20. May 2005 nr. 28.

7. NOU 1984:31 (Straffelovgivningens stedlige virkeområde) p. 7, Ot.prp. nr. 90 (2003-2004) p. 175. *Jo Stigen*, "Lokalisering av straffbare handlinger". Tidsskrift for Strafferett 2011-2, pp. 142-145 also comments on other authors' views as well as positions in preparatory works.

8. Supreme Court case Rt. 2010 p. 1217 where the lack of jurisdiction lead to acquittal of the case (*frifinnelse, ikke hjemmel å straffe forholdet i Norge*). See also on the contrary view the case of the Supreme Court Rt. 2003 p. 179 where the case was dismissed (*avvist*).

9. Similar *Stigen* (2011), p. 145.

10. NOU 1984:31, p. 7, NOU 1992:23 (Ny straffelov – alminnelige bestemmelser), p. 38 and *Johs Andenæs*, Alminnelig strafferett, 5th edition, published by *Magnus Matningsdal and Georg Fredrik Rieber-Mohn*, Universitetsforlaget 2004, p. 556 and *Magnus Matningsdal and Anders Bratholm*, Straffeloven med kommentarer, Bind I, 2nd edition, Universitetsforlaget 2003, p. 45. However, see also Ot.prp. nr. 20 (1962-63), p. 6-7.

11. The Norwegian Constitution, Kongeriget Norges Grundlov, given in Rigsforsamlingen paa Eidsvold, 17. May 1814. See also *Anders Bratholm*, Strafferett og samfunn, Universitetsforlaget 1980, p. 372.

The expression *"according to law"* has been considered meaning Norwegian law.[12]

The provisions on jurisdiction have been subject to amendments over time, but apart from extending the extraterritorial jurisdiction, they have not changed significantly from their original form.[13] The Norwegian Criminal Code has been subject to a major amendment in 2005.[14] The whole Code has been thoroughly revised and a new Criminal Code has been introduced. When entering into force, the new SL will have a big impact on Norwegian criminal law in general. It will also amend the Norwegian provisions on jurisdiction, however in relation to the overall changes; the impact here will be somewhat lesser. The new SL has not yet entered into force and it is unclear when this will take place. Where relevant, changes in the new SL will be mentioned in this article, but the starting point is the current provisions.

1.2. Outline of the principles of the law on jurisdiction

In essence, jurisdiction is based on the principle that the State exercises jurisdiction over offences committed in its territory. This *territoriality principle* also constitutes the point of departure for the application of Norwegian criminal law. This is clear from the main rule in section 12(1)(1) SL, where it states that Norwegian criminal law applies to acts committed in the realm (*riket*). The realm as such is not defined, but the Norwegian legislator has considered it necessary to elaborate further on which parts or installations should be considered as being part of the realm. This principle will in the new SL be expressed in the new section 4(1) and 4(2)a).[15]

Norwegian jurisdiction has been considered applicable to Norwegian vessels and aircrafts. The *flag state principle* is therefore applicable and section 12(1)(1) letters d) and e) SL regulate offences connected to Norwegian vessels or aircrafts. Section 4(2)c) will express this principle in the new SL.[16]

Norwegian law applies to an offence committed outside of Norway by a Norwegian citizen, or by persons domiciled in Norway. The *active personality principle* is laid down in section 12(1)(3) SL. This applies, with some fur-

---

12. *Andenæs, Matningsdal and Rieber-Mohn* (2004), p. 556, who also state that this was considered being the case already in 1896. Section 96 first part in Norwegian: "Ingen kan dømmes uden efter Lov, eller straffes uden efter Dom."
13. See especially NOU 1984:31 and NOU 1992: 23.
14. See also NOU 2002:4 (Ny straffelov), p. 197-207 on jurisdiction.
15. This principle is dealt with in 2.1.
16. This principle is dealt with in 2.2.

ther restrictions, regardless of where the offence was committed. In the new SL, section 5 will express this principle.[17]

The *passive personality principle* is not, contrary to other Nordic legislation, expressed in the Norwegian Criminal Code.[18] Therefore, it is not applicable *per se*. Offences directed at Norwegians can be punished either in combination with the *active personality principle* or the *principle of universal jurisdiction* (either under section 12(1)(3) SL, when the offence is committed abroad by a Norwegian national or a person domiciled in Norway, or under section 12(1)(4) SL, when the act is committed by a foreigner with some further conditions). Contrary to the current provisions, section 5(5) in the new SL will express this principle.[19]

In addition, important interests of the Norwegian State are protected and these are included in different provisions. Section 12(1)(4)a can to some extent, be considered an expression of the *principle of state protection.* This section states that Norwegian law is applicable to offences committed outside Norway, for instance when these are directed at important Norwegian state interests (*kvalifiserte realprinsipp*).[20] Section 12(1)(3)b SL states that Norwegian criminal law is applicable to acts committed abroad by a Norwegian national, or to a person residing in Norway, when the act is an offence directed against the Norwegian State or Norwegian State authority. In the new SL, the new section 5(1)6) will express this principle.[21]

The *principle of universal jurisdiction* is based on the premise that some offences are so serious that they must not go unpunished. States can therefore pursue such offences regardless of where they were committed. The rules of international law generally restrict the application of this principle. Section 12(1)(4) SL lays down the principle and some restrictions to it. This principle will in the new SL, be expressed in sections 5(1)1), 5(3), 5(4) and 6.[22]

The *principle of representational jurisdiction* (also called the *principle of vicarious jurisdiction*) is not clearly expressed in the Norwegian Criminal

17. This principle is dealt with in 2.3.
18. Straffrättslig jurisdiktion i Norden, Nord 1992:17, p. 51.
19. This principle is dealt with in 2.4.
20. *Matningsdal and Bratholm* (2003), p. 47. See also 2.6. which deals with the *principle of universal jurisdiction*.
21. This principle is dealt with in 2.5.
22. This principle is dealt with in 2.6.

Code. This will also be the case with the new SL, as it contains no clear expression of this principle.[23]

1.3. The relationship between jurisdictional rules and the scope of the criminal provisions

As a starting point, the Norwegian provisions on jurisdiction apply to all offences. This follows from section 1(1) SL, which states that the general part of the SL (including the provisions on jurisdiction) is applicable to all criminal acts, unless otherwise stated. This has been considered to include all criminal offences, both in SL and in other legislation.[24]

However, some offences require a closer connection to Norway. This concerns mainly offences committed on Norwegian territory or offences connected to Norwegian interests. Outside the SL, Norwegian jurisdiction is usually restricted to offences committed in Norway and this can follow directly from the acts themselves.[25] Offences connected to acts on public administration are typical examples of where the offence should be committed in Norway, as Norwegian administrative law as a starting point only applies in Norway.[26] In addition offences regulated in the Road Traffic Act have been considered to apply only when committed in Norway.[27] In the opposite direction, examples of legislation outside the SL where the Norwegian jurisdiction applies for offences committed abroad are section 11 of the Military Criminal Code (explicitly applies for offences committed abroad) and section 3 of the Act on polar bear hunting (considered applying also for offences committed abroad).[28]

In the SL, some offences can only be committed in Norway or against Norwegian interests. This can be read out of the statutory definition of the offence. This applies for offences in chapter 8 SL, which concerns offences against the independence and security of the state, state meaning Norway. This further applies in relation to chapter 9 SL, which regulates offences

23. This principle is dealt with in 2.7.
24. NOU 1984:31 p. 15 and *Matningsdal and Bratholm* (2003), p. 1.
25. NOU 1984:31 p. 15 and preparatory works SKM I 1896 – Udkast til almindelig borgerlig Straffelov med Motiver. Udarbeidet av Straffelovkommisjonen fra 1885 (Kristiania 1896), p. 15.
26. *Andenæs, Matningsdal and Rieber-Mohn* (2004), p. 562 and *Bratholm* (1980), p. 384.
27. This Act may also apply to Norwegian jurisdiction for road traffic offences committed by Norwegians abroad; see *Andenæs, Matningsdal and Rieber-Mohn* (2004), p. 563 and Supreme Court case Rt. 1969 p. 509.
28. Militær Straffelov, Act 22 May 1902 no. 13 and Lov om fredning og fangst av isbjørn [isbjørnloven], Act 22 March 1957 no. 04.

against the Norwegian Constitution and Head of State.[29] Certain other statutory definitions include the requirement of the offence being committed in the realm, such as defamation of character pursuant to section 254 SL, return to the realm after being expelled pursuant to section 342 SL (especially letter a)), misleading persons to emigrate from the realm pursuant to section 141 SL and summary offences relating to using or showing scenes of gross violence pursuant to section 382 SL.

Some of the offences that are listed in SL have been included in the specific provisions in relation to the *active personality principle* and the *principle of universal jurisdiction*. These offences can therefore be committed abroad by a Norwegian or a foreigner. Nevertheless, the definition of the offence cannot be extended solely on the basis of the jurisdiction provisions (meaning for example, for offences against the Norwegian state that the offence can be committed by anyone and wherever, but it needs to be directed at the Norwegian state and not a foreign state).[30]

1.4. Impact of foreign law

The *double criminality principle* is expressed in sections 12(1)(3)c) and 12(1)(4)b) SL. Double criminality is therefore required for Norwegian criminal law to be applied when the offence is committed abroad by a Norwegian national or person residing in Norway. Double criminality is furthermore required when the offence is committed abroad by a foreigner. The offence is then to be punishable in that state and the offender is to be resident or staying in Norway. The *double criminality principle* applies *in abstracto* in relation to the *active personality principle* and *in concreto* when the offence is committed abroad by a foreigner.[31] In both cases, the penalty the offender would have been sentenced to in the place of commission should be taken into account and the penalty imposed should furthermore not exceed the penalty that is prescribed by law in the place of commission.[32] This means that the principle of *lex mitior* is applicable in relation to double criminality.

There are however significant exceptions to the applicability of the *double criminality principle*. As sections 12(1)(3)c) and 12(1)(4)b) are options within possible situations where Norwegian criminal law is applicable, all other

29. See NOU 2003:18, pp. 34-44.
30. See 2.3. and 2.6.
31. NOU 1984:31 p. 12, *Andenæs, Matningsdal and Rieber-Mohn* (2004), pp. 562, 564, and *Bratholm* (1980), pp. 379, 381.
32. See also *Sverre Tønnesen*, Internasjonal strafferettspleie, Manuskript December 1975 Universitetet i Bergen 1975, pp. 4.99-4.103.

situations, that is the letters a), b) and d) to i) of section 12(1)(3) SL and letters a), c) and d) of section 12(1)(4) SL, are not subjected to the *double criminality principle*.[33]

In the new SL, the *double criminality principle* will be a first condition for the application of Norwegian jurisdiction to offences committed abroad. Section 5(1)1 will lay this requirement down. This section will state that Norwegian criminal law applies when an offence is committed by a Norwegian national, a person with permanent residence in Norway or a Norwegian company when an offence:

1. is also criminalized by law in the state where the act has been committed

This will however only be a first condition, whereas points 2 to 10 list offences for which the requirement will not apply.[34] The new section 5(6) will furthermore apply the *lex mitior* principle. It will state that:

(6) For the prosecution under this section, the sentence may not exceed the statutory maximum penalty for the same offence in the country where the offence has been committed.

1.5. Impact of foreign judgments

Based on the European cooperation in relation to the transfer of prosecution and convicted persons, section 12a was added to the SL. This section regulates the principle of *ne bis in idem* and states the following:

Section 12a
When a legally enforceable judgment has been passed on a person pursuant to
1. Act of 20 July 1991 no. 67 relating to the transfer of convicted persons,
2. Act of 25 March 1977 no. 22 relating to the transfer of a prosecution from or to another European country or
3. an international agreement within the Schengen area of co-operation, no criminal proceedings may be instituted or sentence passed in Norway for the same criminal offence if
   a)   he has been acquitted;
   b)   he has been found guilty but no sanction has been imposed;
   c)   the sanction imposed has been fully executed or is in the process of execution; or
   d)   the sanction imposed has ceased to apply according to the rules of the adjudicating country.
Unless the prosecution in the adjudicating country was instituted on the application of the Norwegian authorities, the first paragraph shall not apply to such cases as are referred to in no. 1 and no. 2 of the first paragraph,

33. See 2.3. and 2.6. on these provisions.
34. These are mentioned in relation to relevant principles of jurisdiction, see 2.3. and 2.6.

a) when the act is committed in this realm, cf. section 12, first paragraph, no. 1 and the second paragraph;
b) when the perpetrator at the time of committing the act was resident in Norway or was a Norwegian national, and the prosecution is required in the public interest;
c) when the act was directed against a person holding a Norwegian public office or a public institution or something else of a public character in this realm, or the perpetrator himself held a Norwegian public office;
d) when the act was hijacking of an aircraft or some other international crime under international law; or
e) in so far as otherwise follows from an extradition treaty or a multilateral international agreement.

Unless the prosecution in the adjudicating country was instituted on the application of the Norwegian authorities, the first paragraph shall not apply to such cases as are referred to in no. 3 of the first paragraph, when

a) the act on which the foreign judgment was based was wholly or partly committed in Norway. If the act was only partly committed in Norway, the exception shall not, however, apply if the act was partly committed on the territory of the party to the convention where the judgment was pronounced;
b) the act on which the foreign judgment was based is punishable in Norway pursuant to chapter 8, 9 or 14 of this code or the Act of 18 August 1914 no. 3 relating to defence secrets; or
c) the act on which the foreign judgment was based was committed by a Norwegian official and was in breach of his official duties.

The section 12a(1) starts with listing those conventions that regulate the *res judicata* effect of judgments and decisions in Norway. These include the international, European and Schengen conventions. The Nordic cooperation is regulated in a separate Act.[35] The section lists the requirements for when criminal proceedings cannot be instituted or a sentence passed in Norway for the same offence which was decided on with a foreign judgment. The rule is that when a case has been finally decided on in another state, this prohibits the prosecution and sentencing in Norway.[36]

The section then has two exceptions to this main rule. The first exception in relation to the conventions, except the Schengen convention, is found in section 12a(2) and states that the restriction in 12a(1) does not apply in situations where the offence is connected to Norway, unless prosecution in the other state was instituted on the application of the Norwegian authorities. The

35. Act on execution of Nordic judgments etc., Lov om fullbyrding av nordiske dommer på straff m.v., Act 15 November 1963. For information on which states have ratified the conventions listed in section 12a (1), see *Matningsdal* and *Bratholm* (2003), pp. 68-70.
36. See the Appeal Committee of the Supreme Court case HR-1994-1888-s and the Appellate Court case LB-2005-148662.

offence is connected to Norway when it is committed in Norway, the perpetrator is a Norwegian national or resident in Norway or the offence was directed against a Norwegian public office or the perpetrator held such office (letters a) to c)). In these situations national interests may speak for prosecution in Norway.[37] The same exception applies furthermore in situations of the offence being hijacking of an aircraft or another international crime or if it otherwise follows from an extradition treaty or multilateral agreement (letters d) and e)). These situations are based on international agreements, which prescribe universal jurisdiction for relevant offences.[38]

The second exception is found in section 12a(3) and regulates situations in relation to international agreements within the Schengen area. Similarly, as the first exception, it states that the restriction in 12a(1) does not apply when the offence was committed in Norway (partly or wholly), directed at the Norwegian state or committed by a Norwegian official, unless prosecution in another Schengen state was instituted on the request of Norwegian authorities. This provision was added to the section 12a SL when Norway became part of the Schengen area, and it was considered important to list the exceptions in the act.[39] It corresponds to article 55 CISA, which allows the states to restrict the application of article 54 CISA. The explicitly mentioned offences are considered to be of importance for Norway, which explains the preservation of jurisdiction and prosecution in such cases.

Section 13(4) SL also states that in situations where a person has been sentenced abroad and is convicted of the same offence in Norway;

the penalty already served shall as far as possible be deducted from the sentence imposed.

Only the penalty served is to be taken into account by the court and based on the circumstances in the case.[40] This section is in line with article 56 CISA.

The current section 12a will essentially be forwarded with section 8 SL in the new SL. Some minor adjustments will be made, but these will not influence the content of the section.[41] The current section 13(4) will be found in the new section 84 SL. Only language adjustments will be made here, but the

---

37. *Matningsdal and Bratholm* (2003), p. 71.
38. Ibid.
39. Ot.prp. nr. 56 (1998-1999), pp. 89-90. See also *Jon Petter Rui*, Forbudet mot gjentatt straffeforfølgning, Universitetsforlaget 2009, p. 203-204.
40. See Supreme Court cases Rt. 1996 p. 561, Rt. 1985 p. 1325, Rt. 1981 p. 46, and Rt. 1977 p. 399.
41. NOU 2002:4, pp. 206-207.

section is moved to the chapter regulating determination of sentence (*reaksjonsfastsettelse*), which was considered systematically more coherent.[42] It now states that reactions, and not only penalties, should be deducted.[43]

The new section 8 in the new SL will, when entering into force state the following:

Section 8
Power to prosecute matter adjudicated abroad.

(1) When a final judgment was rendered abroad, falls under
a) Law no. 22 of 25 March 1977 on the transfer of prosecution by or to another European country or
b) Law no. 67 of 20 July 1991 on the transfer of sentenced persons or
c) an international agreement within the framework of the Schengen cooperation criminal proceedings or judgment can not be instituted in Norway for the same offence, when,
    1.   the person was acquitted or found guilty without any sanction imposed or
    2.   the sentence imposed is fully served, is being served or has been annulled according to the judicial rules of the country.

(2) If the prosecution has not taken place in the country at the request of Norwegian authorities, criminal matters within the meaning of subsection 1, letters a and b, can be prosecuted in Norway, when
a) the offence was committed in an area as mentioned in Section 4, cf. Section 7,
b) the offender at the time of the crime was a resident in Norway or a Norwegian citizen and public interest requires prosecution,
c) the act was directed against a person in a Norwegian public office or against a public institution or against something else of a public nature in Norway or the offender held a Norwegian public office themselves, or
d) Norway is entitled or obliged under international law to prosecute.

(3) If the prosecution has not taken place in the country at the request of Norwegian authorities, criminal matters within the meaning of subsection 1, letter c, can be prosecuted in Norway, when
a) the offence is committed in whole or in part in Norway. Has the act only partially been committed in Norway, the exception does not apply if the act was partially committed in the territory of the Contracting State in which the judgment was rendered,
b) the act is criminalised in Norway as war crimes, genocide, crime against the independence and security of the state, crime against the constitution and the political system,

---

42. NOU 2002:4, pp. 267-268.
43. This could in principle include also deduction for detention (varetektsfradrag), as envisaged in NOU 1992:23, p. 55, however not commented on in NOU 2002:4, p. 268. To include reductions and not only penalties generally seems to be based on article 56 CISA in fine.

hijacking, sabotage against infrastructure, serious drugs offence, unlawful dealing with plutonium and uranium or serious arson or other particularly dangerous destruction, or

c) the act was committed by a Norwegian official and was a violation of that person's official duties.

1.6. Restrictions on prosecution

The *principle of discretionary prosecution* is applicable in Norwegian criminal procedure.[44]

Section 13(1) SL has a specific rule in relation to prosecution and the *principle of universal jurisdiction*. It regulates in relation to letters a) and b) in section 12(1)(4), which concern offences committed abroad by foreigners, either listed in letter a) or falling under the *double criminality principle* in letter b) that prosecution can only be instituted when the King so decides. This restriction of applying Norwegian jurisdiction in these cases is based on the fact that prosecuting foreigners for offences committed abroad raises some questions of international law and foreign policy. In practice, it is the Government that decides on instituting prosecution in such cases and restricting the competence has been considered leading to a better assessment of different aspects in such cases.[45] Such an institution of prosecution has been considered to overrule the general possibility to waive prosecution (*påtaleunnlatelse*) pursuant to section 69 of the Norwegian Criminal Procedural Code (Strpl.).[46]

Section 13(2) SL includes a further restriction in cases dealt with in section 12(1)(4)b), which are those of Norwegian jurisdiction being based on the *principle of universal jurisdiction*, falling under the *double criminality principle* and the offender being present in Norway. A prosecution may not take place in such a case;

---

44. Sections 69 and 70 of the Norwegian Criminal Procedural Code, Lov om rettergangsmåten i straffesaker (Straffeprosessloven, Strpl.), Act 22 May 1981 no. 25 and *Johs Andenæs*, Norsk straffeprosess, 4. utgave ved *Tor-Geir Myhrer*, Universitetsforlaget 2009, pp. 364-365. On the history of the principle of discretionary prosecution in Norwegian criminal procedure, see *Rolf Thoresen*, Påtaleunnlatelse i teori og praksis: anvendelsen av opportunitetsprinsippet i norsk straffeprosess, Juristforbundets forlag 1997, pp. 15-24.

45. NOU 1984:31 p. 40 and *Matningsdal and Bratholm* (2003), p. 73. See Supreme Court case Rt. 2003 p. 1770, where the fact that such a decision did not exist did not lead to dismissal of the case, as the offence was considered committed also in Norway, based on section 12(2) SL.

46. See *Hans Kristian Bjerke, Erik Keiserud og Knut Erik Sæther*, Straffeprosessloven, Kommentarutgave, 4. utgave, Bind I, Universitetsforlaget 2011, p. 298.

unless there is also power to impose a penalty according to the law of the country in which the act was committed. Nor may a more severe penalty be imposed than is authorized by the law of the said country.

This means that the *double criminality principle* is absolute in relation to prosecuting the offence in Norway and the requirement applies *in concreto*, as the penalty imposed cannot be more severe than in the state of commission.

In the new SL, applying Norwegian criminal law for offences committed abroad, both in situations of the offender being a Norwegian national or a foreigner, prosecution shall only be commenced if the public interest so requires (*allmenne hensyn tilsier det*). This will be stated in section 5(7):

Prosecution under this section is raised only when public interest so requires.

This applies also in situations of the new section 6 on a specific basis for prosecution based on international law.[47] This requirement of public interest will be a restriction in relation to prosecution and the *principle of discretionary prosecution*, but will not be a significant change in todays practice, as the application of the *principle of universal jurisdiction* is fairly restricted. The restriction of the institution of prosecution in relation to offences committed abroad by foreigners will be moved into a new section 65(1)4 Strpl. and the Director of Public Prosecutions (*Riksadvokaten*) will have this competence.[48] It was considered a better systematic approach to include the provision in the Strpl. with the other provisions regulating prosecution competence of the Director of Public Prosecutions.[49]

2. The Rules on Jurisdiction in Detail

2.1. Territoriality principle

Section 12(1)(1) SL states that Norwegian criminal law applies to acts committed in the realm (*riket*). This main rule applies both to offences in the SL

---

47. See 2.6. on this.
48. When the decision to prosecute may affect Norwegian foreign relations, the director should confer with the Ministry of Foreign Affairs, see Ot.prp. nr. 90 (2003-2004), p. 487 and *Erling Johannes Husabø:* Fighting terrorism through multilevel criminal legislation, Martinus Nijhoff Publishers 2009, p. 339.
49. NOU 2002:4, p. 204 and Ot.prp. nr. 90 (2003-2004), pp. 186, 487 and 514. On the different prosecution competences, see *Andenæs and Myhrer* (2009), pp. 35-50.

and in other legislation.[50] This rule will also be found in the new provisions on jurisdiction. The new section 4(1) SL will state that criminal legislation applies to acts committed in Norway.

2.1.1. Localisation

The place of commission is regulated in section 12(2) SL, which states:

> In cases in which the criminality of the act depends on or is influenced by any actual or intended effect, the act shall be regarded as committed also where such effect has occurred or is intended to be produced.

The place of commission is therefore defined as both the place where the act was committed and, if necessary, where the consequence contained in the statutory definition of the offence became apparent.[51] Although the provision does not expressly state that the place of commission is also the place where the act was committed, this is considered implied with the word "also" in the section 12(2).[52] The place of commission is based on the *principle of ubiquity* and includes firstly offences committed through active conduct. In cases of continued offences (*fortsatt forbrytelse*) Norway is considered the place of commission, even if only part of the continued offence has taken place in Norway.[53]

The definition of the place of commission secondly includes offences of omission, although this is not expressly stated. This follows from Section 4 SL, which defines offences and includes offences of omissions as offences, unless otherwise stated. The place of omission is in such situations considered to be where the perpetrator should have acted and where the consequence contained in the statutory definition of the offence became apparent.[54] An example of this is a case where a father was sentenced for having deprived his children of parental care in Norway. The case concerned two children whose mother was Norwegian and the father foreign. The father failed to return the children to Norway as agreed, which resulted in the children being deprived of their mother's care. Based on the section 12(2) SL and the

---

50. NOU 1984:31, p. 15 and *Andenæs, Matningsdal and Rieber-Mohn* (2004), p. 559.
51. Already stated in preparatory works SKM I 1896 – Udkast til almindelig borgerlig Straffelov med Motiver. Udarbeidet av Straffelovkommisjonen fra 1885 (Kristiania 1896) p. 19, see also *Stigen* (2011), p. 141 and Supreme Court case Rt. 2003 p. 1770.
52. *Stigen* (2011), p. 149, *Andenæs, Matningsdal and Rieber-Mohn* (2004), p. 565 and the Supreme Court case Rt. 2003 p. 1770 no. 26.
53. *Andenæs, Matningsdal and Rieber-Mohn* (2004), p. 367 and Supreme Court cases Rt. 1996 p. 654 and Rt. 1951 p. 498.
54. *Andenæs, Matningsdal and Rieber-Mohn* (2004), p. 565 and *Stigen* (2011), p. 160.

fact that the omission lead to the children not being cared for in Norway, resulted, in the commission being in Norway because the children were to be handed over to the mother in Norway.[55]

In relation to attempt, the last part of Section 12(2) SL, states that the act shall be considered committed also where the effect is intended to be produced. Apparently, both the place where the attempt was made and where its effects would have occurred qualify as a place of commission. As the section states "intended", it is clear that intent (*forsett*) is required.[56]

There is no provision in the SL in relation to the place of commission and complicity. There is furthermore no general provision on criminal responsibility in relation to complicity in the SL.[57] The criminal provisions of the special part in the SL either include the criminal responsibility of complicity or not, such as theft pursuant to section 257 SL, which includes persons who aid or abet such an offence.[58] The place of commission defined as with the offence, and deemed to be where the act of complicity was committed and where the offence by the main offender is deemed to have been committed.[59] This follows from the principal offence being regarded as an effect of complicity.[60]

There are no specific rules in the SL in relation to cybercrimes, where the offence is committed on the internet. Regulating the place of commission in relation to such offences was discussed, and an amendment was even put for-

---

55. Case of 22 February 2007 of Trondheim district court. The case was appealed and the appeal dismissed by the Supreme Court in Rt. 2007 p. 1002, but not in relation to the jurisdiction part. Deprivation of parental care is criminalized in section 216 SL.
56. *Stigen* (2011), p. 158 and *Andenæs, Matningsdal and Rieber-Mohn* (2004), p. 565.
57. The current section 58 SL only regulates sentencing in relation to complicity. This will, with the new SL, be amended, as the new section 15 will rule that a penal provision also covers any person who aids or abets the crime, unless otherwise provided (in Norwegian: Et straffebud rammer også den som medvirker til overtredelsen, når ikke annet er bestemt). See *Erling Johannes Husabø*, "The regulation of complicity, attempts and preparatory acts in the new Norwegian Penal Code (2005), seen in a historical and European perspective", in *Sözüer* (ed.), Congress on the Criminal Law Reforms in the World and in Turkey 26 May-4 June 2010, Istanbul 2013, p. 419-420 on the new section.
58. See further *Husabø* (2013), p. 420-422 on this question.
59. See further *Erling Johannes Husabø*, Straffansvarets periferi. Medvirkning, forsøk, førebuing, Universitetsforlaget 1999, p. 255-261. See further Supreme Court case Rt. 1927 p. 513.
60. *Husabø* 2009, p. 319.

ward,[61] but the Government's view was that defining the place of commission is sufficiently clear from the current section 12(2) SL (and new section 7 SL).[62]

Section 7 in the new SL will apply the same approach as the current regulation and will transfer the current section 12(2) into the new SL. This section will state:

If the criminality of an act is dependent or influenced by an actual or intended result, the act is also regarded as committed there, where the result has occurred or its induction was intended.

2.1.2. Definition of Norway

The realm is not defined in the legislation, but it is considered to include what is generally considered part of the realm, the mainland, islands, the water territories and air territories.[63] Norwegian criminal law also applies in the Norwegian custom zone, the fishing zone and the economic zone.[64] Svalbard and Jan Mayen are furthermore part of the realm.[65]

In section 12(1)(1) SL, the legislator has included some other installations or constructions that are to be included in the Norwegian realm. These are:

61. In NOU 2007:2, p. 142 and 177 a new sentence was suggested to regulate the matter. In Norwegian: *"Er et datasystem eller elektronisk kommunikasjonsnett i Norge rammet eller forsøkt rammet av en handling som er straffbar etter kapitlet om "Vern av data, databasert informasjon og datasystemer", anses virkningen inntrådt i Norge."*
62. Ot.prp. nr. 22 (2008-2009), p. 27. See furthermore *Stigen* (2011), p. 178-187 and the Supreme Court case Rt. 2004 p. 1619 and the Appellate Court case RG 2001, p. 219.
63. NOU 1984:31, p. 7-8. Critically on the lack of definition of the realm already in 1975, see *Tønnesen* (1975), p. 7.74.
64. NOU 1984:31, p. 8. These are based on sections 1-3 and 1-4 of the Customs Act, Lov om toll og vareførsel (tolloven), Act 21 December 2007 no. 119, section 1 of the Act on the Economic Zone, Lov om Norges økonomiske sone (økonomiske soneloven) Act 17 December 1976 no. 91 and the Act on territorial waters, Lov om Norges territorialfarvann og tilstøtende sone (territorialfarvannsloven) Act 27 June 2003 no. 57. The economic zone will be included in the new section 4(2)b) of the new SL.
65. This is often further specified in legislative work or commentaries, but there is no such specification in the legislation. See e.g. NOU 1984:31, p. 8. The new section 4(1) of the SL will include a specific mentioning of Svalbard and Jan Mayen as well as Norway's dependent territory (*"biland"*) as belonging to the Norwegian realm. A dependent territory is a part that is not considered to be part of the Norwegian State, but falling under its jurisdiction, see the Act on dependent territory, Lov om Bouvetøya, Peter I's øy og Dronning Maud Land m.m. (bilandsloven), Act 27 February 1930 no. 03. See further *Matningsdal and Bratholm* (2003), pp. 50-52.

a) any installation or construction placed on the Norwegian part of the continental shelf and used for exploration for or exploitation or storage of submarine natural resources
b) constructions for the transport of petroleum resources connected with any installation or construction placed on the Norwegian part of the continental shelf
c) the security zone around such installations and constructions as are mentioned under a and b above.

Letters a) b) and c) are a result of the Norwegian oil industry. They proclaim that oil installations and platforms on the Norwegian continental shelf are considered part of Norwegian realm. These rules were added to the SL in the 1970s following a case that was heard by the Norwegian Supreme Court, where the question was whether the Norwegian jurisdiction applied on such installations.[66]

In essence, these points are included in the new SL, in section 4(2)a). This letter will state that for acts committed on installations on the Norwegian part of the continental shelf that is used for exploration, exploitation or storage of submarine natural resources, and on pipe structures and other permanent transport structures connected to such installations, including when these are outside the Norwegian part of the continental shelf, the Norwegian jurisdiction applies, as these are included in the Norwegian realm. Furthermore, the application of Norwegian jurisdiction in the economic zone will be included in section 4(2)b). The new section 4(2) will state:

(2) The criminal law also applies to acts that have been carried out
a) on facilities on the Norwegian Continental Shelf for the exploration or exploitation, or storage of submarine natural resources and on pipelines and other fixed transportation facilities associated with such devices even when they are outside the Norwegian Continental Shelf,
b) in the area of jurisdiction established by Law, 17 December 1976, no. 91 on the Economic Zone of Norway, the acts violating the interests safeguarded by Norwegian jurisdiction.

2.2. Flag state principle
In section 12(1)(1) SL, the *flag state principle* is expressed in letters d and e, those places are considered part of the Norwegian realm:

d) any Norwegian vessel (including a Norwegian drilling platform or similar mobile installation) in the open sea, and

---

66. Case Rt. 1974 p. 897. The amendments were made by the Act of 10 June 1977, and detailed discussions can be found in the *travaux préparatoires* Ot.prp. nr. 50 (1976-1977).

e) any Norwegian aircraft outside such areas as are subject to the jurisdiction of another state.

What is to be included in the term vessel or aircraft is not defined in the SL. Vessel is intended to have a broad definition and to encompass the definitions in the Norwegian Maritime Code and the Act on the Norwegian international ship register.[67] The term aircraft is to be defined in accordance with the Civil Aviation Act.[68] Focus should be on whether the vessel or aircraft is registered in Norway.[69]

Furthermore, section 12(1)(2) SL states that Norwegian criminal law applies to acts committed:

on any Norwegian vessel or aircraft wherever it may be, by a member of its crew or any other person travelling on the vessel or aircraft; the term vessel here also includes a drilling platform or similar mobile installation.

This provision applies the so-called "French system" and entails the *flag state principle* first of all in relation to persons travelling or working on the vessel or aircraft.[70] This means that if an offence is committed on board the vessel or aircraft by a visitor, this does not as a starting point fall under Norwegian jurisdiction.[71] This provision also includes drilling platforms and similar installations. This is again relevant for Norway, as the exploitation of submarine natural resources is widespread.

The new section 4(2)c) SL will have the same approach as the current provisions and will transfer and comprise these provisions into a single point. This section will state that Norwegian criminal law applies to offences committed:

c) aboard Norwegian vessels or aircraft, on drilling platforms or other similar movable facility. On vehicles or facilities located in the territory of another State, the criminal law applies only to acts of passengers or people belonging to the crew of the vehicle or facility.

---

67. Lov om sjøfarten (sjøloven), Act 24 June 1994 no. 39, Lov om norsk internasjonalt skipsregister (NIS-loven), Act 12 June 1987 no. 48, see also *Matningsdal and Bratholm* (2003), p. 55.
68. Lov om luftfart (luftfartsloven), Act 11 June 1993 no. 101.
69. NOU 1984:31, p. 10.
70. See Supreme Court case Rt. 2000 p. 803.
71. *Andenæs, Matningsdal and Rieber-Mohn* (2004), p. 560.

2.3. Active personality principle

This principle is expressed in section 12(1)(3) SL. This states that Norwegian criminal law shall be applicable to acts committed:

(3) abroad by any Norwegian national or any person domiciled in Norway when the act

a) is one of those dealt with in chapters 8, 9, 10, 11, 12, 14, 17, 18, 20, 23, 24, 25, 26 or 33, or paragraphs 135, 141, 142, 144, 145 second subparagraph, 145b, 147a, 147b, 162c, 169, 192 to 199, 202, 202a, 203, 204a, 222 to 225, 227 to 235, 238, 239, 242 to 245, 291, 292, 294 number 2, 317, 326 to 328, 330 last subparagraph, 338, 342, 367 to 370, or 423,

b) is an offence or a summary offence against the Norwegian State or Norwegian state authority,

c) is also punishable according to the law of the country in which it is committed, or

d) is committed in relation to the EFTA Court of Justice and is included among those dealt with in section 163, cf. section 167 and section 165, of this code, or sections 205 to 207 of the Courts of Justice Act;

e) is punishable pursuant to section 5 of Act of 6 May 1994 no. 10 relating to the implementation of the Chemical Weapons Convention,

f) shall be punishable in accordance with Article 113 of the UN Convention on the Law of the Sea of 10 December 1982 (damage to submarine cables and pipelines),

g) is punishable pursuant to section 5 of Act of 17 July 1988 no. 54 relating to the implementation of the Convention on the prohibition of the use, stockpiling, production and transfer of anti-personnel mines and on their destruction, or

h) is punishable pursuant to Act of 15 December 1995 no. 74 relating to a prohibition against female genital mutilation, or

i) is punishable pursuant to section 3 of the Act of 15 May 2009 no. 28 on the implementation of the Convention on Cluster Munitions;[72]

This provision states that Norwegian criminal law applies to acts committed abroad by Norwegian nationals or persons with a permanent residence in Norway. In relation to nationals and persons treated as such, the nationality of the person at the time of the offence is the deciding factor.[73] The section also lists conditions for the application of Norwegian law.

According to a), the act must fall within a certain scope of chapters and sections of the SL. These chapters concern serious acts, which are commonly to be considered punishable by all civilized nations.[74] These chapters concern

---

72. The translation is slightly outdated, so the author has filled in the relevant amendments herself.

73. *Andenæs, Matningsdal and Rieber-Mohn* (2004), p. 561 and *Matningsdal and Bratholm* 2003, p. 57.

74. Expressed in the preparatory works SKM I 1896 – Udkast til almindelig borgerlig Straffelov med Motiver. Udarbeidet av Straffelovkommisjonen fra 1885 (Kristiania

offences against the independence and security of the State, offences against the Norwegian constitution and Head of State, offences concerning the exercise of civil rights, offences in the public service and offences against the public authority. These offences could naturally be considered expressions of the principle of state protection.[75] Furthermore, they include offences against public safety, counterfeiting of money, forging of documents, offences concerning family relationship, defamations, embezzlement, extortion, fraud and summary offences (*forseelser*) in the civil service.

The specific provisions include endangering general order, misleading persons to emigrate from the realm, insults or contempt for creed or religion, revealing secrets confided in persons due to their position (such as defence councils), unlawfully obtaining data by electronic means, disseminating access data, terrorist offences and financing of terrorism (the latter two are already included in Chapter 14 on offences against public safety, and are therefore already included in the scope of offences). In addition, it includes participating in an organised criminal group, false accusation, certain sexual offences, also in relation to sexual abuse of children, certain offences in relation to prostitution (including promoting the engagement of other persons in prostitution and enabling oneself or others of sexual benefits, especially in relation to persons under 18 years), certain offences against personal liberty, certain offences against another person's life, body and health including negligent injuring with weapons, rendering other people helpless, unlawful abortion (not applying to the women themselves), certain offences of vandalism, receiving the proceeds of crime and some summary offences against the public authorities. Lastly, encouragement of offences, unlawfully entering a marriage, unlawful return into the realm, some summary offences against public confidence and unlawful carrying of freight or a Norwegian flag by a shipmaster is included in the provision listed.

The scope of offences included is rather large. Most of the offences are indeed of such seriousness that claiming jurisdiction for Norwegian nationals and permanent residents seems well-motivated. Norwegian criminal jurisdiction has recently been applied, in relation to the purchasing of sexual services. This is criminalised in section 202a SL, and included in the letter a) of section 12(1)(3) SL and therefore applicable to Norwegians abroad. A member of the Norwegian Parliament (Stortinget) was exposed as having pur-

---

1896), p. 15, see also *Andenæs, Matningsdal and Rieber-Mohn* (2004), p. 561 and *Tønnesen* (1975), pp. 7.74-75.

75. See 2.5.

chased sexual serviced from a prostitute in Latvia and as a result he agreed to pay a fine of NOK 25,000.[76]

The second possibility for Norway to apply its jurisdiction when an act is committed by a Norwegian national or a person residing in Norway applies in letter b) when the act is an offence against the Norwegian State or Norwegian state authority. This letter is to cover offences specifically related to Norway, which are not usually covered by foreign criminal law, such as tax offences against the Norwegian State or customs-related offences.[77] This could naturally be considered an expression of the *principle of state protection.*[78]

The third possibility is pursuant to letter c) if the act is also punishable in the place of commission. The *double criminality principle* applies generally, but not in relation to those offences listed in letter a).[79] The *double criminality principle* seems to apply *in abstracto*, as the act is to be criminalised, but the circumstances of the case, such as time-limitation, are not taken into consideration. It is however pointed out that in situations where the offender could not have been sentenced for the offence in the place of commission, sentencing in Norway should be used with caution.[80] When jurisdiction is based on letter c), the penalty the offender would have been sentenced to in the place of commission should be taken into account.[81]

---

76. Section 202a entered into force in 2009. This was the first case where a Norwegian national agreed to a fine for purchasing sexual services abroad. The case resulted in significant media impact, perhaps mainly due to the fact that a TV company had followed the member to Latvia and filmed him, in case "something illegal" would happen. It was further unclear what sort or services were in fact bought. The case has further launched a debate on the media functioning as provoking such situations. For other examples of applying jurisdiction in accordance with letter a), see Supreme Court cases Rt. 2002 p. 190, Rt. 1997 p. 1637 and Rt. 1977 p. 242.
77. *Andenæs, Matningsdal and Rieber-Mohn* (2004), p. 562 and Appellate Court case RG 2001 p. 1110.
78. See 2.5.
79. Therefore, when deciding on the sentence in situations falling under letter a), only Norwegian sentencing provisions are relevant. This was stated by the Supreme Court in case Rt. 1983 p. 510.
80. NOU 1984:31, p. 12, *Andenæs, Matningsdal and Rieber-Mohn* (2004), p. 562 and *Bratholm* (1980), p. 379.
81. Stated by the Norwegian Supreme Court in cases Rt. 2008 p. 116, Rt. 2000 p. 803, Rt. 1993 p. 1489, Rt. 1987 p. 1355, Rt. 1977 p. 779, and Rt. 1959 p. 509, also NOU 1984:31, p. 12 and *Bratholm* (1980), p. 379. On deciding on the penalty, when the offence has been committed on board a vessel, see Supreme Court case Rt. 2000 p. 803. See also Supreme Court case Rt. 1995 p. 104 and Rt. 1986 p. 1318.

Letters d) to h) in section 12(1)(3) SL contain provisions on the applica-tion of Norwegian jurisdiction as a result of Norway's international obliga-tions. These have been amended through the years, as Norway has concluded new agreements, which have presupposed that Norway extends its jurisdic-tion in relation to acts covered by the international conventions.[82] This could of course also be considered an expression of the *principle of universal juris-diction*.

The letters a), b), c) and h) are transferred into the new section 5(1) SL. This section will systematise the current rules and consist more of general rules, instead of giving a list of offences. Generally, the *active personality principle* will apply in relation to Norwegian nationals and persons permanently resid-ing in Norway as well as for Norwegian legal persons.[83] The *double criminal-ity principle* will be the first precondition, which means that extraterritorial jurisdiction will be more limited than today. This will be expressed in the fol-lowing way in section 5:

(1) Outside the scope of Section 4, the criminal law applies to acts committed
a) by a Norwegian citizen
b) by a person resident in Norway or
c) by a registered company in Norway, provided the acts
    1.   are also criminalized by law in the state, where the act has been committed
    2.   are considered as war crimes, genocide or crimes against humanity,
    3.   are regarded as a violation of the international laws and customs of war
    4.   are regarded as child marriage or forced marriage,
    5.   are regarded as genital mutilation,
    6.   are directed against the Norwegian State or Norwegian State authority,
    7.   are committed outside an area of sovereignty of any State and is punishable by imprisonment,
    8.   are considered as evasion of care,
    9.   are covered by Section 257, Sections 291-296, Sections 299-306 or Sections 309-316 or
    10. are regarded as trade to influence third parties.

The *double criminality principle* is therefore applicable, but with some ex-ceptions, for example offences directed against Norway, offences of genital mutilation and some international core crimes. The *active personality princi-*

---

82. For more details, see *Matningsdal and Bratholm* (2003), pp. 61-63.
83. A legal person is considered Norwegian, when it is registered in Norway. See NOU 2002:4, p. 202.

ple will not require double criminality in these situations.[84] This section also includes some parts of the *principle of universal jurisdiction.*[85]

The new section 5(2) will also regulate situations where the person has become a Norwegian national (or acquired another equivalent status) after the offence has been committed. This section will state the following:

(2) Subsection 1 shall apply mutatis mutandis to acts that have been committed
a) by a person, who after the fact has acquired Norwegian citizenship or taken up residence in Norway,
b) by a person who is a citizen or resident, or after the fact takes up citizenship or residence, in another Nordic State and who is staying in Norway, or
c) on behalf of a foreign entity, which after the fact has transferred its overall operations to an enterprise registrered in Norway.

This is an extension in relation to the current rules, as today the nationality of the person at the time of the offence is the decisive factor.[86]

2.4. Passive personality principle

As mentioned above, in chapter 1.2., there is no existing provision regulating the *passive personality principle* in the SL. This currently means that for Norwegian jurisdiction to apply to offences directed at Norwegians, they need to fall under either section 12(1)(3), where the offence is committed abroad by a Norwegian national or a person domiciled in Norway, or under section 12(1)(4), where the act is committed by a foreigner and the *principle of universal jurisdiction* applies.

In the preparatory works for the new SL, the current protection of Norwegian nationals was considered insufficient.[87] A new provision, section 5(5) was then added which concerns offences directed at Norwegian nationals or persons permanently resided in Norway. In the new section 5(5) SL, the *passive personality principle* will be expressed in the following way:

(5) The criminal law also applies to acts that have been committed abroad by persons other than those covered by Subsections 1-4, if the offence is punishable by a maximum sentence of 6 years' imprisonment or more and is directed against a Norwegian citizen or a resident of Norway.

---

84. See further Ot.prp. nr. 90 (2003-2004), pp. 401-404.
85. See chapter 2.6. below on the *principle of universal jurisdiction.*
86. See further Ot.prp. nr. 90 (2003-2004), p. 403.
87. Ot.prp. nr. 22 (2008-2009), p. 397.

2.5. Principle of state protection

Generally, the SL has not been considered to include a general provision in relation to protecting Norwegian state interests. Section 12(1)(4)a) SL could however be considered as expressing the *principle of state protection*, although it is generally considered an expression of the *principle of universal jurisdiction*.[88] The section states that Norwegian law is applicable to offences committed outside Norway when these are directed at important state interests of Norway (*kvalifiserte realprinsipp*). This follows from sections 83, 88, 89, 90, 91, 91a, 93, 94, 98 to 104a, and 110 to 132 SL, which are listed in letter a). These include offences against the independence and security of the State, offences against the Norwegian constitution and Head of State, offences within and against any public authority, and offences against public safety.

Section 12(1)(3)b) SL, states that Norwegian criminal law is applicable to acts committed abroad by a Norwegian national, or a person residing in Norway, when the act is an offence directed against the Norwegian State or Norwegian State authority. This letter naturally covers those offences already listed in letter a) but includes further offences in other legislation than the SL, such as national tax- and expense offences.[89]

In the new SL, the new section 5(1)6) will express this principle. This section will state that Norwegian jurisdiction will apply to offences, that are directed against the Norwegian State or Norwegian State authority.

2.6. Principle of universal jurisdiction

Section 12(1)(4) lays down the *principle of universal jurisdiction*. Pursuant to this section, Norwegian criminal law is applicable to acts committed

(4) abroad, by a foreigner when the act either
a) is one of those dealt with in sections 83, 88, 89, 90, 91, 91a, 93, 94, 98 to 104a, 110 to 132, 147a, 147b, 148, 149, 150, 151a, 152 first cf. second paragraph, 152a, 152b, 153 first to fourth paragraphs, 154, 159, 160, 161, 162c, 169, 174 to 178, 182 to 185, 187, 189, 190, 192 to 195, 217, 220 second and third paragraph, 221, 222 to 225, 227 to 229, 231 to 235, 238, 239, 243, 244, 256, 258, 266 to 269, 271, 276 to 276c, 291, 292, 324, 325, 328, 415 or 423 of this code, or sections 1, 2, 3 or 5 of the Act relating to defence secrets,
b) is an offence also punishable according to the law of the country in which it is committed, and the offender is resident in the realm or is staying therein, or

---

88. *Andenæs, Matningsdal and Rieber-Mohn* (2004), p. 564 and *Matningsdal and Bratholm* (2003), p. 47.
89. Ot.prp. nr. 90 (2003-2004), p. 181.

c) is committed in relation to the EFTA Court of Justice and is included among those dealt with in section 163, cf. section 167 and section 165, of this code, or sections 205 to 207 of the Courts of Justice Act, or

d) comes under Act of 13 June 1997, no. 47, relating to the implementation of the Council of Europe Agreement of 31 January 1995 on illicit traffic by sea, implementing Article 17 of the UN Convention against illicit traffic in narcotic drugs and psychotropic substances.

Like the provision on *active personality principle*, a) includes a long list of offences that are included within the scope of the *principle of universal jurisdiction*. Firstly, these include some offences against the independence and security of the State and offences against the Norwegian constitution and Head of State. These can be considered an expression of the *principle of state protection* (see chapter 2.5.). Secondly, offences within and against public authority are included, as are offences against public safety, and terrorism and organised crime included here. Thirdly, offences concerning false accusation, counterfeiting of money and forging of documents are also covered. Fourthly, some sexual offences, offences concerning family relationships, offences against personal liberty and against other person's life, body and health as well as some forms of embezzlement and theft are included. Fifthly, extortion and robbery, fraud, vandalism, certain summary offences against the civil service and public authorities and the summary offence of unlawful carrying of freight or a Norwegian flag by a shipmaster are also covered. For most of these specific offences, Norwegian jurisdiction applies to the aggravated forms of the offences.

An alternative requirement pursuant to b), is that the act is an offence (not a summary offence) which is punishable also in the state of commission and the offender is a resident of Norway or is staying in Norway. Therefore, the offender needs to be present in Norway when the prosecution is initiated, because extradition based on this provision is not possible.[90] The *double criminality principle* applies in this case *in concreto*, as section 13(2) SL expressly requires in these cases that the offender could have been sentenced for the offence in the place of commission.[91] In addition, the penalty imposed should not exceed the penalty that is prescribed by law in the place of commission.[92]

---

90. NOU 1984: 31, p. 13. This could also be considered an expression of the *active personality principle* because the foreigner must be present in Norway (and apparently not extradited).

91. Similarly *Matningsdal and Bratholm* (2003), p. 64.

92. *Andenæs, Matningsdal and Rieber-Mohn* (2004), p. 564 and *Bratholm* (1980), p. 381.

Jurisdiction based on letters a) and b) does not seem to have been applied very often.[93] Section 13(1) SL has a further requirement in relation to letters a) and b) in section 12(1)(4). It states that prosecution can only be instituted when the King so decides. As mentioned above, in chapter 1.6., this is mainly based on the fact that prosecuting foreigners for offences committed abroad raises some questions of international law and foreign policy and in practice, it is the Government that decides on instituting prosecution of such cases.[94]

Letters c) and d) in section 12(1)(4) SL regulate the application of Norwegian jurisdiction following from Norway's obligations based on conventions, in situations where a foreigner has committed the offence abroad. The actualisation of Norwegian jurisdiction based on these letters seems fairly farfetched and no case law exists. It follows from section 1(2) SL that Norwegian criminal law applies with restrictions from agreements with other states or international law generally.[95] This entails that if such a situation would arise, where Norwegian jurisdiction would be contrary to international law, the relevant provision would not be applicable. As these expressions of the *principle of universal jurisdiction* are seldom applied, this does not seem very likely to occur.[96]

Although the Norwegian provisions relating to the *principle of universal jurisdiction* are rather broad, these should be seen in relation to the rather strict Norwegian policy as regards extradition.[97] The *aut dedere aut judicare*

93. Stated in NOU 1984: 31, p. 40 and *Matningsdal and Bratholm* (2003), p. 63. On case law in relation to letter a), see Supreme Court cases Rt. 2011 p. 514 (where jurisdiction was applicable) and Rt. 2010 p. 1217 (where jurisdiction was not applicable), and as a curiosity case Rt. 2011 p. 531 (which was a civil case, but the question was nevertheless relevant) and in relation to letter b) Supreme Court cases Rt. 2010 p. 1271, and more generally Rt. 1964 p. 374 (which concerned offences committed by a British national in Sweden and Denmark). A case, TBERG-2011-194827 was decided on by the Bergen District Court where six Rumanian nationals were prosecuted for several offences in a crime hurdle, including amongst other human trafficking and several sexual offences. The offences had taken place in Sweden, Norway or Rumania. Jurisdiction was based on section 12(1)(4)a) where the offence has not taken place in Norway. On the original motivations for applying the *principle of universal jurisdiction*, see preparatory works SKM I 1896 – Udkast til almindelig borgerlig Straffelov med Motiver. Udarbeidet av Straffelovkommisjonen fra 1885 (Kristiania 1896), p. 17.
94. See *Husabø* (2009), p. 339. Section 13(1) SL also refers to section 64 Strpl., which regulates the procedure of the Government (Kongen i stratsråd) deciding.
95. In Norwegian: *"Straffelovgivningen gjelder med de begrensningene som følger av overenskomst med fremmed stat eller av folkeretten for øvrig."*
96. *Matningsdal and Bratholm* (2003), p. 47.
97. *Jo Stigen*, "Universaljurisdiksjon – en kritisk analyse.", Tidsskrift for Rettsvitenskap 1/2009, p. 34.

principle leads to the Norwegian rules being extensive although these usually are not applied when the connection to Norway is unessential.[98]

In the new SL, the *principle of universal jurisdiction* will be furthered in the new section 5(1)1), where double criminality is laid down as a first condition (the new section 5 applies the same approach to the *principle of universal jurisdiction* as it does with the *active personality principle*).[99] Some exceptions from the *double criminality principle* are stated in points 2 to 10 of section 5(1), the most relevant being offences directed at Norway, offences of genital mutilation and some international core crimes. Based on either section 5(3) or 5(5), Norwegian criminal law applies when a foreigner is in Norway and the penalty for the offence is at least 1 year of imprisonment, or where the penalty for the offence is at least 6 years of imprisonment and the offence is directed at a Norwegian national or a person residing in Norway. The new section 6 SL will also state a specific basis for prosecution based on international law. In situations outside the scope of sections 4 and 5, Norwegian criminal law will apply to acts that Norway is obliged to prosecute because of international agreements or international law.[100] The *principle of universal jurisdiction* will continue to have a broad scope of application, and although the European Arrest Warrant, when also applicable to Norway, would lead to easier prosecution and extradition of person (including Norway) a solution that prevents Norway from becoming a safe haven for offences committed abroad was preferred.[101]

The relevant parts of the new section 5 in the new SL will state the following:

Section 5
Application of criminal law to acts abroad.
(1) Outside the scope of Section 4, the criminal law apply to acts committed
a) by a Norwegian citizen
b) by a person resident in Norway or
c) by a registered company in Norway, provided the acts
   1.   are also criminalized by law in the state, where the act has been committed,
   2.   are considered as war crimes, genocide or crimes against humanity,
   3.   are regarded as a violation of the international laws and customs of war,

---

98. NOU 1984:31, pp. 22-23.
99. This will affect applying jurisdiction on terrorism offences, see *Husabø* (2009), pp. 338-339.
100. In Norwegian: *"Utenfor virkeområdet etter §§ 4 og 5 gjelder straffelovgivningen også for handlinger som Norge etter overenskomster med fremmende stater eller etter folkeretten for øvrig har rett eller plikt til å strafforfølge."*
101. Ot.prp. nr. 90, pp. 174-175.

4. are regarded as child marriage or forced marriage,
5. are regarded as genital mutilation,
6. are directed against the Norwegian State or Norwegian State authority,
7. are committed outside an area of sovereignty of any State and is punishable by imprisonment,
8. are considered as evasion of care,
9. are covered by Section 257, Sections 291-296, Sections 299-306 or Sections 309-316 or
10. are regarded as trade to influence third parties.

(2) Subsection 1 shall apply mutatis mutandis to acts that have been committed
a) by a person, who after the fact has acquired Norwegian citizenship or taken up residence in Norway,
b) by a person who are a citizen or resident, or after the fact takes up citizenship or residence, in another Nordic State and who is staying in Norway, or
c) on behalf of a foreign entity, which after the fact has transferred its overall operations to an enterprise registrered in Norway.

(3) Subsection 1, no. 1, 2, 3, 6, 7 and 8 shall apply mutatis mutandis to acts committed by persons other than those covered by Subsections 1 and 2 if the person if physically present in Norway and the act is punishable with a maximum penalty of more than 1 years' imprisonment.

(4) For acts in the meaning of Subsection 1, no. 2, Subsection 2 and 3 shall only apply if the act is regarded under international law as genocide, crimes against humanity or war crimes.

(5) The criminal law also applies to acts that have been committed abroad by persons other than those covered by Subsections 1-4, if the offence is punishable by a maximum sentence of 6 years' imprisonment or more and is directed against a Norwegian citizen or a resident of Norway.

The new section 6 of the new SL will state:

Section 6
Special basis for prosecution in international law

(1) Outside the scope of sections 4 and 5, the criminal law applies to acts, where Norway, by conventions with foreign states or under international law in general, has a right or duty to prosecute.

(2) Section 5, subsection 7 applies correspondingly.

2.7. Principle of representational jurisdiction

The *principle of representational jurisdiction* is not clearly found in the SL. The already mentioned section 12(1)(4) could to some extent also be considered as expressing the *principle of representational jurisdiction*, but this is not stated in any of the preparatory works or the literature.

Section 13 SL however regulates the instigation of prosecution in relation to universal jurisdiction. In 13(1) it is stated that the King institutes prosecutions, which is the general rule (although once again, it is the Government which decides). This rule does not apply when prosecution in Norway is based on an agreement with another state on transfer of criminal proceedings, based on section 13(3) SL. There are no further provisions on this in the SL, but there is an Act regulating the transfer of prosecution to or from another European state.[102] It was not considered necessary to include such provisions in the SL.[103] Norway can however, and has applied representational jurisdiction based on this act.[104]

There will be no equivalent to section 13(3) in the new SL. It would nevertheless seem that prosecution in Norway is still possible in such cases, as the international conventions justifying the current status will also be applicable when the new SL applies.The new section 6 SL (quoted above) seems to imply this, as it states that outside the scope of sections 4 and 5, the Norwegian criminal law applies to offences which Norway due to international treaties or pursuant to international law otherwise is obliged to prosecute.

3. Abbreviations

CISA   Convention Implementing the Schengen Agreement, Official Journal L 239/19, 22 September 2000
New SL   New Norwegian Criminal Code, Straffeloven of 20 May 2005 no. 28
NOU   Official Norwegian Reports (Norges offentlige utredninger)
Ot.prp. nr. Proposition to the Odelsting
Rt.   The register of Supreme Court judgments (Norsk Retstidende)
RG   The register of the Appellate Courts (Rettens gang)

---

102. Lov om overføring av straffeforfølgning fra eller til annet europeisk land, Act 25 March 1977 no. 22.
103. Ot.prp. nr. 7 (1976-1977), p. 18.
104. See case Rt. 2011 p. 31.

SL   Norwegian Criminal Code (Straffeloven) 22 May 1902 no. 10
Strpl.   Norwegian Criminal Procedural Code (Straffeprosessloven) 22
            May 1981 no. 25

4. English translation of the Norwegian Criminal Code[105]

Chapter 1

Section 12
Unless it is otherwise specially provided, Norwegian criminal law shall be applicable to
acts committed:
1. in the realm, including
    a) any installation or construction placed on the Norwegian part of the continental
       shelf and used for exploration for or exploitation or storage of submarine natural
       resources
    b) constructions for the transport of petroleum resources connected with any installa-
       tion or construction placed on the Norwegian part of the continental shelf
    c) the security zone around such installations and constructions are mentioned under
       a) and b) above
    d) any Norwegian vessel (including a Norwegian drilling platform or similar mobile
       installation) in the open sea, and
    e) any Norwegian aircraft outside such areas as are subject to the jurisdiction of an-
       other state;
2. on any Norwegian vessel or aircraft wherever it may be, by a member of its crew or
   any other person travelling on the vessel or aircraft; the term vessel here also includes a
   drilling platform or similar mobile installation;
3. abroad by any Norwegian national or any person domiciled in Norway when the act
    a) is one of those dealt with in chapters 8, 9, 10, 11, 12, 14, 17, 18, 20, 23, 24, 25, 26
       or 33, or paragraphs 135, 141, 142, 144, 145 second subparagraph, 145b, 147a,
       147b, 162c, 169, 192 to 199, 202, 202a, 203, 204a, 222 to 225, 227 to 235, 238,
       239, 242 to 245, 291, 292, 294 number 2, 317, 326 to 328, 330 last subparagraph,
       338, 342, 367 to 370, or 423,
    b) is a felony or misdemeanour against the Norwegian State or Norwegian state au-
       thority,
    c) is also punishable according to the law of the country in which it is committed, or
    d) is committed in relation to the EFTA Court of Justice and is included among those
       dealt with in section 163, cf. section 167 and section 165, or this code, or sections
       205 to 207 of the Courts of Justice Act;
    e) is punishable pursuant to section 5 of Act of 6 May 1994 no. 10 relating to the
       implementation of the Chemical Weapons Convention,

---

105. This is the unofficial translation of the Norwegian Ministry of Justice. In some sec-
     tions, the author had added some parts, to update the text.

f)   shall be punishable in accordance with Article 113 of the UN Convention on the Law of the Sea of 10 December 1982 (damage to submarine cables and pipelines),

g)   is punishable pursuant to section 5 of Act of 17 July 1988 no. 54 relating to the implementation of the Convention on the prohibition of the use, stockpiling, production and transfer or anti-personnel mines and on their destruction, or

h)   is punishable pursuant to Act of 15 December 1995 no. 74 relating to a prohibition against female genital mutilation,

i)   is punishable pursuant to section 3 of the Act of 15 May 2009 no. 28 on the implementation of the Convention on Cluster Munitions;

4.   abroad, by a foreigner when the act either

a)   is one of those dealt with in sections 83, 88, 89, 90, 91, 91a, 93, 94, 98 to 104a, 110 to 132, 147a, 147b, 148, 149, 150, 151a, 152 first cf. second paragraph, 152a, 152b, 153 first to fourth paragraphs, 154, 159, 160, 161, 162c, 169, 174 to 178, 182 to 185, 187, 189, 190, 192 to 195, 217, 220 second and third paragraph, 221, 222 to 225, 227 to 229, 231 to 235, 238, 239, 243, 244, 256, 258, 266 to 269, 271, 276 to 276c, 291, 292, 324, 325, 328, 415 or 423 of this code, or sections 1,2,3 or 5 of the Act relating to defence secrets,

b)   is a felony also punishable according to the law of the country in which it is committed, and the offender is resident in the realm or is staying therein, or

c)   is committed in relation to the EFTA Court of Justice and is included among those dealt with in section 163, cf. section 167 and section 165, of this code, or sections 205 to 207 of the Courts of Justice Act, or

d)   comes under Act of 13 June 1997, no. 47, relating to the implementation of the Council of Europe Agreement of 31 January 1995 on illicit traffic by sea, implementing Article 17 of the UN Convention against illicit traffic in narcotic drugs and psychotropic substances.

In cases in which the criminality of an act depends on or is influenced by any actual or intended effect, the act shall be regarded as committed also where such effect has occurred or is intended to be produced.

Section 12a

When a legally enforceable judgment has been passed on a person pursuant to

1.   Act of 20 July 1991 no. 67 relating to the transfer of convicted persons,

2.   Act of 25 March 1977 no. 22 relating to transfer of a prosecution from or to another European country or

3.   an international agreement within the Schengen area of co-operation, no criminal proceedings may be instituted or sentence passed in Norway for the same criminal offence if

a)   he has been acquitted;

b)   he has been found guilty but no sanction has been imposed;

c)   the sanction imposed has been fully executed or is in the process of execution; or

d)   the sanction imposed has ceased to apply according to the rules of the adjudicating country.

Unless the prosecution in the adjudicating country was instituted on the application of the Norwegian authorities, the first paragraph shall not apply to such cases as are referred to in no. 1 and no. 2 of the first paragraph,
a)   when the act is committed in this realm, cf. section 12, first paragraph, no. 1 and the second paragraph;
b)   when the perpetrator at the time of committing the act was resident in Norway or was a Norwegian national, and the prosecution is required in the public interest;
c)   when the act was directed against a person holding a Norwegian public office or a public institution or something else of a public character in this realm, or the perpetrator himself held a Norwegian public office;
d)   when the act was hijacking of an aircraft or some other international crime under international law; or
e)   in so far as otherwise follows from an extradition treaty or a multilateral international agreement.

Unless the prosecution in the adjudicating country was instituted on the application of the Norwegian authorities, the first paragraph shall not apply to such cases as are referred to in no. 3 of the first paragraph, when
a)   the act on which the foreign judgment was based was wholly or partly committed in Norway. If the act was only partly committed in Norway, the exception shall not, however, apply if the act was partly committed on the territory of the party to the convention where the judgment was pronounced;
b)   the act on which the foreign judgment was based is punishable in Norway pursuant to chapter 8, 9 or 14 of this code or the Act of 18 August 1914 no. 3 relating to defence secrets; or
c)   the act on which the foreign judgment was based was committed by a Norwegian official and was in breach of his official duties.

Section 13
In the cases dealt with in section 12, no. 4 (a) and (b), a prosecution can only be instituted when the King so decides.

In the cases dealt with in section 12, no. 4 (b), a prosecution may not take place unless there is also power to impose a penalty according to the law of the country in which the act was committed. Nor may a more severe penalty be imposed than is authorized by the law of the said country.

The first and second paragraphs shall not apply when a criminal prosecution in this country take place in accordance with an agreement with a foreign State concerning the transfer of criminal proceedings.

In every case in which a person who has been punished abroad is convicted of the same offence in this country, the penalty already served shall as far as possible be deducted from the sentence imposed here.

5.   English translation of the new Criminal Code[106]

Part One: General Provisions Chapter 1 Scope of criminal law
Section 1
Scope of the General Provisions
The provisions in part one apply to all offences, unless otherwise provided by or pursuant to law or required by interpretation.

Section 2
Limitations by international law
The Criminal Code applies with the limitations imposed by conventions with foreign states or under international law in general.

[Section 3]
[Temporal scope of criminal law]

Section 4
Application of criminal law to acts in Norway and Norwegian territories, among others.
(1) The criminal law applies to acts committed in Norway, including Svalbard, Jan Mayen and the Norwegian dependencies cf. Law no. 3 of 27 February 1930.

(2) The criminal law also applies to acts that have been carried out
  a)   on facilities on the Norwegian Continental Shelf for the exploration or exploitation, or storage of submarine natural resources and on pipelines and other fixed transportation facilities associated with such devices even when they are outside the Norwegian Continental Shelf,
  b)   in the area of jurisdiction established by Law 17 December 1976, no. 91 on the Economic Zone of Norway, the acts violating the interests safeguarded by Norwegian jurisdiction, and
  c)   aboard Norwegian vessels or aircraft, on drilling platforms or other similar movable facility. On vehicles or facilities located in the territory of another State, the criminal law applies only to acts of passengers or people belonging to the crew of the vehicle or facility.

Section 5
Application of criminal law to acts abroad.
(1) Outside the scope of Section 4, the criminal law applies to acts committed
  a) by a Norwegian citizen
  b) by a person resident in Norway or
  c) by a registered company in Norway, provided the acts
     1.   are also criminalized by law in the state, where the act has been committed,
     2.   are considered as war crimes, genocide or crimes against humanity,

106. Unauthorised translation

3. are regarded as a violation of the international laws and customs of war
4. are regarded as child marriage or forced marriage,
5. are regarded as genital mutilation,
6. are directed against the Norwegian State or Norwegian State authority,
7. are committed outside an area of sovereignty of any State and is punishable by imprisonment,
8. are considered as evasion of care,
9. are covered by Section 257, Sections 291-296, Sections 299-306 or Sections 309-316 or
10. are regarded as trade to influence third parties

(2) Subsection 1 shall apply mutatis mutandis to acts that have been committed
a) by a person, who after the fact has acquired Norwegian citizenship or taken up residence in Norway,
b) by a person who are a citizen or resident, or after the fact takes up citizenship or residence, in another Nordic State and who is staying in Norway, or
c) on behalf of a foreign entity, which after the fact has transferred its overall operations to an enterprise registered in Norway.

(3) Subsection 1, no. 1, 2, 3, 6, 7 and 8 shall apply mutatis mutandis to acts committed by persons other than those covered by Subsections 1 and 2 if the person if physically present in Norway and the act is punishable with a maximum penalty of more than 1 years' imprisonment.

(4) For acts in the meaning of Subsection 1, no. 2, Subsection 2 and 3 shall only apply if the act is regarded under international law as genocide, crimes against humanity or war crimes.

(5) The criminal law also applies to acts that have been committed abroad by persons other than those covered by Subsections 1-4, if the offence is punishable by a maximum sentence of 6 years' imprisonment or more and is directed against a Norwegian citizen or a resident of Norway.

(6) For the prosecution under this section, the sentence may not exceed the statutory maximum penalty for the same offence in the country where the offence has been committed.

(7) Prosecution under this section is raised only when public interest so requires.

Section 6
Special basis for prosecution in international law
(1) Outside the scope of sections 4 and 5, the criminal law applies to acts, where Norway, by conventions with foreign states or under international law in general, has a right or duty to prosecute.

(2) Section 5, subsection 7 applies correspondingly

Section 7
Localisation of an act at multiple locations
If the criminality of an act is dependent or influenced by an actual or intended result, the act is also regarded as committed there, where the result has occurred or its induction was intended.

Section 8
Power to prosecute matters adjudicated abroad.

(1) When a final judgment was rendered abroad, falls under
a) Law no. 22 of 25 March 1977 on the transfer of prosecution by or to another European country or
b) Law no. 67 of 20 July 1991 on the transfer of sentenced persons or
c) an international agreement within the framework of the Schengen cooperation criminal proceedings or judgment cannot be instituted in Norway for the same offence, when,
    1. the person was acquitted or found guilty without any sanction imposed or
    2. the sentence imposed is fully served, is being served or has been annulled according to the judicial rules of the country.

(2) If the prosecution has not taken place in the country at the request of Norwegian authorities, criminal matters within the meaning of subsection 1, letters a and b, can be prosecuted in Norway, when
a) the offence was committed in an area as mentioned in Section 4, cf. Section 7,
b) the offender at the time of the crime was a resident in Norway or a Norwegian citizen and public interest requires prosecution,
c) the act was directed against a person in a Norwegian public office or against a public institution or against something else of a public nature in Norway or the offender held a Norwegian public office themselves, or
d) Norway is entitled or obliged under international law to prosecute.

(3) If the prosecution has not taken place in the country at the request of Norwegian authorities, criminal matters within the meaning of subsection 1, letter c, can be prosecuted in Norway, when
a) the offense is committed in whole or in part in Norway. Has the act only partially been committed in Norway, the exception does not apply if the act was partially committed in the territory of the Contracting State in which the judgment was rendered,
b) the act is criminalised in Norway as war crimes, genocide, crime against the independence and security of the state, crime against the constitution and the political system or as hijacking, sabotage against infrastructure, serious drugs offence, unlawful dealing with plutonium and uranium or serious arson or other particularly dangerous destruction, or
c) the act was committed by a Norwegian official and was a violation of that person's official duties.

CHAPTER 5

Sweden

Karin Cornils[1]

1. General Basis

1.1. Systematic classification of the rules on jurisdiction

Chapter 2 of the Swedish Criminal Code (*Brottsbalken*, BrB)[2] bears the heading "On the Application of Swedish Law". This refers to the provisions of the main and ancillary parts of the criminal law. The chapter heading is imprecise to the extent that the provisions actually relate to the jurisdiction of Swedish courts for domestic and foreign offences. The application of Swedish law is simply a consequence of the jurisdiction of the Swedish criminal courts since Swedish courts always apply Swedish criminal law. By contrast with international private law, the question of which law to apply does not arise here.[3] A current draft bill, to comprehensively reform Chapter 2, provides for a new heading with the more accurate formulation: "On the Jurisdiction of Swedish Courts".[4]

Although the jurisdictional rules are contained in the General Part of the Criminal Code, according to their content, they are regarded as *procedural*

---

1. Revised and expanded version of the country report: *Karin Cornils*, "Internationaler Geltungsbereich des Strafrechts in Schweden". In: Ulrich Sieber/Karin Cornils (eds.), Nationales Strafrecht in rechtsvergleichender Darstellung. Allgemeiner Teil. Volume 2, Berlin 2008, pp. 299-316. That volume contains further country reports on 11 European and Non-European countries.
2. Criminal Code (*Brottsbalken*) of 21 December 1962, SFS 1962:700, last update 23 December 2013, SFS 2013:856.
3. For the impact of foreign law, see 1.4. below.
4. Internationella brott och svensk jurisdiktion. SOU 2002:98. Betänkande av Internationella straffrättsutredningen, Stockholm 2002, p. 34.

provisions and come under so-called international criminal procedural law.[5] The fact that they are set out in the Criminal Code is explained by the fact that the jurisdiction of the Swedish criminal courts represents a direct condition for the application of national criminal provisions and is therefore closely connected to substantive criminal law.[6]

The procedural character of the provisions in Chapter 2 BrB becomes particularly clear in the provisions on the requirement for a prosecution order in the case of foreign offences or offences committed by foreigners (Chapter 2, Sections 5, 7 a, 7 b BrB[7]) and in the provisions relating to the effect of a binding foreign Judgment which prevent prosecution for the same offence *(res judicata, ne bis in idem)* (Chapter 2, Section 5 a BrB[8]).

1.2. Outline of the principles of the law on jurisdiction

The subject matter of jurisdictional rules consists of the possible grounds on which domestic jurisdiction in criminal matters may be based, that is the specific links between the offence and Sweden itself, on which the state can base its right to effect criminal prosecution. The relevant factors provided for in this regard are the *locus delicti*, the protected interest which has been violated or put at risk, the nationality of the offender or victim and the type of offence. In addition, the interests of international legal cooperation in criminal matters and other obligations under international law may also play a role.

The *territoriality principle*[9] is accorded a prominent part. According to this rule Sweden has jurisdiction over all criminal offences committed within its territory as well as those in relation to which it is uncertain but where there are grounds for believing that they were committed within its territory (Chapter 2, Section 1 BrB). *The locus delicti*[10] is deemed to be the place where the criminal activity was performed as well as the place where the result of the

---

5. Cf. *Iain Cameron et al.*, International Criminal Law from a Swedish Perspective, Cambridge/Antwerp/Portland 2011, pp. 39, 57; *Petter Asp, Magnus Ulväng and Nils Jareborg*, Kriminalrättens grunder, Uppsala 2010, p. 18; *Petter Asp*, "Svensk jurisdiktion". In: Bengt Lindell (ed.), Straffprocessen, Uppsala 2005, pp. 93-129 (94-97, 100 f.).
6. See *Petter Asp and Jörgen Samuelsson*, "De svenska jurisdiktionsreglerna". In: Nils Jareborg/ Petter Asp (eds.), Svensk internationell straffprocessrätt, Uppsala 1995, p. 25.
7. See below 1.6.
8. See below 1.5.
9. See below 2.1.
10. See below 2.1.1.

offence occurred or, in the case of attempt, where it was intended to occur (*principle of ubiquity*, Chapter 2, Section 4 BrB).

Foreign offences committed on board Swedish ships or aircraft, or by a member of their crew whilst on duty, are also subject to Swedish jurisdiction (Chapter 2, Section 3 no. 1 BrB). This provision corresponds partly to the *flag state principle*[11] and partly goes beyond it.

Otherwise, with respect to offences committed abroad, the main jurisdictional basis arises under the *active personality principle*[12] which, under Swedish law, has a particularly broad scope. This basically extends domestic jurisdiction to offences committed by Swedish nationals or foreigners domiciled in Sweden, and this is true even where nationality or residence is not established until after the offence has been committed (Chapter 2, Section 2, (1), Nos. 1 and 2 BrB). With respect to offences committed in a stateless area, the active personality principle only applies where they are punishable in Sweden by a sanction more severe than a fine (Chapter 2, Section 2, (2) BrB).

Sweden also has jurisdiction over foreign offences committed by nationals of the Scandinavian neighbouring countries, Denmark, Finland, Iceland and Norway, who are present in Sweden (Chapter 2, Section 2, (1), no. 2 BrB). With regard to other foreigners, present but without a permanent residence in Sweden, this only applies insofar as their offence is punishable by more than six months' imprisonment (Chapter 2, Section 2, (1), no. 3 BrB). Both provisions, systematically regulated in the context of the active personality principle, may also be based on the concept of *representational jurisdiction.*[13]

The principle of state protection[14] applies to the endangerment or violation of domestic interests. It places under Swedish jurisdiction offences which are committed abroad and directed against the Swedish state, Swedish local authorities, corporate bodies or public institutions (Chapter 2, Section 3, no. 4 BrB).

The same applies under the *passive personality principle*[15] to offences directed against Swedish nationals, associations and private institutions and against foreigners resident in Sweden insofar as the offence is committed in a stateless area (Chapter 2, Section 3, no. 5 BrB).

11. See below 2.2.
12. See below 2.3.
13. See below 2.7.
14. See below 2.5.
15. See below 2.4.

Under the *principle of universal jurisdiction*,[16] Sweden has jurisdiction over the specific types of offence listed, namely hi-jacking, sabotage of sea or air traffic, airport sabotage, money counterfeiting, criminal offences under international law, the unlawful handling of chemical weapons or mines, giving false testimony before an international court, intentionally or by gross negligence, as well as terrorist offences and those which are directed against the jurisdiction of the International Criminal Court (Chapter 2, Section 3, no. 6 BrB). This principle also gives rise to the so-called four-year rule (Chapter 2, Section 3, no. 7 BrB) under which Swedish jurisdiction applies to foreign offences which, under Swedish law, are punishable with a minimum of four years' imprisonment, irrespective of the nationality, domicile or residence of the offender or victim.

Finally, there is one provision (Chapter 2, Section 3 a BrB), based on the *principle of representational jurisdiction*, which applies exclusively with regard to the signatory states of the 1972 European Convention on the Transfer of Proceedings in Criminal Matters. According to this provision, even in cases where there is no other basis for it, Swedish jurisdiction applies in respect of a foreign offence where the transfer of proceedings has been approved by Sweden on request by the country in which the offence took place and the act – if it had been committed in Sweden – would also be a criminal offence under Swedish law.[17]

1.3. The relationship between jurisdictional rules and the scope of the criminal provisions

One essential requirement for the jurisdiction of the Swedish courts (and the application of Swedish law) is that the act committed must in fact be covered by Swedish criminal law. In this regard, Swedish legal doctrine strictly distinguishes the question of domestic jurisdiction as dealt with under Chapter 2 BrB from the substantive legal aspect of the territorial limits of the national criminal statutes.[18]

The substantive scope of national criminal law is not determined by the jurisdictional rules of Chapter 2 BrB but arises from the respective area of

---

16. See below 2.6.
17. See below 2.7.
18. Cf. SOU 2002:98, pp. 74 ff.; *Nils Jareborg*, Allmän kriminalrätt, Uppsala 2001, pp. 35, 236-253; *Asp, Ulväng and Jareborg* (2010), pp. 197-201.

application of the individual provisions of the Special Part.[19] It is clear from the wording of many offences that their application is restricted to domestic offences or domestic protected interests (for example, tax and customs offences, provisions relating to treason and spying, Chapter 19, Sections 1 and 4 BrB, or to violence against public officials, Chapter 17, Section 1 BrB). With others, there is no doubt that they apply irrespective of national borders (such as the provisions on offences against life and health, Chapter 3, Sections 1-9 BrB, and those relating to most property offences, Chapter 8-10 BrB). In other cases, there is a need for interpretation in this regard. With respect to the offences contained in the Criminal Code, there is an assumption that, in principle, they cover acts and omissions irrespective of the *locus delicti*, whereas other criminal legislation is mainly restricted to offences committed in Sweden.[20] Apart from geographical limitations on the area of application, other limitations may arise from the fact that many criminal provisions are aimed exclusively at Swedish citizens (for example: arbitrary conduct in negotiations with a foreign power, Chapter 19, Section 4 BrB).

1.4. Impact of foreign law

Swedish courts exclusively apply Swedish criminal law. Provisions from a foreign legal system may be consulted, in the case of offences with a foreign component, where this is necessary in order to clarify preliminary questions of civil or administrative law to which Swedish criminal law refers, such as the validity of a marriage or property transfer or the regulation of certain duties of care.[21]

By way of exception, however, foreign criminal provisions must be taken into account where the Swedish judge has to determine whether the act committed is a criminal offence under the applicable law of the *locus delicti.*[22]

---

19. Cf. *Lena Holmqvist et al.*, Brottsbalken. En kommentar. Kap. 1-12. Brotten mot person och förmögenhetsbrotten m.m., Stockholm loose-leaf, updated in January 2011, 2:2 f.; *Asp, Ulväng and Jareborg* (2010), pp. 201-206.
20. Cf. *Alvar Nelson*, "Swedish and Foreign Crimes in the Swedish Criminal Justice System". In: Nils Jareborg (ed.), Double Criminality. Studies in International Criminal Law, Uppsala 1989, pp. 11-42 (16).
21. Cf. *Jareborg* (2001), pp. 105 f., 238; *Asp, Ulväng and Jareborg* (2010), p. 200; *Karin Cornils*, "The Use of Foreign Law in Domestic Adjudication". In: Nils Jareborg (ed.), Double Criminality. Studies in International Criminal Law, Uppsala 1989, pp. 70-83.
22. In general on the requirement of double criminality, see *Per Ole Träskman*, "Should We Take the Condition of Double Criminality Seriously?" In: Nils Jareborg (ed.), Double Criminality. Studies in International Criminal Law, Uppsala 1989, pp. 135-155.

This requirement of double criminality applies in conjunction with the *active personality principle* and the *principle of representational jurisdiction.*[23]

Chapter 2, Section 2 (2) BrB provides that Sweden does not have jurisdiction over foreign offences committed by Swedish nationals or equivalent persons or by foreigners resident in Sweden, if the act is not punishable under the law of the *locus delicti*. The provision was introduced into the Criminal Code in 1972 after Sweden acceded to the European Convention on the International Validity of Criminal Judgments. This stipulated that no prosecution for a foreign offence could be brought in Sweden where the defendant had been acquitted for the same act in another country because the act was not a criminal offence in the *locus delicti* (see below). In addition thereto, the Swedish legislature ruled out prosecution in Sweden for acts not punishable in the *locus delicti* even if the foreign prosecution authorities had not checked punishability under their own law.

Double criminality is regarded as a requirement *in concreto*, which means that it not only depends on the general criminalisation of the respective type of conduct under the foreign criminal law but on the actual possibility of prosecuting the offender for a concrete offence in the country in which it was committed, taking account of objective or subjective defences and other grounds of impunity which apply there and any impediment to criminal procedure, particularly lapse of time.[24]

Offences which fall under the *principle of state protection*, the *passive personality principle* and the *principle of universal jurisdiction*, as well as all offences (by nationals or foreigners) which are punishable under Swedish law by four or more years imprisonment (Chapter 2, Section 3, Nos. 4-7 BrB), are subject to Swedish jurisdiction irrespective of their punishability under the law of the *locus delicti*. The same applies to foreign offences committed on board Swedish ships or aircraft or by a member of their crew whilst on duty (Chapter 2, Section 3, no. 1 BrB). Offences committed by members or employees of the Swedish armed forces, police, customs authorities or coast guard during a deployment abroad are also subject to Judgment by Swedish courts applying Swedish law irrespective of the foreign law of the *locus delicti* (Chapter 2, Section 3, Nos. 2-3 a BrB). A special rule applies to sexual offences against children and young people under the age of 18 and to human trafficking and the production of child pornography (Chapter 2, Section 2 (4) BrB); the requirement of double criminality has been lifted with respect to

23. Cf. *Asp and Samuelsson* (2010), pp. 41-50; *Cameron et al.* (2011), pp. 62-71.
24. Cf. *Karin Cornils* (1989), pp. 73-81; *Cameron et al.* (2011), pp. 63 f.

these offences since 2005, 2010 and 2013 respectively to allow for the more effective prosecution of foreign offences. An additional exception is contained in the special Act on Prohibition of Female Genital Mutilation (*lag om förbud mot könsstympning av kvinnor*, SFS 1982:316). This aims to prevent persons living in Sweden from evading the ban on circumcision by having the operation carried out in a country whose laws allow it.

In cases where the requirement of double criminality applies, the principle of *lex mitior* (Chapter 2, Section 2 (3) BrB) must also be complied with, that is the sentence imposed by the Swedish court may not exceed the maximum punishment provided for by the law of the *locus delicti*:

Chapter 2, Section 2 (3) BrB
In the cases covered by this Section, the sanction imposed may not be more severe than the severest punishment provided for the offence under the law of the *locus delicti*.

In this regard, it is the statutory penalty applicable in the *locus delicti* which is relevant rather than the actual sentence to be expected. This does not prevent the Swedish court from taking account of sentencing practice in the country where the offence took place, particularly if the offence would be subject to a far more lenient sentence there than in Sweden.

1.5. Impact of foreign Judgments
After Sweden's accession to the European Convention on the International Validity of Foreign Judgments (1970) the *ne bis in idem* principle was extended to include foreign Judgments. The Swedish provision not only applies with respect to the other signatory states, however, but to any foreign country if the offence has been adjudged there under the territoriality principle. With respect to the signatory states of certain international conventions, the *res judicata* effect is not linked to the requirement that the offence must have been committed in the country of Judgment itself:

Chapter 2, Section 5 a BrB
(1) If the question of criminal liability for an act has been determined by a Judgment passed res judicata in a foreign state in which the act was committed or which is a signatory to one of the conventions listed under Sub-section 4, the defendant may not be prosecuted again for the same act in Sweden,
1. if he has been acquitted,
2. if he has been convicted of the offence without a sanction having been imposed,
3. if the sanction imposed has been fully enforced or is being enforced, or
4. if the sanction imposed has lapsed under the law of the foreign state concerned.

(2) Sub-section 1 does not apply to the offences covered by Sections 1 and 3 Nos. 4, 6 and 7 unless prosecution took place in the foreign state at the request of a Swedish authority or the person was extradited from Sweden for the purpose of prosecution.

(3) If the question of criminal liability for an act has been determined by a Judgment issued in a foreign state and there is no impediment to prosecution under the foregoing provisions of this Section, the act may only be prosecuted in Sweden by order of the Government or an office authorised by the Government.

[...]

The list of international conventions referred to in Sub-section 1 and contained in Sub-section 4 is continually being extended. It currently includes the European Conventions on the International Validity of Criminal Judgments, on the Transfer of Proceedings in Criminal Matters, on the Protection of the European Communities' Financial Interests with Protocols 1 and 2, on the Fight against Corruption in the EU, on the Implementation of the Schengen Agreement and on Double Jeopardy within the EU.

Sub-section 2 contains a reservation in relation to foreign Judgments for offences committed in Sweden or directed against Sweden or offences which fall under the principle of universal jurisdiction or which are punishable by at least four years' imprisonment under Swedish law. In such cases, the *res judicata* effect depends on the foreign Judgment being preceded by a Swedish request for prosecution or by the extradition of the defendant by Sweden.

Insofar as there is no impediment to prosecution under the foregoing provisions, prosecution for an offence which has been unappealably adjudged in a foreign country may only take place on the order of the Swedish Government or an office authorised by the Government (Sub-section 3). Where sentencing takes place in Sweden, the sanction imposed and enforced abroad must be taken into account in determining the sentence:

Chapter 2, Section 6 BrB
(1) If a person is convicted in Sweden for an act for which he/she has been sentenced abroad, the enforcement of the foreign sentence must be appropriately taken into account in determining the sanction. If he/she should be sentenced to a fine or imprisonment and he/she has been given a sanction involving the deprivation of liberty abroad, this must, insofar as it has been enforced, be offset when determining the sanction.

(2) In cases covered by Sub-section 1, a less severe punishment than that provided for the act may be imposed or a sanction be waived completely.

1.6. Restrictions on prosecution

Restrictions on national jurisdiction in criminal matters arising from codified and customary international law are taken into account by a blanket provision in the Criminal Code:

Chapter 2, Section 7 BrB
With regard to the application of Swedish law and the jurisdiction of the Swedish courts, in addition to the provisions of this Chapter, the restrictions arising out of generally recognised principles of public international law or from special provisions in agreements with foreign states must also be observed.

This rule principally concerns cases of immunity.[25] A restriction on prosecution may arise from the fact that another state has applied to take over prosecution or for the extradition of the defendant and Sweden does not oppose the application. Other restrictions arise in the context of the cooperation with the ICTY, the ICTR and the International Criminal Court.

In addition, for most foreign offences and for certain domestic offences committed by foreigners, it is the case that they may only be prosecuted on the order of the Swedish government or an office authorised by the government, (Chapter 2, Sections 5, 5 a (3), 7 a BrB). This is intended to ensure that a de facto and legitimate interest in a domestic prosecution exists. The government has delegated the authority to issue orders in such cases to the Prosecutor-General (*Riksåklagaren*), the highest prosecuting authority. The order is issued on the basis of a discretionary decision which, in addition to jurisdictional aspects of the individual case, also takes account of various circumstances such as the severity of the offence, its link to Sweden and any interests of foreign states.[26]

2. The Rules on Jurisdiction in Detail

2.1. Territoriality principle

The first rule on jurisdiction of Swedish criminal courts relates to the location in which the offence is committed:

---

25. See *Holmqvist et al.* (2011), 2:57-60; *Cameron et al.* (2011), pp. 89-92; *Asp and Samuelsson* (1995), pp. 63-74.
26. In more detail *Alvar Nelson* (1989), pp. 11-42; *Cameron et al.* (2011), pp. 95-99; *Asp* (2005), pp. 93-129 (125); *Holmqvist et al.* (2011), 2:43-52 b, 2:61-67.

Chapter 2, Section 1 BrB
An offence committed in Sweden shall be adjudged under Swedish law and by a Swedish court. The same applies if it is uncertain where the offence has been committed but there is reason to assume that it was committed in Sweden.

Thus Sweden has jurisdiction in accordance with the *territoriality principle* even where it is not certain that the offence was committed in Sweden but where there is evidence suggesting that it was. Criminal jurisdiction under this principle is unrestricted, that means that it applies irrespective of double criminality and generally without the requirement of a special order for prosecution. Exceptions apply principally with respect to certain offences committed by foreigners on board foreign ships or aircraft within Swedish sovereign territory (Chapter. 2, Section 5 (1) BrB) and to domestic offences committed by foreign officials or civil servants of an inter-governmental organisation in the course of their official duties (Chapter 2, Section 7 a BrB) or by members of foreign armed forces present in Sweden as part of international cooperation (Chapter 2, Section 7 b BrB).

2.1.1. Localisation
The basis of application for the territoriality principle is the location in which the offence was committed. Its identification, that is the localisation of the offence, is therefore of crucial importance and the subject of a special provision in the Criminal Code:

Chapter 2, Section 4 BrB
An offence is deemed to have been committed in the place where the criminal act was perpetrated and also in the place where the offence was accomplished, or, in the case of attempt, where the intended offence was to have been accomplished.

With respect to the localisation of an offence in Sweden, initially it is sufficient if part of the criminal act is carried out in Sweden (*principle of ubiquity*). Thus the killing of a person in another country by means of a letter bomb sent in Sweden is deemed to have been committed in Sweden. In addition, the *locus delicti* is also deemed to be the place in which the offence is accomplished, or, was to have been accomplished in the mind of the offender. In the case of result crimes, this corresponds to the place where the result occurs according to the definition of the offence (*result principle*). By contrast with the other Scandinavian criminal codes, the wording of the Swedish Criminal Code does not refer expressly to the place where the result occurs. This gives rise to problems of interpretation where a distinction is to be drawn – as is usual in Swedish legal doctrine – between the primary effect, as the direct consequence of the criminal act, and the end effect, as the result which indicates the accomplishment of the offence.[27] In the aforementioned example, the letter bomb may be sent in a foreign country and explode there but the victim travels to Sweden and dies there as a result of his/her injuries. On the other hand, the letter bomb may be sent from abroad, explode in Sweden, but the injured victim leaves the country and dies outside Swedish territory. According to the *travaux préparatoires*, to which the traditional view refers, it should depend on the primary effect of the criminal act. Thus, in the first version of the above case, the offence would not have been committed in Sweden. Today, however, another view is gaining ground, based on the wording of the law, which regards the location of the end effect, i.e. the place where the offence is really accomplished, as the *locus delicti*. On that basis, in both versions of the case the act is committed in Sweden. The legal position is still considered to be unclear and the current draft reform bill to amend the Swedish rules on jurisdiction provides for a clarification in this regard which is no longer based on the place where the offence is accomplished but on the place where the result occurs, thus encompassing both the primary and the end effect of the offence.[28]

The prevailing law contains no provision on localisation for crimes by omission. Legal doctrine considers the offence to have been committed in the place where the omitted act should have been carried out, in case of doubt the place where the offender was present when he/she should have acted. In the case of result crimes, the place where the result occurs is also relevant. Thus the evasion of tax by failing to provide information to the Swedish tax authorities is also deemed to be a domestic offence even where the person liable for tax was abroad at the time the crime was committed.[29]

The draft reform bill recommends an express provision not only for omission but also for complicity which, until now, has likewise not been regulated by the rules on jurisdiction in the Criminal Code. According to the draft bill, complicity should – in accordance with the prevailing doctrine – be regarded as having been committed in Sweden if the participant acted in Sweden or, in the case of a crime by omission, should have acted, and also if the main act constitutes a domestic offence. Under the draft bill, any person who, whilst abroad, successfully incites another to commit an offence in Sweden, is sub-

---

27. Cf. *Holmqvist et al.* (2011), 2:38-40; *Cameron et al.* (2011), pp. 59 f.; SOU 2002:98, pp. 95 f.
28. SOU 2002:98, pp. 160 f., 399 f.
29. Cf. *Jareborg* (2001), p. 244; *Holmqvist et al.* (2011), 2:40 f.

ject to Swedish jurisdiction, likewise any person who, whilst in Sweden, incites another to commit a crime abroad.[30]

A special provision on identification of the *locus delicti* in the case of internet crimes is also not included in the Criminal Code. The reform commission expressly refused to go into this problem in more detail. In its report, submitted in 2002, it expressed doubt as to whether this question could be solved on a national level at all.[31]

2.1.2. Definition of Sweden

The definition of Sweden corresponds to that of Swedish sovereign territory over water and land including the airspace above it. Swedish coastal waters extend for 12 nautical miles. The height of the airspace claimed is not precisely defined; it covers at least that part in which conventional aircraft fly.[32]

Under the International Convention of 1958 relating to the continental shelf, Sweden, under a special Act (*lag om kontinentalsockeln*, SFS 1966:314), extended its jurisdiction to cover offences relating to the exploration and exploitation of natural resources in the area of the continental shelf. On the basis of the 1982 UN Convention on the Law of the Sea, a Swedish economic zone of 200 miles was set up (*lag och förordning om Sveriges ekonomiska zon*, SFS 1992:1140, 1992:1226) which, with respect to certain specific offences, is subject to Swedish jurisdiction. Various offences, such as marine pollution from ships, the dumping or burning of waste at sea and the violation of fishing agreements, are expressly designated as criminal offences in the event that they are committed within the economic zone. The corresponding offences are prosecuted, by extension of the *territoriality principle*, like domestic offences.

2.2. Flag state principle

The *flag state principle* represents a traditional addition to the territoriality principle. On the one hand, the Swedish rules on jurisdiction leave no room for doubt that offences committed on board foreign ships or aircraft within Swedish sovereign territory, are treated as domestic offences in relation to which no foreign law has to be taken into account when prosecuting them and for which an order for prosecution is only necessary in certain cases (Chapter

---

30. SOU 2002:98, pp. 161, 400.
31. SOU 2002:98, pp. 97 f. For the localisation of internet crimes, see also *Karin Cornils*, "Lokalisering av brott på internet", Nordisk Tidsskrift for Kriminalvidenskab (NTfK), 86. Årgang (1999), pp. 194-205.
32. Cf. *Cameron et al.* (2011), p. 58.

2, Section 5 (1) BrB). On the other hand, Swedish jurisdiction is extended without restriction to offences committed on board Swedish ships and aircraft in foreign territory:

Chapter 2, Section 3 BrB
An offence committed abroad shall also be adjudged under Swedish law and by a Swedish court in cases other than those set out in Section 2,
1. if the offence was committed on board a Swedish ship or aircraft and otherwise if it was committed in the course of duty by the commander or a crew member of such a vehicle,
[…]

This rule on jurisdiction is founded on the fact that the state, in the context of its "administrative function", has a legitimate interest in ensuring safety and orderly conduct on board ships and aircraft registered under its flag and this applies irrespective of where they are located. With respect to offences by a captain or crew member, Swedish jurisdiction applies even where they are committed in the course of duty outside the vehicle. In this regard, the provision goes beyond the *flag state principle* and is partly attributable to the *principle of state protection.*[33]

In connection with the *flag state principle*, the current draft reform bill also refers, in addition to ships and aircraft, to "facilities" within the Swedish economic zone or in the area of the Swedish continental shelf, by which is meant artificial islands and drilling platforms.[34]

2.3. Active personality principle
Foreign offences may possess a link to Sweden arising from the personality of the offender. The corresponding basis for jurisdiction under the active personality principle has a relatively broad scope under Swedish law:

Chapter 2, Section 2 BrB
(1) An offence committed abroad shall be adjudged under Swedish law and by a Swedish court if it was committed
1. by a Swedish national or a foreigner domiciled in Sweden,
2. by a foreigner, not domiciled in Sweden, who became a Swedish national or took up Swedish domicile after the offence was committed [...]
[...]

---

33. See below 2.5.
34. SOU 2002:98, pp. 163, 403 ff.

(2) Sub-section 1 does not apply if the offence is not subject to criminal responsibility under the law of the *locus delicti* or if it was committed in an area which does not belong to any state and the offence is not punishable under Swedish law by more than a fine.

(3) In the cases covered by this Section, the sanction imposed may not be more severe than the severest punishment provided for the offence under the law of the *locus delicti.*

Under this provision, Swedish jurisdiction generally extends to all offences by Swedish nationals or foreigners with (permanent) domicile in Sweden, and this is also the case where nationality or domicile is only acquired after the offence has been committed.

With respect to an offence committed in a stateless area, the *active personality principle* only applies where the offence is punishable under Swedish law by a custodial sentence. Where the *locus delicti* falls under foreign jurisdiction, however, the punishability of the act, and the severest punishment provided for under the law applicable there, must be taken into account.[35]

In the past, the *active personality principle* used to be based on the duty of a Swedish national to show allegiance to the law of his/her home country.[36] This view is now obsolete however – particularly since the introduction of the requirement for double criminality. Today, far greater weight is placed on the fact that Sweden generally does not extradite its own nationals but, if they committed a criminal offence abroad, guarantees their prosecution in Sweden.[37] The *active personality principle* is thus based, at least in part, on the idea of international solidarity which also forms the basis of the *principle of representational jurisdiction.*[38] A request for judicial assistance or extradition by the country in which the offence took place is not necessary.

Foreigners with a permanent domicile in Sweden are placed on the same footing as Swedish nationals. This so-called *domicile principle* is also connected to Swedish extradition practice which is markedly circumspect in favour of foreigners domiciled in Sweden. In order to avoid offering either these residents or Swedish nationals a "safe haven", Swedish jurisdiction also

---

35. On the requirement of double criminality and the principle of *lex mitior*, see above 1.4.
36. Cf. *Ivar Agge*, Den svenska straffrättens allmänna del i huvuddrag. Häfte 1, Stockholm 1944, p. 72.
37. Cf. *Asp and Samuelsson* (1995), pp. 21-112 (36).
38. See below 2.7.

extends, in the spirit of international solidarity, to their offences committed abroad.[39]

2.4. Passive personality principle

Whereas the active personality principle focuses on the offender, the passive personality principle is based on the victim's relationship to Sweden. Here too, foreigners with (permanent) domicile in Sweden are placed on the same footing as Swedish nationals. These jurisdictional rules do not, however, apply to all foreign offences but only to those committed in a stateless area:

Chapter 2, Section 3 BrB
An offence committed abroad shall also be adjudged under Swedish law and by a Swedish court in cases other than those set out in Section 2,
[...]
5. if the offence was committed in a stateless area and against a Swedish national, a Swedish association or private institution or against a foreigner domiciled in Sweden,
[…]

Having originally been included in a joint jurisdictional provision together with the principle of state protection, in 1972 the *passive personality principle* was separated and its scope restricted. The reason for this change was the widespread criticism which stated that the *passive personality principle* ran counter to the efforts towards international solidarity by indicating a lack of confidence on the part of the home country in the level of protection offered to its citizens and their private interests under the criminal law applicable in the *locus delicti*. In order to avoid giving the impression of such a vote of no confidence in a foreign country's administration of justice, the Swedish legislature restricted the *passive personality principle* to offences committed in an area not subject to any national jurisdiction such as international waters.[40]

The draft reform bill of 2002, on the other hand, provides, once again, for a significant extension of the passive personality principle. It proposes that all offences directed against a Swedish national, a foreigner domiciled in Sweden or a Swedish legal entity, irrespective of the place in which they are committed, are subject to Swedish jurisdiction.[41] Restrictions are placed on

39. Cf. SOU 2002:98, p. 98; *Cameron et al.* (2011), pp. 68 f.
40. *Holmqvist et al.* (2011), 2:32 f.
41. SOU 2002:98, pp. 403, 406 f.

the provision by the requirement of double criminality and a special order for prosecution by the Prosecutor-General.[42]

2.5. Principle of state protection

In addition to such aspects as *locus delicti*, or the offender and victim of the offence, the basis for national jurisdiction may also arise from the link between the state and the public interest which is violated or put at risk by the offence. According to the principle of state protection, Swedish jurisdiction covers acts committed abroad which are directed against the Swedish state, one of its regional authorities or other bodies or public institutions:

Chapter 2, Section 3 BrB
An offence committed abroad shall also be adjudged under Swedish law and by a Swedish court in cases other than those set out in Section 2,
[...]
4. if the offence was committed against Sweden, a Swedish municipal authority or other assembly or a Swedish public institution.
[…]

What is meant by offences against Sweden is subject to some controversy. It is undisputed that it refers principally to offences touching upon the country's external or internal security or relating to Swedish authorities or public officials. Smuggling and violations of the legal provisions on foreign currency and weapons have also been designated as offences against Sweden in the judicial case law.[43]

The punishability of the act according to the law of the *locus delicti* is, in this case, just as irrelevant for Swedish jurisdiction as the nationality of the offender. Where the latter is not from one of the Scandinavian countries, however, prosecution may only be brought on the basis of a special order (Chapter 2, Section 5 (2) BrB).

Sweden's jurisdiction also applies, likewise without reference to the law applicable in the *locus delicti*, to foreign offences committed by specific persons in the Swedish civil service whilst on deployment abroad. The group of persons includes the captain and crew of Swedish ships or aircraft, members or employees of the armed forces, as well as police officers, customs officials and coast guard officials (Chapter 2, Section 3, Nos. 1-3 a BrB). The basis for jurisdiction here arises from the public interest in maintaining order and dis-

---

42. See above 1.4. and 1.6.
43. Cf. *Holmqvist et al.* (2011), 2:30 b–32.

cipline in the ranks of those wielding Swedish sovereign power in the exercise of their duty whilst abroad. The cases therefore fall predominantly under the *principle of state protection* although aspects of the *active personality principle* and the *principle of representative jurisdiction* are also involved.[44]

2.6. Principle of universal jurisdiction

2.6.1. International law agreements

Certain types of offence, of which there is a conclusive list, fall under Swedish jurisdiction due to the *principle of universal jurisdiction*:

Chapter 2, Section 3 BrB
An offence committed abroad shall also be adjudged under Swedish law and by a Swedish court in cases other than those set out in Section 2
[...]
6. if the offence is hijacking, sabotage of sea or air traffic, airport sabotage, money counterfeiting or an attempt to commit such crimes, or is an offence under international law, involves the unlawful handling of chemical weapons, unlawful handling of mines or giving, or negligently giving, false testimony to an international court, constitutes a terrorist offence under Section 2 of the Terrorist Offences Act (2003:148) or an attempt to commit such a crime, or an offence under Section 5 of the same Act, or if the offence was directed against the jurisdiction of the International Criminal Court [...]
[...].

Swedish jurisdiction applies in these cases irrespective of whether the act is a criminal offence under the law of the *locus delicti*. Generally, though, the case may only be prosecuted by special order (Chapter 2, Section 5 (2), Sentence 1 BrB).

Swedish jurisdiction under the *principle of universal jurisdiction* is based, with respect to each of the offences listed in the Code, on an international convention under which Sweden is obliged to provide for jurisdiction over corresponding acts.

In the draft reform bill of 2002, the list of offences was extended to cover torture and incitement to commit genocide.[45] In return, money counterfeiting, unlawful handling of chemical weapons and mines as well as the financing of terrorism were no longer referred to in this connection but placed together

---

44. SOU 2002:98, p. 99; *Holmqvist et al.* (2011), 2:28-30 a.
45. See, in more detail, *Karin Cornils*, "Grundlagen der Strafverfolgung völkerrechtlicher Verbrechen in Schweden". In: Albin Eser/Helmut Kreicker (eds.), Nationale Strafverfolgung völkerrechtlicher Verbrechen. National Prosecution of International Crimes, Volume 2, Freiburg 2003, pp. 183-278 (215-223).

with other types of crime in a new provision exempt from the requirement of double criminality.[46]

2.6.2. *Miscellaneous: The four year rule*
The jurisdictional rule in Chapter 2, Section 3, no. 7 BrB is also considered to be a basis for application of the principle of universal jurisdiction:

[…]

7. if under Swedish law the least severe punishment prescribed for the offence is imprisonment for four years or more.

When it was introduced into the Criminal Code in 1972, this so-called four-year rule was originally intended to be an exemption from the requirement of double criminality under the *active personality principle* and the *principle of representational jurisdiction*. It was to allow for the possibility, in exceptional cases, of prosecuting a serious offence[47] in Sweden even where it did not fulfil the requirement of being a criminal offence under the law of the *locus delicti*. The plan was thus to have a supplementary provision for cases where Swedish jurisdiction was based on one of the traditional principles. In the provision, the legislator failed, however, to express the necessary link with an existing jurisdictional principle. The provision which thus arose therefore seems to be an independent jurisdictional rule based solely on the strictness of the domestic sanction; and that is how it is generally regarded and applied today.[48]

Over and above agreements made under international law, the reform commission does not consider Sweden to have a legitimate interest in prosecuting offences which do not have any domestic connection and has proposed that the four-year rule be struck out. Instead, in accordance with the original intention, only the requirement for double criminality should be lifted for serious offences punishable under Swedish law by at least four years' imprisonment.[49]

---

46. SOU 2002:98, pp. 170-175, 404, 408 f., 412 f.
47. See, for example, murder (Chapter 3, Section 1 BrB), manslaughter (Chapter 3, Section 2 BrB), kidnapping (Chapter 4, Section 1 BrB), aggravated robbery (Chapter 8, Section 6 BrB) and aggravated arson (Chapter, 13, Section 2 BrB).
48. Cf. *Cameron et al.* (2011), pp. 81 f.; *Holmqvist et al.* (2011), 2:36 a; critical *Asp* (2005), pp. 93-129 (98).
49. SOU 2002:98, pp. 174 f., 412-414.

2.7. Principle of representational jurisdiction

The *principle of representational jurisdiction*, also known in Swedish as *"derivative jurisdiction" (härledd jurisdiktion)*, arises *inter alia* where jurisdiction is based on the presence of the offender in Sweden:

Chapter 2, Section 2 BrB
(1) An offence committed abroad shall be adjudged under Swedish law and by a Swedish court if it was committed
[…]
2. by a foreigner, not domiciled in Sweden, who […] is of Danish, Finnish, Icelandic or Norwegian nationality and is present in Sweden, or
3. by another foreigner present in Sweden if the offence is punishable under Swedish law by more than six months' imprisonment.

Generally, a domestic prosecution requires that the offender be present in Sweden. In the cases provided for here, the presence of the offender on Swedish sovereign territory constitutes not only a procedural requirement for jurisdiction but also a material one. This material requirement is not fulfilled where, for example, the offender is in Sweden against his/her will, following extradition.

The provisions are connected with Swedish extradition law. They were introduced in order to ensure that where an offence does not fall under one of the traditional principles on which jurisdiction is based, it does not go unpunished even if the offender is not extradited. Thus the law generally requires a certain level of severity of the offence (No. 3). The special provision for nationals of the neighbouring Scandinavian countries is based on the fact that Sweden wishes to reserve the right to refuse their extradition to third-party countries outside Scandinavia and the EU and therefore sees a need to make up for this.[50] It is of no consequence, in the individual case, whether a request for extradition has actually been made which Sweden has refused.

Following Sweden's accession to the 1972 European Convention on the Transfer of Proceedings in Criminal Matters, an additional provision was incorporated into the Criminal Code which is based on the principle of representational jurisdiction:

Chapter 2, Section 3 a BrB
Pursuant to the provisions of the Act on International Cooperation concerning Proceedings in Criminal Matters (SFS 1976:19), an offence shall also be adjudged under Swedish law and by a Swedish court in cases other than those covered by Sections 1-3.

50. Cf. *Cameron et al.* (2011), p. 69.

The basis for jurisdiction here requires another state to make an application for the transferral of proceedings which is granted by Sweden. The case law, however, also considers it to be sufficient where the offender is extradited to Sweden without a formal transfer procedure.

Under the 2002 draft reform bill, the *principle of representational juris-diction* would be more clearly expressed than previously by way of its own jurisdictional provision. The bill proposes that prosecution in Sweden would require the offender to be present in Sweden and another country to have applied for Sweden to take over prosecution; or a request for extradition from another country to have been rejected; or the act to fall under an international convention under which Sweden is obliged to effect unconditional prosecution, in the event of a failure to extradite.[51]

3. Abbreviations

BrB	Brottsbalken (Swedish Criminal Code)
EC	European Community
EU	European Union
ICTR	International Criminal Tribunal for Rwanda
ICTY	International Criminal Tribunal for the former Yugoslavia
Ch.	Chapter
SFS	Svensk författningssamling (Swedish Law Gazette)
SOU	Statens offentliga utredningar (Official Report on Reform)

4. The Jurisdictional Rules of the Swedish Criminal Code[52] in English translation.

Chapter 2 – On the application of Swedish law
Ch. 2, Section 1
An offence committed in Sweden shall be adjudged under Swedish law and by a Swedish court. The same applies if it is uncertain where the offence has been committed but there is reason to assume that it was committed in Sweden.

---

51. SOU 2002:98, pp. 175-180, 404, 409-411.
52. Criminal Code (*Brottsbalken*) of 21 December 1962, SFS 1962:700, last update 23 December 2013, SFS 2013:856.

Ch. 2, Section 2

(1) An offence committed abroad shall be adjudged under Swedish law and by a Swedish court if it was committed

1. by a Swedish national or a foreigner domiciled in Sweden,
2. by a foreigner, not domiciled in Sweden, who became a Swedish national or took up Swedish domicile after the offence was committed, or is of Danish, Finnish, Icelandic or Norwegian nationality and is present in Sweden, or
3. by another foreigner present in Sweden if the offence is punishable under Swedish law by more than six months' imprisonment.

(2) Sub-section 1 does not apply if the offence is not subject to criminal responsibility under the law of the *locus delicti* or if it was committed in an area which does not belong to any state and the offence is not punishable under Swedish law by more than a fine.

(3) In the cases covered by this Section, the sanction imposed may not be more severe than the severest punishment provided for the offence under the law of the *locus delicti*.

(4) The restrictions on Swedish jurisdiction referred to in Sub-sections (2) and (3) do not apply to offences under Ch. 6, Sections 1-6, 8, 9 and 12, or to the attempt to commit such offences if the offence was committed against a person under the age of 18. Nor do the restrictions apply to offences under Ch. 4, Section 1 a, or Ch. 16, Section 10 a (1), no. 1, and (5) or the attempt to commit such an offence.

Ch. 2, Section 3

An offence committed abroad shall also be adjudged under Swedish law and by a Swedish court in cases other than those set out in Section 2,

1. if the offence was committed on board a Swedish ship or aircraft and otherwise if it was committed in the course of duty by the commander or a crew member of such a vehicle,
2. if the offence was committed by a member of the Swedish armed forces in an area in which a unit of the armed forces was present, or if it was committed by another person in such an area and the unit was present there for a purpose other than an exercise,
3. if the offence was committed in the course of duty abroad by a person employed by the armed forces who is part of an international military deployment or belongs to a foreign unit of the police,
3a. if the offence was committed in the course of duty abroad by a police officer, customs officer or coast guard official, undertaking cross-border duties pursuant to an international convention to which Sweden is a signatory,
4. if the offence was committed against Sweden, a Swedish municipal authority or other assembly or a Swedish public institution,
5. if the offence was committed in a stateless area and against a Swedish national, a Swedish association or private institution or against a foreigner domiciled in Sweden,
6. if the offence is hijacking, sabotage of sea or air traffic, airport sabotage, money counterfeiting or an attempt to commit such crimes, or is an offence under international law, involves the unlawful handling of chemical weapons, unlawful handling of mines or giving, or negligently giving, false testimony to an international court, constitutes a terrorist offence under Section 2 of the Terrorist Offences Act (2003:148) or an attempt to

commit such a crime or an offence under Section 5 of the same Act or where the offence was directed against the jurisdiction of the International Criminal Court

7. if under Swedish law the least severe punishment prescribed for the offence is imprisonment for four years or more.

Ch. 2, Section 3 a

Pursuant to the provisions of the Act on International Cooperation concerning Proceedings in Criminal Matters (SFS 1976:19), an offence shall also be adjudged under Swedish law and by a Swedish court in cases other than those covered by Sections 1-3.

Ch. 2 Section 4

An offence is deemed to have been committed in the place where the criminal act was perpetrated and also in the place where the offence was accomplished, or, in the case of attempt, where the intended offence was to have been accomplished.

Ch. 2, Section 5

(1) With respect to an offence committed in Sweden on board a foreign ship or aircraft by a foreigner who was the commander of the vehicle or a member of its crew or was otherwise travelling on board, and the offence was directed against such a foreigner or against a foreign interest, the prosecution may only be brought by order of the Government or an office authorised by the Government.

(2) With respect to an offence committed abroad, prosecution may only be brought by order pursuant to Sub-section 1. Prosecution may, however, be brought without such an order if the offence consists of giving false testimony before an international court, intentionally or by gross negligence, or if the offence was committed

1. on board a Swedish ship or aircraft or by the commander or a crew-member of such a vehicle in the course of his duty,
2. by a member of the armed forces in an area in which a unit of the armed forces was present,
3. in the course of duty abroad by a person employed by the armed forces who is part of an international military deployment or a member of a foreign unit of the police,
4. in the course of duty abroad by a police officer, customs officer or coast guard official undertaking cross-border duties pursuant to an international convention to which Sweden is a signatory,
5. in Denmark, Finland, Iceland or Norway, or on board a ship or aircraft in regular traffic between places situated in Sweden or in one of the said countries, or
6. by a Swedish, Danish, Finnish, Icelandic or Norwegian national against a Swedish interest.

Ch. 2, Section 5 a

(1) If the question of criminal liability for an act has been determined by a Judgment passed *res judicata* in a foreign state in which the offence was committed or which is a signatory to one of the conventions listed under Sub-section 4, the defendant may not be prosecuted again for the same act in Sweden,

1. if he has been acquitted,
2. if he has been convicted of the offence without a sanction having been imposed,

3. if the sanction imposed has been fully enforced or is being enforced, or
4. if the sanction imposed has lapsed under the law of the foreign state concerned.

(2) Sub-section 1 does not apply to the offences covered by Sections 1 and 3 Nos. 4, 6 and 7 unless prosecution took place in the foreign state at the request of a Swedish authority or the person was extradited from Sweden for the purpose of prosecution.

(3) If the question of criminal liability for an act has been determined by a Judgment issued in a foreign state and there is no impediment to prosecution under the foregoing provisions of this Section, the act may only be prosecuted in Sweden by order of the Government or an office authorised by the Government.

(4) The conventions covered by Sub-section 1 are
1. the European Convention of 28 May 1970 on the International Validity of Criminal Judgments,
2. the European Convention of 15 May 1972 on the Transfer of Proceedings in Criminal Matters,
3. the Convention of 26 July 1995 on the Protection of the European Communities' Financial Interests, but only insofar as the act falls under the convention,
4. the Protocol of 27 September 1996 to the Convention on the Protection of the European Communities' Financial Interests, but only insofar as the act falls under the convention,
5. the Convention of 26 May 1997 on the Fight against Corruption Involving Officials of the European Communities or Officials of the Member States of the European Union, but only insofar as the act falls under the convention,
6. the Convention of 19 June 1990 on the Implementation of the Schengen Agreement of 14 June 1985,
7. the Convention of 25 May 1987 between the Member States of the European Communities on Double Jeopardy, and
8. the second Protocol of 19 June 1997 to the Convention on the Protection of the European Communities' Financial Interests, but only insofar as the act falls under the convention.

(5) If an offence is committed partly in Sweden and partly also in the sovereign territory of the Member State in which the Judgment was issued, Sub-section 1 applies if the act falls under the conventions listed in Sub-section 4, Nos. 3-5 or 8, or if the Judgment was issued in a state which is signatory to one of the conventions listed in Sub-section 4, no. 6 or 7.

Ch. 2, Section 6
(1) If a person is convicted in Sweden for an act for which he/she has been sentenced abroad, the enforcement of the foreign sentence must be appropriately taken into account in determining the sanction. If he/she should be sentenced to a fine or imprisonment and he/she has been given a sanction involving the deprivation of liberty abroad, this must, insofar as it has been enforced, be offset when determining the sanction.

(2) In cases covered by Sub-section 1, a less severe punishment than that provided for the act may be imposed or a sanction be waived completely.

Ch. 2, Section 7
With regard to the application of Swedish law and the jurisdiction of the Swedish courts, in addition to the provisions of this Chapter, the restrictions arising out of generally recognised principles of public international law or from special provisions in agreements with foreign states must also be observed.

Ch. 2, Section 7 a
If a foreign national has committed an offence in the exercise of an office or duty comprising a general position held on behalf of another state or international organisation, prosecution for the offence may only be brought on order of the Government. This does not apply if the offender has attempted, by way of misleading information, disguise or other means, to conceal the capacity in which he was acting.

Ch. 2, Section 7 b
(1) A foreigner who is not domiciled in Sweden but deployed there in the course of international military cooperation or for dealing with an international emergency, and who falls under an agreement applicable with respect to Sweden, may only be prosecuted for an offence he or she has committed while in Sweden, by order of the Government.

(2) The provision in Sub-section 1 also applies to a Swedish national or a foreigner domiciled in Sweden who is in the service of a foreign state's armed forces.

Ch. 2, Section 7 c
Prosecution for an offence contrary to the judicial case law of the International Criminal Court may only be brought by order of the Government or by an office authorised by the Government.

Ch. 2, Section 8
(1) Special provisions apply with respect to extradition for a criminal offence.

(2) Conditions stipulated in connection with surrender or extradition from a foreign state to Sweden must be complied with in Sweden.

CHAPTER 6

Nordic trends of jurisdiction
– An international perspective

Thomas Elholm & Birgit Feldtmann

1. Introduction – why jurisdiction from a Nordic perspective?

The reader might want to know why it is appropriate and relevant to write a book about the rules on jurisdiction in all five Nordic countries. The Nordic countries have a close historical and cultural relationship. Iceland and Norway were part of the realm of the Danish king for centuries; Finland was a part of Sweden, while Norway and Sweden formed a personal union in 1814-1905 (the United Kingdoms of Sweden and Norway). Although there are many differences between the five countries, they have in a number of ways a common Nordic heritage and culture. They also have – to some extent at least – a common language. There has been a close legislative and procedural cooperation in legal matters between the Nordic countries, not only regarding criminal law and criminal procedure, but within many legal disciplines.[1] In the field of criminal law this results in certain similarities concerning criminal justice, but there are also major differences, for example concerning concepts of attempt or participation in crimes. The cooperation between the Nordic countries is visible within *travaux préparatoires*. Indeed, it is visible in their legislation, for example the Nordic countries have a special agreement, extending the scope of the active personality principle. Thus, the Nordic countries have jurisdiction under this principle, not only with regard to their own citizens who commit criminal acts abroad, but also with regard to citizens

1. *Karin Cornils*, "Strafrechtliche Zusammenarbeit zwischen den nordischen Ländern", in V. Greve/K. Cornils: Studien zum dänischen Strafrecht/Studies in Danish Criminal Law, Copenhagen 2011, p. 67 ff.

from other Nordic countries, who happen to be in the country. Thus, if a Dane has committed a crime in France and this act is punishable according to Norwegian law, the Dane can be prosecuted in Norway, if he moves to Norway or goes on holiday in Norway. The extensive rule on the principle of active personality is a result of the close relationship between the Nordic countries and the mutual trust in criminal matters between these countries and in addition, practical needs are a motivating factor.[2]

The Nordic Committee for Criminal Law (NCCL, *Nordiska Straffrätts-kommittén*) was established in 1960 by four Nordic Ministers of Justice (Iceland joined three years later). It was the task of NCCL to make proposals for legislation, which would harmonise the criminal laws of the Nordic countries. The NCCL made a number of reports. The last report was made in 1992 (Nord 1992:17), and it concerns jurisdiction. In the report, NCCL makes a number of recommendations for the national legislators. For example the NCCL recommends that rules concerning *principles on state protection and passive personality* are conceived as clear and precise as possible in order to avoid conflicts between national jurisdictions. Another very interesting example in light of the current development is the recommendation to limit the principle of passive personality to offences, which are punishable in both countries (double criminality requirement).

Finland reformed the rules on jurisdiction in 1996, mainly as a result of the recommendations made by NCCL. A commitment to implement the recommendations is also seen in a *travaux préparatoires* from Sweden in 2002 (SOU 2002:98), in which a coming reform of the Swedish rules on jurisdiction is based. However, in the Danish *travaux préparatoires*, which were the foundation for the Danish 2008 reform on the rules of jurisdiction, the recommendations from NCCL were neglected.[3] In the new Norwegian criminal code, which was adopted in 2005, but which has not yet come into force, the Norwegians have taken a position that in fact lies between the Danish and the Finnish approach. Thus, it can be seen that the impact of the report from NCCL is quite different in the Nordic countries. NCCL was dissolved after 1992.

The practical legal cooperation between the five countries is visible in the rules on jurisdiction which apply between the Nordic countries. A Nordic ar-

2. *Vagn Greve et al.*, Kommenteret Straffelov, Almindelig Del, 10th ed., Copenhagen 2013, p. 164.
3. Critical to the Danish approach is *Per Ole Träskman*, "'In dubio pro Dania'. Några reflexioner över dansk straffrättslig jurisdiktion", in T. Elholm et al. (eds), Ikke kun straf ... Festskrift til Vagn Greve, Copenhagen 2008, pp. 563-590, p. 590.

rest warrant and extensive rules on extradition (both for prosecution and for execution of sentences), as well as special rules of jurisdiction between the Nordic countries have existed for decades. The Nordic Arrest Warrant from 1970 has – so it seems – been a source of inspiration for the European Arrest Warrant. The decades of close practical cooperation between the Nordic countries makes a Nordic perspective on jurisdiction highly interesting. We are not going to take a detailed look at the rules on extradition in this book. However, extradition and jurisdiction are related issues, and the close cooperation between the Nordic countries regarding extradition must be kept in mind.

Before engaging in an analysis of some selected issues related to jurisdiction, we would like to offer a few practical guidelines to the reader. The present considerations are not meant to be a summary of the country reports. It is a thematic article that aims to discuss and clarify certain relevant issues on jurisdiction. Our choice of topics is based on findings in the country reports, where 1) the Nordic countries' systems differ significantly, or 2) there are some ambiguities regarding the interpretation of the law or 3) where the issue might be of potential political importance in the years ahead. We are not trying to provide the reader with definitive answers, but instead we are trying to raise questions and highlight tendencies within the Nordic countries.

By jurisdiction, we mean the competence of a court in a certain country to initiate criminal proceedings against an offender under domestic law.

2. Nordic trends – widening the scope of jurisdiction?

When comparing the five country reports on criminal jurisdiction from Denmark, Finland, Iceland, Norway and Sweden with the above mentioned report *Nord 1992:17,* a number of trends are evident. Some of these will be scrutinised below.

Within the last two or three decades, the Nordic countries – and probably many other legal systems – have adopted rules widening the scope of jurisdiction in criminal matters. This has been done by adopting more extensive concepts and application of the jurisdictional principles.

First of all, giving up the requirement of double criminality in certain situations seems to be a general feature. The tendency is especially evident in Danish law. Double criminality is no longer a requirement in some cases, where both perpetrator and victim are Danish or residing in Denmark. Intentional bodily harm inflicted on a Danish person whilst abroad by another Danish person is named as an example of its application.[4] All the Nordic countries have given up the requirement of double criminality within the *active personality principle* for certain offences, especially female genital mutilation and some sexual offences against children.[5]

Secondly, widening the scope of the principle of the *active personality principle* is another way to broaden the scope of jurisdiction. The scope of jurisdiction can also be widened by applying a broader concept of the persons falling under the *active personality principle*. As mentioned above, in all of the Nordic countries the *active personality principle* also covers nationals and residents of the other Nordic countries. In Denmark, an already relatively large group of people falling under the *principle of active personality* was further extended by the reform of 2008, and now includes foreigners living in Denmark who have permanent residency status or the like (for example students staying in Denmark for a longer period of time).[6] The new provisions also cover persons who have been awaiting a decision on their residency permit for a long time or against whom extradition has been ordered but which has not yet been executed.

Thirdly, when analysing the development in the Nordic countries, we can see that one of the tendencies occurring concerns the *passive personality principle*, e.g. the protection of national citizens or residents independently of where they are at the time when they are subjected to a criminal offence. The *Danish Commission on Jurisdiction* concludes in its report that there is little support in the legal literature and international practice to accept the *passive personality principle* in situations where an act is committed on another state's territory. The argument put forward in this instance is that the state whose citizen was victimised cannot argue that it has a bigger interest in prosecuting the offence than the territorial state. The commission therefore assumes that it *"cannot be ruled out"* that the use of the *passive personality principle* might be somewhat *"difficult to combine with the principles of international law"*.[7] Spiermann, a Danish professor in international law, subse-

---

4. See Section 2.3. of the Danish country report.
5. See Section 1.4. of the country reports from Denmark, Finland, Iceland, Norway and Sweden (concerning Norway see Section 5(6) of the new Criminal Code).
6. See section 2.3. of the Danish country report.
7. Betænkning no. 1488/2007, pp. 181 f. (original in Danish: *"kan det ikke udelukkes"* and *"vanskeligt foreneligt med folkeretlige principper"*).

quently called this assumption an *"outstanding understatement".*[8] Spiermann argues further that newer state practice might indicate a move towards a less strict attitude towards the *passive personality principle* but that the *Danish Commission on Jurisdiction* seems to overrate those tendencies by indirectly assuming that the general ban on the *passive personality principle* today is replaced by a system of the weighting of different interests. By doing so, Spiermann concludes that the Commission is ahead of a possible trend that might be underway but which is far from complete, and he questions whether it was the Commission's intention to contribute towards such a development.[9]

Spiermann categorises the *passive personality principle* as being closer to the concept of the *principle of universal jurisdiction* than to the concept of the *active personality principle*, due to the weak connection to the state which extends its jurisdiction into another state's territory.[10]

The *Danish Commission on Jurisdiction* suggested in its report that Danish jurisdiction should be extended on the basis of the *passive personality principle* and limited by criteria concerning the types of crimes and minimum sentencing levels (penalty scale minimum). Furthermore, the Commission stresses the importance of the requirement of double criminality in this particular context.[11] Subsequently, the suggestions of the Commission were codified to a large extent and the considerations concerning the *passive personality principle* were codified in § 7 a of the Danish Criminal Code. However, the question remains as to whether this extension of jurisdiction can be used. Looking at Spiermann's reasoning, it can be argued that the extended jurisdiction is restricted again by § 12 of the Danish Criminal Code, which limits the Danish rules of jurisdiction by the *"exceptions in international law".*[12]

As mentioned in the Finnish country report, the considerations on the limits of the *passive personality principle* through international law were a decisive factor in restricting the scope of Finnish jurisdiction in this context. However, the *passive personality principle* is still upheld for certain serious offences, punishable with more than 6 months' imprisonment. The Finnish jurisdiction in those cases is, however, restricted by the requirement of double criminality.

---

8. *Ole Spiermann,* "Dansk straffemyndighed i folkeretlig belysning", Ugeskrift for Retsvæsen (UfR) B 2007, p. 225 (original in Danish: *"enestående underdrivelse").*
9. Ibid., p. 225.
10. Ibid., p. 226.
11. Betænkning no. 1488/2007, p. 282 ff.
12. *"ved de i folkeretten anerkendte undtagelser", Spiermann* (2007), p. 226.

Norway has chosen an even more restrictive approach and has not codified the *passive personality principle* as such. This means that offences directed against Norwegians can only be punished in Norway in combination with the *active personality principle* or under the *principle of universal jurisdiction*.[13] Also Iceland has chosen a restrictive approach only applying the *passive personality principle* as an exception in a very limited scope, e.g. only outside the jurisdiction of other states.[14]

An opposite approach is taken by Sweden, as shown in the Swedish country report. The 2002 draft reform bill provides a significant extension to the passive personality principle. It proposes that all offences directed against a Swedish national, a foreigner domiciled in Sweden or a Swedish legal entity, irrespective of the place in which they are committed, are subject to Swedish jurisdiction. Restrictions are placed on the provision by the requirement of double criminality and a special order for prosecution by the Director of Public Prosecution.[15]

Fourthly, the country reports show another clear tendency: The influence of international criminal law on domestic rules of jurisdiction. The rapid development of international criminal law in the 1990s, culminated with the establishment of the International Criminal Court (ICC) in The Hague and this has had an impact on legislation in the Nordic countries. All five countries are party to the Rome Statute and have subsequently regulated the question of jurisdiction for cases concerning international crimes/crimes under the Rome Statute. This can be seen as a necessary result of the *principle of complementarity* (art.17 of the Rome Statue), establishing the ICC as a last resort; only proceeding with a case if domestic proceedings have not been initiated or have been insufficient. However, the way in which the Nordic countries have approached this topic differs slightly: Denmark, for example, has established jurisdiction for cases under the Rome Statue if the suspected person at the time of the charge ("*sigtelse*") is a Danish citizen, is resident in Denmark or is in Denmark for a longer period. Furthermore, Danish jurisdiction is also established in those cases if a person, with no further connection to Denmark is present in Denmark at the time of the charge ("*sigtelse*"). For example, this would be the case if the suspected person is charged while being in the transit-areas of the Copenhagen Airport.[16] The new Norwegian provision also includes persons who are physically present in Norway. Sweden has a general

---

13. See Section 2.4. of the Norwegian country report.
14. See Section 2.4. of the Icelandic country report.
15. See Section 2.4. of the Swedish country report.
16. See *Greve et al.* (2013), p. 178.

provision establishing jurisdiction for international crimes. However, a prosecution order is a precondition to proceed with the case. In Finland the *principle of universality* is defined in section 7 of the Criminal Code. Before the revision of 1996, the relevant offences were listed in the provision. After the revision, and due to the constantly changing nature of international law, it was considered sufficient to include the relevant offences in a Decree, which is easier to amend if necessary. Iceland has no specific regulation concerning international crimes.

Besides influencing the rules of jurisdiction, the establishment of the ICC affected the Nordic countries' legal systems in other ways. For example, in Denmark in 2002, a specialised division of the Prosecution Service ("*Statsadvokaten for særlige internationale straffesager*") was established and this predominantly (but not exclusively) worked with crimes under the Rome Statute. In 2012, this Prosecutors Office was merged with the specialised Prosecutors Office for serious economic crimes under a general reform of the Danish Prosecution Service.[17]

Finally, when analysing the development in the Nordic countries, the question of the precision of rules on jurisdiction also becomes evident. The lack of precision of the rules on jurisdiction presents the courts (or the prosecutor) with a fair degree of leeway when it comes to interpretation. This is indirectly or potentially a way to widen the scope of jurisdiction. For example, the possible wide formulation of the *principle of protection of state interests.*[18]

Generally speaking, the tendency described above might be characterised as showing that the *principle of territoriality* is still predominant in the Nordic countries, but increasing weight is being given to principles, such as the *active* and *passive personality principles*. Where these principles apply, the requirement of double criminality still prevails in the Nordic countries. However, the requirement has increasingly – within the last 10 years – been abandoned for certain crimes, especially in Denmark.

It is striking that there is no unity concerning this issue in the Nordic countries' approach. Finland has taken quite another approach, limiting the juris-

---

17. See *Lene Rosenmeier*, "Anklagemyndigheden opruster med reform", Advokaten no. 8/2012, p. 18 ff. and Statsadvokaten for særlig økonomisk og international kriminalitet (SØIK): http://www.anklagemyndigheden.dk/Sider/statsadvokaten-for-saerlig-oekonomisk-og-international-kriminalitet.aspx (last visited 10.10.2013).
18. See for example Nord-1992:17, p. 116, where the Commission recommends a detailed and strict formulation of the principle of protection of state interests, and *Iain Cameron*, "Straffrättslig jurisdiktion i Norden", NTfK 1993, pp. 221-234.

dictional rules, which previously were relatively wide. The provisions in the first chapter of the Finnish Criminal Code were thoroughly revised in 1996.[19] The revision restricted the scope of application of Finnish criminal law, including requiring double criminality and a separate prosecution order to a greater extent than before in regard to offences committed outside Finland. This last revision was motivated by considerations of previous provisions being problematic in relation to international law and the risks for conflicts of jurisdiction with other states.

Before the revision of 1996, the *passive personality principle* was unrestricted and did not require double criminality. Today, it applies pursuant to offences committed outside Finland, if these are directed at a Finnish citizen, a Finnish legal entity or a foreigner permanently resident in Finland, but only if the offence under Finnish law is punishable by imprisonment for more than six months and the requirement of double criminality is fulfilled. Thus, Finland has taken another approach, one that differs from Denmark or (the proposal from) Sweden.

3. Jurisdictional rules – part of substantive or procedural criminal law?

One of the first questions dealt with in each of the chapters on Denmark, Finland, Iceland, Norway, and Sweden is whether rules on jurisdiction are regarded as being part of substantive criminal law or criminal procedure. The question might seem academic with little practical significance and it is somewhat neglected in Nordic literature on jurisdiction.[20] However, it could have fundamental and practical implications. Thus, for example, the principle of legality normally has different implications in terms of substantive criminal law and criminal procedure. Also, the consequences of a lack of jurisdiction will often depend on the nature of the jurisdictional rules. If the jurisdictional rules are regarded as part of substantive criminal law, acquittal is often the consequence. If jurisdictional rules are regarded as procedural, lack of jurisdiction will often result in dismissal of the case. The following is a brief summary of the country reports and therefore there are no references (see the country reports).

19. See Government Bill, Regeringens Proposition till Riksdagen med förslag till revidering av lagstiftningen om tillämpningsområdet för finsk straffrätt, RP 1/1996.
20. See recently however, Dan Helenius, Straffrättslig Jurisdiktion, Helsinki 2014, p. 141 ff.

3.1. The five country reports

In Denmark, it is the predominant view of legal researchers that rules on jurisdiction should be classified as procedural provisions, but certain writers treat them as substantive legal norms or as a mixture of procedural and substantive law. However, the literature consistently draws a clear distinction between jurisdictional rules and the question of the territorial scope of Danish criminal law, which undisputedly forms part of substantive law. This view was recently confirmed by the Supreme Court. Lack of jurisdiction will sometimes result in dismissal of the case or sometimes in acquittal – Danish case law is not consistent.

In Finland, the predominant view is that provisions on jurisdiction are part of substantive criminal law (although some consider the rules to be principles of international procedural law). According to the doctrine, a person should be acquitted in the case of lack of jurisdiction, because no offence has taken place. There is no case law on this issue. In some situations however, the provisions are also considered part of procedural law, but this applies only in situations of representational jurisdiction.

In Iceland, researchers writing about criminal jurisdiction have not directly stated whether the rules are viewed as substantive or procedural rules. Scholarly Criminal Law discusses criminal jurisdiction as part of general criminal law. To that degree they are substantive rules. It is not completely clear whether failure to fulfil the conditions for criminal jurisdiction constitutes grounds for acquittal or dismissal from court, but it is more likely that it will lead to acquittal.

In Norway, it is somewhat unclear whether jurisdictional rules are considered part of substantive or procedural criminal law. However, they seem mainly to be regarded as part of substantive criminal law (even though in some cases they might be regarded as procedural). This position is in line with most recent case law of the Norwegian Supreme Court, although there is some previous case law from the Supreme Court stating otherwise. Lack of jurisdiction is grounds for acquittal, and not for dismissal of the case.

In Sweden, the rules on jurisdiction are regarded as *procedural provisions* and come under so-called international criminal procedural law. The fact that they are set out in the Criminal Code is explained by the fact that the jurisdiction of the Swedish criminal courts represents a direct condition for the application of national criminal provisions and is therefore closely connected to substantive criminal law. Lack of jurisdiction results in dismissal.

To summarise: In all of the Nordic countries – except from Sweden – it is somewhat unclear as to whether the provisions on jurisdiction are considered part of substantive or procedural criminal law. However, it is the general or prevailing view in Iceland, Finland and Norway that they are part of substantive criminal law. In Denmark, the prevailing view is that they are part of procedural law. In Sweden there is no doubt that the jurisdictional rules are regarded as being part of criminal procedure.

3.2. The Criminal Code or the Administration of Justice Act
How does one know, whether jurisdictional rules in a country are part of substantive criminal law or procedure? It would be too formalistic to answer the question by referring to the act or statute in which the rules occur. In all of the Nordic countries, the rules on jurisdiction are to be found in the criminal code. However, they are not necessarily regarded as part of substantive criminal law.

In Denmark and Sweden, where the rules are regarded as procedural, they are still to be found in the criminal code. This has probably to do with the fact that traditionally there was a close connection between jurisdictional rules and the question which substantive criminal provisions apply in a specific case. Thus, it is important to draw a clear distinction between jurisdictional rules (part of procedural law) and the question of the territorial scope of criminal law provisions (part of substantive criminal law).

In the following, we will try to discuss some of the aspects stemming from the distinction between substantive and procedural rules in a Nordic perspective.

3.3. Acquittal or dismissal
A criminal case is normally dismissed if the procedural requirements are not fulfilled. On the other hand, a person is acquitted if the requirements of substantive criminal law are not fulfilled. The distinction is crucial in a number of ways.

In Finland, the jurisdictional rules are generally regarded as substantive criminal law and according to the doctrine a person is acquitted if the requirements are not met. However, there is no case law on this issue. In Denmark, the prevailing view is that jurisdictional rules are procedural. However, the courts do not always dismiss a case due to a lack of jurisdiction. There are examples of cases where a person was acquitted because the jurisdictional requirements were not fulfilled. This seems to be the result in cases where the question of jurisdiction was only answered by the end of the trial. Thus, it seems to be the stage of the process – rather than the actual question of substantive or procedural matter – which is decisive. Norway also had a certain degree of divergence in case law, but the most recent case law is consistently in favour of acquittal. The conclusion must be that there is not necessarily a connection between the matter of substantive/procedural law and acquittal/dismissal. In systems – like the Danish system – where the jurisdictional provisions are predominantly regarded as procedural, you might find cases that resulted in acquittal because of a lack of jurisdiction. In Finland, there seems to be no doubt according to the doctrine that a lack of jurisdiction leads to acquittal. However, this has never been tested and sanctioned by the courts. In Iceland and Norway (today) lack of jurisdiction will probably also lead to acquittal. In Sweden, jurisdictional rules are without doubt regarded as procedural rules and lack of jurisdiction results in dismissal of the case.

3.4. Ne bis in idem
The Finnish solution seems commendable in the sense that it is clear and provides a secure legal basis for the individual, but what about the principle of *ne bis in idem*? Normally, an acquittal would have *ne bis in idem* effect, while a dismissal would not. In many cases, it would it be inappropriate to exclude a new trial in another country just because there is a lack of jurisdiction in the first country. It is exactly in such cases recommendable that another country tries the case. Thus, the Danish and Swedish systems, where cases (sometimes) are dismissed because of lack of jurisdiction, seem to provide a better solution. There is normally no *ne bis in idem* effect, if a case is dismissed. However, it is possible to regulate this question in a way that would not exclude a retrial, namely by saying that a new trial is not excluded, if the substance of the case has not been tried.

Another similar question might be that of compensation – both for victims and (wrongly) accused persons. A dismissal might not give the accused a right to compensation, but in some cases an acquittal gives the formerly accused person grounds for compensation.

3.5. Principle of legality – in general
Rules of substantive criminal law would normally be covered by the requirement of legality. There are many aspects to the *principle of legality*, only some are focused on here. The *legality principle* requires that norms of criminal law provisions are conceived in a clear and unambiguous way (*lex certa*). Thus, countries which regard jurisdictional rules as substantive criminal law might be more cautious about the *lex certa* requirement than countries that regard jurisdiction as a procedural matter. Of course this might not necessarily be so. In addition, countries where jurisdiction is regarded as a procedural matter might be very careful and conceive jurisdictional rules in a clear and unambiguous way (and countries, which regard jurisdiction as a matter of substantive criminal law, might not be cautious about the formulation of the

rules). Thus, there might not be any difference between the two kinds of jurisdictional concepts. There are reasons to believe that jurisdictional rules should respect the principle of legality – at least at the legislative level. It was recommended in the Council of Europe Report from 1990 (hereinafter 1990-report) that jurisdictional provisions should respect the *lex certa* requirement, be clear and provide a predictable basis for application of the law.[21]

It was concluded in the Norwegian country report that jurisdiction was mainly regarded as a matter of substantive criminal law. However, Section 5 of the new Norwegian Criminal Code (not yet in force) about jurisdiction of Norwegian courts for acts committed outside the Norwegian territory was deliberately conceived in a way that leaves a margin of appreciation to the courts. It even says in the *travaux préparatoires* that the margin of appreciation is "broad".[22] This could normally provide problems of inconformity with the requirement of *lex certa*.

The new Danish jurisdictional rules, which were conceived in the 2008 reform, were drawn in a somewhat ambiguous way. The 2008 reform widened the scope of jurisdiction on the basis of the *active and passive personality principle* and abandoned the requirement of double criminality in some cases. The new rules were criticised for being too far-reaching and in conflict with public international law. The *Danish Jurisdiction Committee* was aware of this when they conceived the new rules. Thus, according to Section 12 of the Danish Criminal Code, rules on jurisdiction must be interpreted in the light of the Danish obligations according to international public law. However, it is unclear where the borderline between the far reaching jurisdictional rules and public international law obligations should be drawn.[23]

In addition, the Danish provision in Section 8, no. 5 of the Danish Criminal Code, is very broad by referring to any international convention etc. This section simply says that Denmark has jurisdiction whenever obliged to have so according to international law.

The five country reports do not give a clear picture of whether the categorisation of jurisdiction as substantive or procedural is reflected in the case law concerning the requirement for the legal basis for punishment in concrete cases. In general, regarding jurisdiction as a matter of substantive criminal law would enhance the requirement for a clear legal basis for conviction. The

---

21. This might even be a requirement stemming from international public law, see Council of Europe, Extraterritorial criminal jurisdiction, European Committee on Crime Problems, Strasbourg 1990, p. 24.
22. Ot.prp. nr. 90, 2003-2004, p. 404.
23. See *Greve et al.* (2013), pp. 202 ff.

vague distinction between these countries is already apparent from the fact that there is some uncertainty to this question even in the national context. The uncertainty about this issue is remarkable in the light of the fact that all Nordic systems are based on the rule of law. In Sweden, it is apparently clear that provisions on jurisdiction are procedural rules and the requirements of the *principle of legality* therefore reduced. In the other countries it might be an issue for prosecutors, defence lawyers and judges in specific cases to determine, if the requirements of the *legality principle* are equally high regarding jurisdictional rules.

3.6. Principle of legality – non-retro activity

Furthermore, the *principle of legality* means a prohibition of retroactivity of norms of criminal law. Thus, in countries where the jurisdictional rules are regarded as substantive criminal law they would not allow new jurisdictional rules to apply to acts previously committed. The opposite may be true for countries, where the rules are regarded as procedural.

In the report of the Danish Jurisdiction Committee (*Betænkning no. 1488/2007*), the question of non-retroactivity has not been analysed. This could mean that the Danish Jurisdiction Committee regarded the answer to the question to be self-evident. However, there are two possible answers to the question of why this is not considered in the report: Either the new rules were considered procedural by the Danish Jurisdiction Committee and therefore no problem of retroactivity occurred or the new rules were considered to be a part of substantive criminal law and therefore the Danish Jurisdiction Committee held it to be self-evident that the *principle of legality*, including non-retro activity, applied. According to Per Ole Träskman, a professor in criminal law and criminal procedure, the Danish Jurisdiction Committee treats the jurisdictional rules as if they were procedural and therefore the question of non-retro activity is disregarded. Per Ole Träskman argues that this is problematic, because the new rules were widening the scope of jurisdiction for Danish courts and *de facto* creating a new criminalisation (criminalising acts, which were not punishable before).[24] Independently of whether the Danish Jurisdiction Committee considered the rules as being procedural or substantive it is striking that – as pointed out by Per Ole Träskman – the question was not dealt with in the Committee's report.

The *principle of non-retro activity* is fundamental in criminal law and a general requirement for states based on the rule of law. It is also a require-

---

24. *Träskman* (2008), pp. 563-590, p. 570.

ment according to ECHR art. 7 and EU Charter art. 49. Thus, whether a country regards the jurisdictional rules as procedural or substantive should not affect the non-retro activity. And this seems to be the solution in Denmark as well. In the proposal for the new Danish rules the provision on the entry into force of the rules actually addresses this issue. According to the proposal for the new legislation the question of non-retro activity has to be decided according to general criminal law principles. It is assumed in the proposal that it would not conflict with these principles if the new rules on jurisdiction were to be applied in situations where the act was criminalised both in Denmark and the country where the act was committed (requirement of double criminality fulfilled).[25]

If double criminality is not required, the changes in jurisdiction would be a *de facto* new criminalisation and hence situations where the non-retro activity is important. The decisive argument – in accordance with ECHR – must be the foreseeability. If the act is punishable in both countries, the accused is able to foresee the criminal liability, but not if double criminality is not a condition. Perhaps this was also the approach of the Danish Jurisdiction Committee.[26]

3.7. Mens rea – in relation to jurisdiction

Another question related to the discussion of substantive or procedural law is whether the requirement of *mens rea* should apply to the jurisdictional rules. Substantive criminal law will normally encompass all the constitutive elements of criminal liability. In many countries, perhaps the majority, the jurisdictional rules are not regarded as constitutive elements of crime. This is the conclusion about jurisdiction in England/Wales, Germany, Greece, Italy, Lithuania, The Netherlands, Poland and Spain:

"In most countries, the provisions about jurisdiction are not considered part of the *actus reus* and, thus, not considered elements of crime. [...] Some reports explicitly state that the jurisdictional provisions constitute so-called 'objective conditions of criminal liability' [...] These are objective elements required for holding a person criminally liable, but they do

25. "Det må afgøres efter almindelige principper, i hvilket omfang de foreslåede lovændringer vil kunne anvendes, hvis det pågældende forhold er begået inden lovens ikrafttræden. Det kan bl.a. ikke antages at være i strid med disse principper at anvende en udvidet straffemyndighed i tilfælde, hvor det pågældende forhold var strafbart både i gerningslandet og i Danmark på gerningstidspunktet." See comments on § 8 of Bill L 16 of 28 November 2007, 2007-08 (2nd).
26. In the Betænkning no. 1488/2007, there are a number of references to the requirement of foreseeability, i.e. in relation to double criminality, pp. 73, 185 and 260.

not form part of the *actus reus* and need not be covered by *mens rea*. Only in England do the principles have an impact on the definition of what is legally wrong […] If a situation is not covered by the jurisdictional principles, then it is not considered an offence. This is summed up in the English report: 'There is no *actus reus* and therefore no offence.'"[27]

Thus, even though jurisdictional provisions are regarded part of substantive criminal law, they are not necessarily conceived as constitutive elements of crime. For example, in Finland provisions about jurisdiction are – by part of the doctrine regarded as – parts of substantive criminal law, but not constitutive elements of crime. In the new Danish jurisdictional rules, the *active and passive personality principles* were combined in the same provision. Thus, if the offender is Danish and the victim as well, there is jurisdiction in Denmark, even though the requirement of double criminality is not fulfilled (Section 7, no. 2, b of the Danish Criminal Code). There is no requirement of *mens rea* in relation to the citizenship of the victim. Thus, this is an objective element required for holding a person criminally liable, but they do not form part of the *actus reus*.[28]

Provisions about jurisdiction are not constitutive elements of crime in any of the Nordic countries and the requirement of *mens rea* does not apply.

3.8. In dubio pro reo

Constitutive elements of crime must be proven beyond reasonable doubt and the principle of *in dubio pro reo* would normally apply to these elements. Therefore, if facts about jurisdiction are considered part of the *actus reus* in a certain country, the next question would be if the high standard of proof applies to facts about jurisdiction. What level of proof is required?

In general, the provisions on jurisdiction are not considered constitutive elements of crime in the Nordic countries. However, the principle of *in dubio pro reo* might still apply. For example, in Finland the high standard of proof applies also to the facts establishing jurisdiction:[29]

"[I]n Finland […] the accused's guilt must be proven beyond a reasonable doubt, and this standard also applies to the facts establishing jurisdiction. However, Finland has a specific

---

27. *Martin Böse, Frank Meyer* and *Anne Schneider*, "Comparative Analysis", in M. Böse, F. Meyer and A. Schneider: Conflicts of Jurisdiction in Criminal Matters in the European Union. National Reports and Comparative Analysis, Baden-Baden, 2013, pp. 407-460, p. 425.
28. See comments on § 7 of Bill L 16 of 28 November 2007, 2007-08 (2nd).
29. For the question of jurisdiction and *actus reus*, see in general *Dan Helenius*, Straffrättslig jurisdiction, Helsinki, 2014 (forthcoming), p. 156 ff.

provision about what happens in cases of doubts about the place of commission. According to S. 10 Para. 4 of the Finnish Criminal Code, the offense is deemed to have been committed in Finland if there is no certainty as to the place of commission, but there is justified reason to believe it was committed in Finland. "Justified reason" is a lower threshold than "beyond reasonable doubt". Accordingly, Finnish jurisdiction can be based on the *territoriality principle* even in cases of reasonable doubt, if there is justified reason to believe the offense was committed in Finland. This means that the *in dubio pro reo principle* does not apply to doubts about the place of commission, but does apply to other aspects on which jurisdiction hinges, such as nationality. The odd result is that prosecution is easier when Finnish jurisdiction is based on territoriality, rather than on some other principle."[30]

3.9. Summed up

The question whether provisions about jurisdiction are part of substantive or procedural criminal law is complex, but two general conclusions can be made. Firstly, whether the provisions are placed in the criminal code or the administration of justice act is not decisive. In all the Nordic countries, the provisions about jurisdiction are parts of the criminal code, but there are different answers to the question of whether they are perceived as procedural or substantive rules.

Secondly, the distinction between procedural and substantive rules does not provide us with the final answer to questions of *mens rea*, acquittal/dismissal and the application of principles like legality, *ne bis in idem* and *in dubio pro reo* in relation to provisions about jurisdiction.

In Sweden, there is no doubt that provisions on jurisdiction are regarded as procedural criminal law. In Norway, they are regarded as part of substantive criminal law. Still, in Sweden the structure of the jurisdictional rules is theoretically elaborated and the Swedish rules about jurisdiction seem to be conceived in a clear and precise way. In Norway, some of the rules on jurisdiction are deliberately conceived in a less precise way. Thus, the principle of legality and the requirement of *lex certa* are not necessarily taken more seriously in countries with a substantive criminal law perspective.

In Denmark, there was no systematic elaboration on the question of substantive or procedural nature of jurisdictional rules, when the latest reform of the jurisdictional rules was implemented in 2008. Denmark and Norway have chosen a (typically) pragmatic Nordic approach, where the issues dealt with above are not linked to the nature of the jurisdictional rules (substantive or procedural), but decided on a "case to case-basis". For example, the new Danish rule, where the requirement of double criminality is sometimes abandoned, is *de facto* a new criminalisation. However, retro activity is not ex-

---

30. *Böse, Meyer and Schneider* (2013), pp. 407-460, p. 431.

cluded. It is assumed by the legislator that the important thing is foreseeability and that it would not conflict with the requirement of foreseeability, if the new rules on jurisdiction were applied in situations, where the act was criminalised both in Denmark and the country, where the act was committed.

4.   Jurisdiction in the context of international cooperation

4.1.   Between sovereignty and non-interference – Domestic interests in investigating and prosecuting acts committed outside own territory

The use of domestic criminal law on acts committed in own state territory is rather uncontroversial and natural part of the execution of state sovereignty. The question of extending domestic jurisdiction in criminal cases outside national territory is, however, more complex and raises a number of issues. Two different settings must be distinguished when considering the question of jurisdiction for acts committed outside national territory. Firstly, the situation concerns the use of domestic criminal law on acts committed on another state's territory. The second situation concerns the use of domestic criminal law on acts committed outside any state's territory, for example the high seas.[31] This situation concerns the question of the rule of the *global commons*,[32] a question we return to further below.

4.2.   Jurisdiction for acts committed on another state's territory

When considering the question of the use of domestic criminal law in connection with acts committed on another state's territory a number of issues are raised. What is the justification for extending own jurisdiction on acts committed in another state's territory? Shouldn't the state on whose territory the acts are committed decide which acts are punishable and what form of punishment should be imposed?

4.2.1.   The question of limitations

It is readily accepted that international law does indeed restrict a state's competence to use criminal law on acts outside its own territory, mainly due to a

---

31.   On the concept of the *"high seas"* see United Nations Convention on the Laws of the Seas (UNCLOS) article 86 ff.
32.   The concept of the *"global commons"* deals with areas under no state sovereignty, which can be described *"free to all and belonging to none"*.

principle of respect for other states' sovereignty.[33] But this does not mean that states are *per se* excluded from establishing and executing domestic criminal jurisdiction on acts committed on another state's territory.[34] In this context, the German authors Werle and Jessberger, both German professors in domestic and international criminal law, concluded that the specific limitations for domestic jurisdiction on acts committed on another state's territory were not quite as clear and that two different lines of argumentation in the legal debate could be distinguished:

The first line of argumentation (the *"traditional opinion"*), assumes that states can extend their domestic jurisdiction on acts committed in other state's territory as long as international law does not directly prohibit it.[35] The notion that *"it is permitted as long as it is not prohibited"* is often based on the decision on the 1927 *"Lotus case"* (concerning the collision of a Turkish and a French ships and subsequently criminal proceedings against a French maritime officer for negligence in Turkey).[36] However, the *"traditional opinion"* is often a second step limiting the state's authority concerning criminal jurisdiction by the consideration that states are restricted by a general principle of *"avoiding interference with another state's internal affairs"*, meaning that it is required that there is a nexus to the interests of the state which wants to use its domestic criminal law on acts committed on another state's territory.[37]

The, newer, second line of argumentation is assuming that states can only extend their criminal jurisdiction on acts committed on another state's territory if this is permitted by international law. The permission to extend domestic jurisdiction can be granted through all kind of sources of international law, e.g. conventions and customary law, but mainly according to principles justifying the extension of domestic jurisdiction (in the German legal debate called *"Geltungsprinzipien"*).[38] Those principles can be divided into two groups: The first group dealing with considerations of the (self-) *protection of the state* (for example acts against the state, protection of its citizens), the second dealing with considerations in connection with the *solidarity between*

---

33. See for example *Gerhard Werle/Florian Jessberger*, "Commentary on § 3 ff of the German Criminal Code (StGB)", in: Laufhütte/Rissing-van Saan/Tiedemann (eds.), Strafgestzbuch; Leipziger Kommentar, 12th edition, first volume, 2007, vor § 3, 20 ff.
34. Ibid., vor § 3, 21.
35. Ibid., vor § 3, 24.
36. The Case of the S.S. Lotus (France vs. Turkey), P.C.I.J. 1927 (Judgment no. 9 of 7 September 1927).
37. *Werle/Jessberger* (2007), vor § 3, 24 and 216.
38. Ibid., vor § 3, 25 and 216 ff.

states (for example protecting others from acts by its citizens, prosecution on the behalf of other states, acts banned by the international community).[39]

As indicated in the brief outline above, the legal debate focuses on the extension of domestic jurisdiction beyond national territory on the perspective/interests of states. Another perspective worth considering in this context is the perspective of the individual: Is it justifiable that individuals are subjected to the criminal law of different states independently from where they are?

This question is not easily answered; considerations on extension of jurisdiction ought to include different interests and arguments. The development of the rules on jurisdiction in the Nordic countries indicates certain tendencies towards "more jurisdiction" ("why not" instead of "why") in some of the countries. This is, as motioned above, a move away from the Nord 1992:17-recommendations, which had a restrictive approach towards the extension of domestic jurisdiction. In the following, we will highlight some selected topics when looking at the development in the Nordic countries.

4.2.2. Council of Europe – report on Jurisdiction

From a (single) state perspective, one might ask why the legislator should not adopt extensive jurisdictional rules and provide the state with as much power as possible. Theoretically, it is possible to make all statutes of a state applicable to anyone, anywhere. So why limit the scope of the jurisdictional rules? The answer seems simply to be that it would infringe upon the sovereignty of other states and create conflicts between states. Thus as outlined above, international public law stipulates some limitations to jurisdiction, although only vaguely. These limitations are based on a number of fundamental principles, including the *principles of non-interference, sovereignty and equality of states.*[40] However, also from the citizens point of view is the question relevant.

The reasons for limiting extraterritorial jurisdiction is further elaborated in the above-mentioned 1990-report from the Council of Europe. The report was prepared by The Select Committee of Experts on Extraterritorial Jurisdiction (hereinafter the Committee), a body that set up in 1984 by the European Committee on Crime Problems (CDPC). The Committee was composed of experts from thirteen Member States, including Denmark and Norway. The

39. *Dietrich Oehler*, Internationales Strafrecht, 2nd edition, 1983, p. 130 ff.
40. *Thilo Marauhn* and *Sven Simon*, "Die völkerrechtlichen Voraussetzungen der Strafgewalt", in A. Sinn (ed.), Conflicts of jurisdiction in cross-border crime situations. A comparative law study on international criminal law, Universitätsverlag Osnabrück, 2012, pp. 21-40, p. 26.

1990-report was titled "Extraterritorial Criminal Jurisdiction". Even the title refers to the dichotomy between territorial and extraterritorial jurisdiction. From the introduction of the report it becomes clear that among other things the Committee was supposed to study the "justification" of extraterritorial jurisdiction and to "examine possible restrictions to be observed" and "make proposals for the prevention and solution of problems". Thus, the *principle of territoriality* is regarded as the point of departure for national jurisdiction and extraterritorial jurisdiction is perceived as something which has conflict potential and needs special justification. In addition, extraterritoriality might also raise problems for the individual, especially if there is no requirement of double criminality.

In the report, the Committee analysed the relationship between public international law and national criminal law. According to the Committee, public international law might impose restrictions – albeit vaguely – on national criminal law:

"The basic concepts of sovereignty and equality imply that states have to observe certain limitations if their conduct is not to qualify as an infringement on the sovereignty and equality of other states and thus constitute an inadmissible intervention in the internal affairs of such other states."

According to the Committee, public international law has three main objectives. The first objective is the delimitation of jurisdiction. This is based on the acknowledgement of the fact that there exist several states with jurisdiction internationally and therefore there must be (mutual) limits to jurisdiction. The second objective is the protection of persons, including their property and living conditions. It is interesting that this is regarded as an objective of public international law. In many ways it seems to be a traditional objective of national criminal law (criminal law is the *"magna carta"* of the citizens). However, the Committee devotes this objective to public international law.[41] The third objective is the furtherance of international co-operation.

In the 1990 report, page 26, the Committee categorises the different jurisdictional principles according to the dichotomy between purely national interests and international solidarity:

---

41. Likewise in the Danish debate about the new jurisdictional rules from 2008, where the criticism of the wide scope of the new Danish rules came from both criminal law and public international law scholars. See below.

A. International solidarity	B. Protection of a state's own interests
– Restricted active personality principle (including double criminality) – Representation principle – Universality principle (for specific, agreed, offences)	– Unrestricted active personality principle – Passive personality principle – Unrestricted principle of state protection

By this categorisation, it becomes clear that the recent development in some of the Nordic countries, especially Denmark, is not in the interest of international solidarity and cooperation. It is also apparent that the Council of Europe report is very much in line with the Nordic Committee for Criminal Law, the 1992:17-report.

The important question asked previously by politicians and legal researchers seems to have been "Why should we have jurisdiction over acts committed abroad"? The requirement of double criminality was regarded as a fundamental principle, and there had to be extraordinary good reasons for neglecting it. For example, this approach is taken by the Commission of the Nord 1992:17 report and also by the Select Committee of Experts on Extraterritorial Jurisdiction from the European Council.[42]

However, over the last 10 years there seems to have been changing attitudes towards the requirement of double criminality and increasing emphasis on the *active and passive personality principles*. This seems to follow the trend of an increasing level of repression in many European countries during the last two or three decades. The requirement of double criminality has become less fundamental and new arguments for abandoning the requirement have been accepted. The question "Why should we have jurisdiction over acts committed abroad" is apparently much easier to answer now than 20-30 years ago. This is especially true for Denmark, but the same tendency is visible in Sweden and Norway. The development is partly due to the international development, i.e. conventions appealing to better protection of certain victims (children, women etc.).[43]

The Finnish tendency – according to which jurisdiction was limited in the 1996 reform – is especially noticeable in comparison to the many new extensive provisions in the Danish Criminal Code and the proposed Swedish Criminal Code. The new Danish rules were criticised by criminal law scholars[44]

---

42. For a recent in depth discussion of this from a Nordic and international perspective, see Dan Helenius, Straffrättslig Jurisdiktion Helsinki 2014, p. 257 ff.
43. Betænkning no. 1488/2007, p. 260.
44. *Träskman* (2008), pp. 563-590.

and public international law experts[45] for being too far-reaching and in conflict with public international law. In its advisory opinion on the 2008 Danish reform of the jurisdictional rules, the Danish Jurisdiction Committee, which proposed the expansion (*passive personality principle*), did not rule out the possibility that the application of the new jurisdictional rules might in certain cases be "difficult to reconcile with international law principles". On the other hand, the examples – which seemed to have been convincing for the Committee – were situations where a father (a Danish citizen) has intercourse with his daughter during a vacation outside Denmark or where a boy from high school rapes his girlfriend (both from Denmark) during a school excursion abroad.

The earlier restrictions on domestic jurisdiction were based on the effort to avoid what looked like a vote of no confidence in a foreign country's administration of justice. It was feared that extending national jurisdiction to offences committed abroad by foreigners against Danish citizens could run counter to international solidarity.[46]

"The continuing trend unilaterally to enlarge the scope of application of national criminal law, which has also been stimulated by international conventions, seems to further a development which runs counter to the traditional objectives of public international law [...] It is hoped that this report will make some contribution towards reconsidering this trend."[47]

4.2.3. The question of sovereignty and international criminal law
Another perspective of the question of the tendency to extend national jurisdiction on an activity in another state's territory is the perspective of international criminal law. As described above; the development of international criminal law and the demands of the Rome Statute have had an impact on the rules on jurisdiction in the Nordic countries. However, in this context the argument of disrespect of another state's sovereignty and the *principle of non-interference* are somewhat opposed. The general idea of international criminal law is in its essence that certain crimes are so severe and unacceptable that it is the responsibility of all states to respond. This argument is in reality challenged by the fact that some major countries, e.g. USA, Russia and China, are not part of the Rome Statue. When accepting the general idea of inter-

45. *Ole Spiermann*, "Personalhøjhed", in T. Baumbach et al. (eds), Festskrift til Jørn Vestergaard, Copenhagen 2008, pp. 441-464.
46. See Section 2.4. of the Danish country report.
47. Council of Europe, Extraterritorial criminal jurisdiction, European Committee on Crime Problems, Strasbourg 1990, p. 39.

national criminal law, one could also add that those crimes are often connected to states or parties in a larger conflict and it is therefore not certain that the territorial state (on which the atrocities occur), has a genuine interest in prosecuting the responsible persons in an acceptable way.

Another aspect in the context of international criminal law and its influence on domestic rules on jurisdiction, is that one of the central arguments for non-interference is not quite accurate when talking about international crimes: The crimes in question are not primarily defined by individual states and their own interests (even if some states have implemented the concepts of those international crimes in their domestic criminal law in their own words) but by international law. Thus, prosecuting those crimes is primarily not an expression of imposing own values on acts committed on another state's territory but expression of solidarity towards the international community's shared values. However, the development of the rules of jurisdiction in this context can also be seen from another perspective: The decision to have jurisdiction in those cases was also connected to the (former) refusal to extradite own citizens to criminal proceedings in another country.

4.3. Jurisdiction for acts committed outside any state's territory

It seems obvious that the extension of national jurisdiction on acts committed in another state's territory is a source of potential conflict between states and one might come to the hasty conclusion that the potential for conflicts is somewhat lower when talking about jurisdiction for acts committed outside any state's territory, e.g. acts committed on what can be called the global commons. The global commons are domains or areas that lie outside any state's territorial sovereignty. International law identifies four global commons namely: The high seas, the airspace, Antarctica and (outer) space.[48] Furthermore, cyberspace is often perceived as part of the global commons.[49]

The question of jurisdiction for acts committed in connection with the internet/cyberspace poses certain specific challenges. One of those challenges is whether the traditional concepts of criminal law, for example where a criminal act is committed, are sufficient when talking about activities on the internet/in online forums. The country reports show that the different Nordic

---

48. See for example United Nations Environment Programme's webpage: http://www.unep.org/delc/GlobalCommons/tabid/54404/Default.aspx (last visited 10.10.2013).
49. See for example the Multinational Experiment 7 (MNE7), MNE7 Access to the Global Commons Outcome 3 Cyber Domain: mne.oslo.mil.no:8080/Multinatio/.../35CyberCon (last visited 10.10.2013).

countries have developed diverse approaches towards the challenges posed by cyberspace. Denmark has introduced a specific regulation, the decisive (limiting) factor is whether the act/content in question has a particular connection to Denmark, for example due to language or a specific target group.[50] The other Nordic countries have no specific regulation: The Finnish approach is that this question is dealt with under the existing concepts and that the decisive factor is the question of where the server is placed.[51] Also Iceland has no specific regulation; the decisive question is here seen as one concerning the consequences of an unlawful act.[52] In Norway the question of whether specific regulation is necessary or not was discussed and dismissed. The approach in Norway is to deal with cyber-related questions within the existing legal concepts.[53] The same is true for Sweden, here the question of cybercrimes was considered by the reform Commission which expressed doubt as to whether this question could be solved on a national level.[54]

But the more traditional areas outside state territory also pose certain challenges. Those can especially be shown in connection with the oceans. The governance of the oceans and the question of law enforcement at sea are of particular importance to all Nordic countries, mainly due to the fact that they all are coastal states with a genuine interest in the protection, use and exploitation of the oceans. International law provides a general framework for the governing of the oceans, mainly through the UN Convention on the Law of the Sea (UNCLOS) which, however, to a very large extent is a codification of customary international law. All Nordic countries are party to UNCLOS.[55] UNCLOS provides a system, which in short, grants the right of sovereignty to the territorial sea (up to 12 nautical miles) and extends certain rights of law enforcement to the contiguous zone (further 12 nautical miles) and, somewhat more limited, in connection with the exploitation, managing etc. of resources to the exclusive economic zone (EEZ).[56] The question of the coastal state's right to perform certain acts of law enforcement in the EEZ is current-

---

50. See Section 2.1.1. of the Danish country report.
51. See Section 2.1.1. of the Finnish country report.
52. See Section 2.1.1. of the Icelandic country report.
53. See Section 2.1.2. of the Norwegian country report.
54. See Section 2.1.1. of the Swedish country report.
55. See United Nations: Chronological lists of ratifications of, accessions and successions to the Convention and the related Agreements as at 20 September 2013: http://www.un.org/depts/los/reference_files/chronological_lists_of_ratifications.htm (last visited 10.10.2013).
56. UNCLOS art. 2 ff., 33 ff., 55 ff. See also *James Crawford*, Brownlie's principles of public international law, eighth edition 2012, p. 255 ff.

ly discussed in connection with the boarding and detention of the Greenpeace vessel *Arctic Sunrise* (flying the flag of the Netherlands) by Russian forces.[57] Similar questions have, however, also been raised in the Nordic context, the Supreme Court of Norway (*Høyesterett*), for example, has ruled on different aspects of the question of law enforcement in the EEZ in connection with Greenpeace's protest actions against Norwegian installations.[58]

In addition, the right to exercise criminal jurisdiction on board foreign vessels passing through territorial waters is not unlimited (UNCLOS art. 27), international law only accepts interference on foreign vessels under certain circumstances, mainly when there is a nexus of the interests of the costal state. The UNCLOS provision on the exercise of criminal jurisdiction in national territorial waters illustrates a rather crucial point: The exercise of national jurisdiction (even within territorial waters) has to be weighted with another state's interests, in the specific context, the flag state's right to undisturbed innocent passage through territorial waters. The right to exercise jurisdiction for own territorial waters and own vessels is reflected in all Nordic rules on jurisdiction which are very similar concerning this particular point. However, in this context some interesting aspects should be noted: Firstly, all Nordic countries link flag state jurisdiction for acts committed on national vessels in foreign waters to the acting person who has to be a crew member or passenger (or in the Finnish context, another person on board). Secondly, it is interesting to note that some Nordic countries, e.g. Denmark, Sweden, claim quite extensive rights of jurisdiction for acts committed on national vessels (*flag state principle*) also in foreign waters but at the same time do not require considerations on flag state regulation when exercising own jurisdiction on foreign vessels in own territorial waters. Finally, the question of the extension of the *active personality principle* on acts committed on foreign vessels on the high seas is a topic of discussion. In Denmark, it seems that the intention of the Danish Jurisdiction Committee (and subsequently of the "lawmakers") is that the *active personality principle*, without the limitation of the requirement of double criminality (but with a certain limitation concerning the severe character of the crime) establishes Danish jurisdiction for acts committed on foreign vessels on the high seas.[59]

Also on the high seas, the right of the flag state to govern national vessels is a central principle and the general *principle of non-interference* by other

---

57. See BBC news: Dutch take legal action over Greenpeace ship in Russia: http://www.bbc.co.uk/news/world-europe-24395769 (last visited 10.10.2013).
58. See Rt-1993-1567 and Rt-2002-1271.
59. See Betænkning no. 1488/2007, p. 379 and *Greve et al.* (2013), p. 162.

states applies. However, some crimes which can be conducted on the high seas are perceived as a shared responsibility; one of those crimes is piracy.[60] In the 21st century, piracy has developed into a serious threat towards maritime navigation and some of the Nordic countries are actively participating in counter-piracy operations in the Horn of Africa region. However, the current counter-piracy efforts have also demonstrated some challenges and shortcomings. International law, with UNCLOS at its centre, provides some specific rights to any state to combat piracy (including, for example, the right to board and seize foreign ships under the suspicion of piracy and to arrest suspected pirates). However, there is no clear obligation to establish universal jurisdiction for cases of piracy, nor an obligation to ensure prosecution of suspected pirates. This has led to a situation where a number of countries (e.g. Denmark) have exercised a "catch and release" strategy in situations where criminal proceedings in "willing countries" in the region (for example Kenya) could not be secured.[61]

4.4. Summarising: Globalisation and symbolic value of criminal law

Centuries ago, jurisdictional rules were linked to persons. It was the lord/landowner, who had the jurisdiction over his people – no matter where they went. During the 19th and 20th century this focus shifted. The nation state emerged and territory became the most important parameter for jurisdiction. Looking at the changes to jurisdictional rules in the Nordic countries in the last 20-30 years, this focus might again be changing. Shifting back from territories to persons, the *principles of active and passive personality* becomes more important.

But why? Why do Nordic countries (and many other countries) widen the scope of their jurisdiction? Apparently the development in the Nordic countries and in other countries is driven – at least partly – by the many international conventions requiring jurisdiction (for example the ICC, as mentioned above). But the question then is why do we see this international development? One explanation could be the globalisation. The increased mobility of persons, information and goods across borders has increased interdependence between states. A nation's citizens relatively freely and frequently travel abroad. The internet makes it possible to commit crimes all over the world.

---

60. UNCLOS art. 100 ff.
61. See *Birgit Feldtmann*, "Should we rule out criminal law as a means of fighting maritime piracy? – An essay on the challenges and possibilities of prosecuting Somali pirates", in U. Anderson et al. (eds.), Festskrift till Per Ole Träskman, Norstedts Juridisk 2013, p. 179 ff.

There seems to be an international political desire (EU, UN, Council of Europe etc.) not to allow persons escape criminal liability by moving from one country to another. No doubt, one central issue for the rules on jurisdiction is to ensure that crime does not pay. The international conventions – which have contributed to the development – are exponents for the same attitude: Some crimes are regarded as global and slip past borders with ease, not exclusively linked to the territory of one state. Thus, globalisation and interdependence between states has increased the importance of the *principle of representation*.[62] However, the *principle of representation* is a symbol of solidarity. On the contrary, the *principles of active and passive personality* are – especially combined with the abandonment of double criminality – troublemakers for international solidarity.

Even though globalisation could explain the increased focus on persons and thus the *active and passive personality principles* instead of the *principle of territoriality*, it does not seem to explain the abandonment of double criminality. This development seems to run counter to international solidarity and thus to the trend of globalisation. Furthermore, the Finnish approach is an example of the fact that globalisation does not necessarily call for more extensive jurisdictional rules.

Thus, it is reasonable to believe that the tendency to widen the jurisdictional scope follows on from something else than practical needs. For example, that the new rules are the result of moral rather than practical needs. Perhaps the reasoning is that "our own" moral codes are right and should be respected no matter where people living in our country go? Legislators in many countries increasingly seem to refer to the "common sense of justice" as grounds for enacting new legislation. The argument of "common sense of justice" is irrational, based on moral beliefs (very often the moral beliefs of the politician, not empirical research on the common sense of justice of the population) and based on political considerations. It seems as if the widening of the scope of jurisdiction within the last 10-15 years has been based on arguments of "common sense of justice", for example in Denmark.[63] The logic seems to be: Some acts are fundamentally and universally wrong and should be punished by persons belonging to our country, no matter where the act was

---

62. *Vagn Greve*, "Strafzumessung im internationalen Strafrecht", in J. Arnold et al. (eds.): Menschengerechtes Strafrecht. Festschrift für Albin Eser zum 70. Geburtstag, München 2005, pp. 751-763, p. 762.
63. See *Thomas Elholm*, "The symbolic purpose of criminal Law – A Danish perspective", in Reindl-Krauskopf et al. (eds.): Festschrift für Helmut Fuchs, Wien 2014 (forthcoming).

committed and no matter if the act was punishable in that country. However, the new jurisdictional rules do not only cover very serious crimes. For example the widening of the Danish rules also covers a 15-year-old Danish girl having sexual intercourse with her 14-year-old boyfriend in a country, where the age of consent is 14 years (and even though the boyfriend is a citizen of the state concerned!). In Denmark the *principle of opportunity applies*, so the girl might not be prosecuted, but the rules on jurisdiction actually cover her behaviour.

In practice, it is often difficult handling criminal cases based on the *active or passive personality principle*, because investigation and the proof of the guilt in these cases are difficult. Combined with the moral element mentioned above, one wonders if the prime function of the new jurisdictional rules in some cases is symbolic:

"Judging from the replies to the questionnaire with respect to the quantitative application of various forms of extraterritorial criminal jurisdiction, the legislature in many member states may well have overestimated the "tensile force" (the potential) of their national criminal justice systems. Indeed, one wonders to what extent some of the established forms of extraterritorial criminal jurisdiction have no more than symbolic value."[64]

5. Jurisdiction and the EU

The EU wants to create *one* area of freedom, security and justice for all. This is stated in the very beginning of the EU treaty, art. 3(2). The EU is also very serious regarding criminal law cooperation and is currently trying to improve cooperation across borders. A number of framework decisions have been adopted and lately, directives aimed at an approximation of national criminal law of the EU Member States.

The harmonisation of substantive criminal law on an EU level could be regarded as an effort to overcome jurisdictional problems. Just to mention one example: The problems related to the requirement of double criminality are redressed by the harmonisation of criminalisation. On the other hand the harmonisation might also create jurisdictional problems by obliging two or

---

64. Council of Europe, Extraterritorial criminal jurisdiction, European Committee on Crime Problems, Strasbourg 1990, p. 38 f.

more EU Member States to have (overlapping) jurisdiction in the same cases.[65]

Apart from this aspect, the legal acts adopted by EU do not focus very much on the jurisdictional problem. The legal acts adopted by EU will normally contain only a few provisions on jurisdiction. The provisions can be categorised into two groups: 1) Some provisions requiring the EU Member States to make sure that they have jurisdiction in certain cases and 2) Some provisions about coordination in cases of jurisdictional conflicts.

Regarding the provisions requiring jurisdiction of the Member States the legal acts from EU legislation can be categorised as follows:

Legal acts based on territoriality and active personality principles	Legal acts based on more than territoriality/active personality	Legal acts with no provisions on jurisdiction
– *Framework decision on Racism* – *Framework decision on Organised Crime* – *Framework decision on Drug Trafficking* – *Framework decision on Corruption* – *Framework decision on Unauthorised Entry (smuggling of people)* – *Directive on Trafficking in Human Beings* – *Framework decision on Non-Cash Means of Payment* – *Framework decision on Information*	– *Framework decision on Counterfeiting (proposed directive)* – *Framework decision on Terrorism* – *PIF Convention (financial interests of EU) (proposed directive)* – *Framework decision on Ship-Source Pollution* – *Framework decision on Environment* – *Directive on Sexual Exploitation of Children*	– *Framework decision on Money Laundering* – *Directive on the Protection of the Environment*

As shown above, most of the legal acts from the EU are based on the principle of territoriality and active personality. Thus, the EU Member States shall take the necessary steps to ensure their jurisdiction in cases where: a) the of-

65. See about EU and jurisdiction in criminal matters generally and specifically on this issue *Frank Zimmermann*, Strafgewaltkonflikte in der Europäischen Union. Ein Regelungsvorschlag zur Wahrung materieller und prozessualer strafrechtlicher Garantien sowie staatlicher Strafinteressen, 2014 (forthcoming).

fence is committed in whole or in part within their territory; or (b) the offender is one of their nationals. Furthermore, the EU generally also requires national jurisdiction where the crime has been committed (c) for the benefit of a legal person that has its head office in the territory of that Member State. Some of the legal acts encompass other jurisdiction principles, mainly the *flag state principle* and the *state protection principle.*

Some of the legal acts mentioned above "allow" for the Member State to use other jurisdictional principles, for example the *passive personality principle* (see art. 10 of the directive on trafficking and art. 17 of the directive on sexual exploitation of children). However, the *passive personality principle* is not recommended (explicitly) by the EU and there are in the EU legislation – except from the European Arrest Warrant, which is a slightly different matter – no examples of abandonment of the double criminality principle in combination with the *passive personality principle*. In the directive on sexual exploitation of children, the requirement of double criminality is abandoned in relation to the *active personality principle.*

The rules on jurisdiction in the EU legal acts are minimum rules: EU Member States are allowed to use more far-reaching jurisdictional rules. There is nothing in the EU system prohibiting the Member States from using, for example, jurisdictional rules based on the *passive personality principle.* Thus, there are plenty of possibilities, where conflicts could occur.

Having the goal of creating one area of justice within EU, the EU legislator may be interested in avoiding jurisdictional conflicts or at least trying to create a framework for settlement of such conflicts. Thus, a special legal act on jurisdictional conflicts has been adopted: The framework decision on the prevention and settlement of jurisdictional conflicts in criminal proceedings.[66] The scope of the decision is restricted in the sense that it requires EU Member States only to inform each other and negotiate in cases of conflicts of jurisdiction. There are no binding or even guiding rules to regulate the choice of jurisdiction. Interestingly, in the original proposal by the EU Commission on the framework decision, the *principle of territoriality* played a significant role. This principle was proposed to regulate conflicts of jurisdiction. It seems to be a very natural way for the EU to regulate jurisdiction, because it creates a certain type of unity conforming to the goal of creating a single area of justice. This is illustrative by an example: Three men commit a crime in an EU Member State A. One is arrested immediately, the two others

---

66. The Council framework decision of 30 November 2009 on the prevention and settlement of conflicts of exercise of jurisdiction in criminal proceedings (2009/948/JHA).

flee, one to Member State B, another to Member State C.[67] Most likely, the three persons will face very different sentences for the same offence, committed in the same country (in one of the countries, the offence might not even be criminalised). From a federal perspective, in the interest of creating one area of justice, where persons can move freely across borders, this seems problematic. The European Arrest Warrant (EAW) has made it easier to have people extradited, and thus the problem is diminished. But there are still cases, where people have already been prosecuted and convicted (for example by a fine) in one state and therefore cannot be convicted in another.[68] It is easy to understand, why the Commission did propose the *territoriality principle* as the turning point. It will be interesting to see, if the tendencies described above will continue in the future for those of the Nordic countries that are members of the EU. Increased applicability of the *active and passive personality principle*, especially without the requirement of double criminality, does not seem to be in accordance with the goal of the Union.

In the future the EU might create stronger bonds – also in the field of criminal law – between the Member States. This could pave the way for using other jurisdictional principles than the *principle of territoriality*. Notable is the jurisdictional rule in the Nordic countries, which makes it possible to use the active personality principle on perpetrators from other Nordic countries. This approach underlines a special and close relationship between the Nordic countries. Jurisdictional rules based on the *active personality principle* normally symbolises close bonds between the state and the citizens:

"The underlying rationale of this principle [*active personality principle*] differs from state to state. According to the prevailing (traditional) understanding, the principle is based on the special bond of loyalty between a state and its citizens. [...] More generally, the *principle of active personality* allows for prosecuting persons who have brought shame and disgrace upon their home country (e.g. by committing sexual offences abroad)."[69]

However, in case of the Nordic systems this is not all true. For example, a Norwegian citizen present in Denmark (e.g. as a tourist) might be prosecuted in Denmark for acts committed abroad due to the fact that the *principle of active personality* applies to all Nordic citizens. Does this show a certain bond between citizens of all Nordic countries and all the Nordic states? On a Euro-

---

67. See also *Greve* (2005), pp. 751-763.
68. See judgment on *ne bis in idem* from Court of Justice of the European Union of 11 February 2003, C-187/01 and C-385/01.
69. *Böse, Meyer and Schneider* (2013), pp. 407-460, p. 416.

pean level the same question might be relevant in the future: Does the European citizenship create a bond between the EU citizens and the EU Member States, which makes it appropriate to apply the *active personality principle* to all?

A special regional level in the application of jurisdictional rules is also visible in another sense. As mentioned above there is a clear distinction in Danish and Swedish legal theory between jurisdictional rules and the question of the territorial scope of criminal law. Thus, in cases of acts committed abroad, a Danish judge will have to find out, firstly, if there is jurisdiction in Denmark, secondly, if the criminal provision in question covers acts abroad. Traditionally the categorisation would be twofold: The provision was either limited to acts committed on Danish territory or universal applicable. Today, the categorisation must be threefold. There might be jurisdiction in cases of acts committed outside Denmark, but within the EU. There might even be an obligation – stemming from EU law – to prosecute in such situations. Therefore, the territorial scope of the Danish criminal law is threefold: Danish territory, EU territory and universally.[70]

6. Some concluding remarks: From international to interregional criminal law?

The question of jurisdiction is one of the core aspects of any domestic system of criminal justice. It is also a rather crucial question with regard to cooperation and potential conflicts between different states. The view on the rules on jurisdiction in the Nordic countries shows that they are based on a common heritage but that there are also significant differences and it seems that the Nordic cooperation in the field of criminal law has in the last decades decreased in influence. For some of the Nordic countries, those who are members of the European Union (Denmark, Sweden, Finland), it seems, a new frame of reference has taken over: The development in the field of criminal law in the EU.

Taking the development within the European Union into account, it is reasonable to assume that substantive, national criminal law will be harmonised considerably in the future. It is also reasonable to assume that the importance of mutual recognition and mutual trust will increase. Thus, the level of mutu-

---

70. See *Greve et al.* (2013), p. 190, and *Vagn Greve*, "Straffebestemmelsernes interlegale gyldighed", TfK 2010, pp. 502 ff.

al trust between the EU Member States will be greater than between EU Member States and third countries. A higher level of mutual trust between the Member States is even required by EU. On this basis, is it reasonable to ask if the traditional principles of international criminal law and criminal procedural law should still prevail between EU Member States.

In most countries, when it comes to questions of international criminal law, the national criminal court will apply the principle of *lex fori* in determining criminal liability and sentencing. Even though a national criminal court does not only use *lex fori* – for example when it comes to the requirement of double criminality, the national criminal court will have to take criminal law of the foreign country (*lex loci delicti*) into account – there is a significant difference between international criminal law and international private law, where the principle of *lex fori* does not prevail.

So, *lex fori* is the point of departure in international criminal law, but if a national criminal court in region X is judging a case from another part of the country, region Y, where the substantive criminal law is different, *lex fori* is normally not the point of departure. In these situations the court in region X would apply the law of region Y. This could be called "interlocal" criminal law.[71]

What would happen, if the prevailing principles of international criminal law were abandoned and substituted with the principles of interlocal criminal law inside the EU? A number of advantages might occur. In the above-mentioned example of three persons committing a crime on the territory of state X, the first person, A, is caught and convicted in state X, the second person B flees and is caught and convicted in state Y and the same happens to the third person C in state Z. At present the principles of international criminal law are used and thus the criminal law of *lex fori* applies. This leads to different punishment for A, B and C – there may be even no punishment, for example person C. If interlocal principles were used instead, they would all be treated the same way and punished according to *lex loci delicti*. This would in some cases diminish the use of an arrest warrant and transfer of persons to trial in foreign countries (and thus diminish the need for pre-trial detention on the ground of risk for escape). It would also have the advantages that the accused person would have a trial in his own language. Furthermore, it would make it easier for the European Public Prosecutor's Office, because

---

71. The term is directly translated from Danish, cf. *Vagn Greve*, Det strafferetlige ansvar, 2nd edition, 2004, Copenhagen, pp. 101 f.

they would have to prepare a trial only according to the substantive criminal law of one country.

Where the principles of interlocal criminal law apply, the big problem facing a structure like the one mentioned, is the cultural aspect. There might be situations where it runs against fundamental moral beliefs in state X to convict and sentence according to state Y. Even between the Nordic countries, where the cultural difference are relatively few and the trust in the other systems high, *lex fori* applies. Thus, it seems quite obvious that it is not the time for EU to introduce a principle like this.

The cooperation within the EU is rather different from the cooperation of the Nordic countries and the difference can in its essence be summarised as follows:

In the Nordic countries, the common rules and cooperation are the product of a cultural community and of mutual trust. In the EU, the common rules and cooperation are the product of a political demand, stressing the common cultural heritage, the need for mutual recognition and mutual trust.